FORM AND IDEA

THE MACMILLAN COMPANY
NEW YORK • CHICAGO
DALLAS • ATLANTA • SAN FRANCISCO
LONDON • MANILA

THE MACMILLAN COMPANY
OF CANADA, LIMITED
TORONTO

FORM AND IDEA

THIRTY ESSAYS FOR COLLEGE STUDY

MORTON W. BLOOMFIELD

The Ohio State University

and

EDWIN W. ROBBINS

The Ohio State University

New York

THE MACMILLAN COMPANY

PREFACE

This collection of essays has been designed for use in college courses in composition. Among the several factors governing our selection of specific essays, literary excellence was foremost. We have tried to avoid the essay that is drably written, sensational, or cheaply popular. Not all our selections, of course, are of equal quality. Occasionally other considerations have dictated the choice of an essay which does not represent a truly high literary level. But we feel that on the whole this collection includes the kind of material that will not only provide the student with good models but will introduce him as well to the excitement produced by first-rate exposition.

A second factor in our choice of essays was our desire to cover a wide range of subject matter so that the total collection might constitute a kind of introduction to academic experience. Because of the limitations of space, we have been forced to exclude some areas of knowledge, but we have been able to include essays on astronomy, geology, anthropology, biology, psychiatry, sociology, political science, journalism, education, linguistics, creative writing, aesthetic criticism, religion, music, the architectural arts, ballet, and the motion pictures. In our selecting, we have been careful to choose essays which demand no specialized knowledge for their understanding.

In many instances, we have ruled out admirable pieces because of our desire not to exceed certain limits of length. We have chosen relatively short essays upon the theory that the best models for the student are those which he can grasp as a whole. The problems of organization and scope involved in essays of the length here represented are much the same as the problems the student will face in his own writing. The shorter essay is also more suitable for assignments, for the student can more easily comprehend in a single reading the article of under 4000 words than one of two or three times that length. We have used essays of more than 4000 words, but three-fourths of the selections are under that length. Of thirty essays, two are 500 words long, four range between 1000 and 2000 words, ten between 2000 and 3000 words, six between 3000 and 4000 words, five between 4000 and 5000 words, and three between 5000 and 6000 words. Thus, while striving generally to avoid the overly long essay, we have endeavored to achieve considerable range in length.

In addition to seeking variety of subject matter and variety in length, we have sought variety in form and approach. In this collection the student will find the direct factual essay, the argumentative essay of opinion, the character sketch, the descriptive essay, the whimsical, evocative personal essay, the book review essay, and the critical essay. He will find essays of definition, of analysis, of classification, and of process. He will find great variety in tone between the exuberance of de Mille, the calm reasonableness of Madison, the delicate sophistication of Aldous Huxley, the biting satire of Swift, the gentler whimsical mockery of E. B. White, the puckish fun of Thurber, the brooding mystery of Carson, the eeriness of Eiseley, the fierce intensity of D. H. Lawrence, and the fervid romanticism of Conrad.

A glance at the Table of Contents will reveal no obvious system of arrangement. We have not grouped these essays in terms of issues, for we are concerned primarily with collecting good essays, not with debating issues. For the same reason, we have not arranged our selections as types of exposition. Vital issues are represented in this collection, as are the various types of exposition, but we prefer not to conceal under any single system of categories the several kinds of variety we have achieved. Instead we have chosen to place first the simpler, more direct essays and have followed them with the more involved selections. What this arrangement means in terms of subject matter is that, with some exceptions, the essays on science precede the generally more subtle, more difficult ones on the humanities. We regard this arrangement as one largely of convenience. Respecting the wish of teachers to order their materials in terms of their own methods, we have designed our apparatus so that the essays may be taught in any order whatever.

The study questions following the essays are offered for the teacher who may find them useful. As a rule, the questions deal with both form and content. In the questions on form we have tried to cover every phase of composition as taught in college courses. In the questions on content, we have aimed at asking the student not so much what he has read as the implications of what he has read. When possible, we have related these content questions to his immediate experience. Throughout, we have been guided by the principle of the interrelation of form and content. We believe that the purpose of this collection is to help the student learn the intricate process of writing, not merely to provide him with a mass of miscellaneous information; and that the problem of learning to write effectively is largely a problem of acquiring a formal mastery of content.

The theme assignments accompanying the essays represent topics growing out of the essays, and therefore should enable the student to avoid the problem of writing in a vacuum. Teachers and students alike may think of additional, better topics, for we have by no means exhausted the possibilities. Many of the topics, even though not assigned as themes, can be used for fruitful class discussion, as is also true of many of the study questions. Individual teachers will no doubt wish to widen or narrow the theme assignments to fit their own tastes.

The biographical headnotes are provided largely to give the student a very brief introduction to each author and to suggest additional books for the student who may wish to read more of any one author. The footnotes are designed to give information not given in *The American College Dictionary* or *Webster's Collegiate Dictionary*.

Our total purpose has been to provide the teacher with a collection of excellent essays together with the necessary teaching aids. We realize fully, however, that finally the task of instruction belongs to the teacher. It is he who must guide the student into the fair uplands of good and satisfying prose. We believe that this collection can help him as far as a textbook can. The rest is up to him.

In our labors of compilation we have been aided and comforted by the encouragement, both witty and grave, of our colleagues, to whom we here extend our thanks. We wish to note expressly our debt of gratitude to Professor Glenn H. Leggett of the University of Washington and Professor Robert Christin of Saint Ambrose College for their helpful criticisms and suggestions. Full responsibility for the finished product is, of course, ours alone.

TABLE OF CONTENTS

FORM AND IDEA

Anna Pavlova*

AGNES DE MILLE (1908–   ), *daughter of William de Mille, film producer, and niece of Cecil B. de Mille, the director, is also prominent in the entertainment world, as a choreographer and dancer. Miss de Mille took thorough training in classical ballet, but she has devoted herself to solo character sketches of a comic cast and to ballets on American themes. Her most successful uses of Americana were* Rodeo, *or* The Courting at Burnt Ranch (1942), *a cowboy ballet depicting a cowgirl's struggle to win the love of a champion roper; and the choreography for the musical comedy* Oklahoma (1943). *She has been highly praised for popularizing the ballet without sacrificing its artistic values. The selection printed here from her autobiography* Dance to the Piper *is given in the form in which it appeared in* The Atlantic Monthly *of October, 1951.*

(1) Anna Pavlova! My life stops as I write that name. Across the daily preoccupation of lessons, lunch boxes, tooth brushings, and quarrelings with Margaret [1] flashed this bright, unworldly experience and burned in a single afternoon a path over which I could never retrace my steps. I had witnessed the power of beauty, and in some chamber of my heart I lost forever my irresponsibility. I was as clearly marked as though she had looked me in the face and called my name. For generations my father's family had loved and served the theater. All my life I had seen actors and actresses and had heard theater jargon at the dinner table and business talk of box-office grosses. I had thrilled at Father's projects and watched fascinated his picturesque occupations. I took a proprietary pride in the profitable and hasty

[1] Miss de Mille's sister.

growth of "The Industry." But nothing in his world or my uncle's prepared me for theater as I saw it that Saturday afternoon.[2]

(2) Since that day I have gained some knowledge in my trade and I recognize that her technique was limited; that her arabesques were not as pure or classically correct as Markova's, that her jumps and *batterie*[3] were paltry, her turns not to be compared in strength and number with the strenuous durability of Baronova or Toumanova.[4] I know that her scenery was designed by second-rate artists, her music was on a level with restaurant orchestrations, her company definitely inferior to all the standards we insist on today, and her choreography mostly hack. And yet I say she was in her person the quintessence of theatrical excitement.

(3) As her little bird body revealed itself on the scene, either immobile in trembling mystery or tense in the incredible arc which was her lift, her instep stretched ahead in an arch never before seen, the tiny bones of her hands in ceaseless vibration, her face radiant, diamonds glittering under her dark hair, her little waist encased in silk, the great tutu balancing, quickening and flashing over her beating, flashing, quivering legs, every man and woman sat forward, every pulse quickened. She never appeared to rest static, some part of her trembled, vibrated, beat like a heart. Before our dazzled eyes, she flashed with the sudden sweetness of a hummingbird in action too quick for understanding by our gross utilitarian standards, in action sensed rather than seen. The movie cameras of her day could not record her allegro. Her feet and hands photographed as a blur.

(4) Bright little bird bones, delicate bird sinews! She was all fire and steel wire. There was not an ounce of spare flesh on her skeleton, and the life force used her body until she died of the fever of moving, gasping for breath, much too young.

(5) She was small, about five feet. She wore a size one and a half slipper, but her feet and hands were large in proportion to her height. Her hand could cover her whole face. Her trunk was small and stripped

[2] Miss de Mille's father, William C. de Mille, began his career as a playwright but switched to directing motion pictures with his brother, Cecil B.
[3] A type of dance movement in which the dancer beats his feet together or beats one against the other.
[4] Famous ballerinas.

of all anatomy but the ciphers of adolescence, her arms and legs relatively long, the neck extraordinarily long and mobile. All her gestures were liquid and possessed of an inner rhythm that flowed to inevitable completion with the finality of architecture or music. Her arms seemed to lift not from the elbow or the arm socket, but from the base of the spine. Her legs seemed to function from the waist. When she bent her head her whole spine moved and the motion was completed the length of the arm through the elongation of her slender hand and the quivering reaching fingers. Without in any way being sensual—being, in fact, almost sexless—she suggested all exhilaration, gaiety, and delight. She jumped, and we broke bonds with reality. We flew. We hung over the earth, spread in the air as we do in dreams, our hands turning in the air as in water—the strong forthright taut plunging leg balanced on the poised arc of the foot, the other leg stretched to the horizon like the wing of a bird. We lay balancing, quivering, turning, and all things were possible, even to us, the ordinary people.

(6) I have seen two dancers as great or greater since, Alicia Markova and Margot Fonteyn, and many other women who have kicked higher, balanced longer, or turned faster. These are poor substitutes for passion. In spite of her flimsy dances, the bald and blatant virtuosity, there was an intoxicated rapture, a focus of energy, Dionysian in its physical intensity, that I have never seen equaled by a performer in any theater of the world. Also she was the *first* of the truly great in our experience.

(7) I sat with the blood beating in my throat. As I walked into the bright glare of the afternoon, my head ached and I could scarcely swallow. I didn't wish to cry. I certainly couldn't speak. I sat in a daze in the car, oblivious to the grownups' ceaseless prattle. At home I climbed the stairs slowly to my bedroom and, shutting myself in, placed both hands on the brass rail at the foot of my bed; then, rising laboriously to the tips of my white buttoned shoes, I stumped the width of the bed and back again. My toes throbbed with pain, my knees shook, my legs quivered with weakness. I repeated the exercise. The blessed, relieving tears stuck at last on my lashes. Only by hurting my feet could I ease the pain in my throat.

(8) It is a source of sadness to me that few of our contemporary

ballet dancers ever saw Anna Pavlova. At the time of which I write, her name was synonymous with the art—Pavlova, the Incomparable, was an internationally known slogan. She was as famous as Caruso and her position as unique. No one today approaches her power over the popular imagination. She half-hypnotized audiences, partaking almost of the nature of a divinity.

(9) My life was wholly altered by her—so I wonder, casting about in vain for similar dazzling influences, what first drove Kaye, Alonso, Fonteyn, Toumanova, and Helpmann to the *barre*.[5]

(10) She danced *The Dying Swan*. Everyone has danced *The Swan*. What was it? A series of *pas de bourrées* [6] around and around the stage with flutterings and undulations of the arms interspersed with broken staggers until the final collapse and folding away. Nothing else. Fokine composed it in half an hour for a charity performance, and it is probably the most famous solo in the history of dancing. When she trembled onto the stage it was a death agony, the voice in the dark, the final anonymous cry against annihilation. And when she lay doubled up and the last shudder passed through feathers and broken bones, drawing as an afterbeat when all was finished the shivering inert hand across her face in a gesture of final decency, everyone sat stricken. Death was upon each of us.

(11) Death came to Anna Pavlova in 1931, when she was fifty. She had not stopped touring for a single season. Her knees had sustained some damage, but she would not rest, and she was in a state of exhaustion when the train that was carrying her to Holland was wrecked. She ran out into the snow in her nightgown and insisted on helping the wounded. When she reached The Hague she had double pneumonia. Her last words were: "Get the *Swan* dress ready."

(12) Standing on Ninth Avenue under the El, I saw the headlines on the front page of the New York *Times*. It did not seem possible. She was in essence the denial of death. My own life was rooted to her in a deep spiritual sense, and had been during the whole of my growing up. It mattered not that I had only spoken to her once and that my

---

[5] A horizontal bar used in ballet exercises.
[6] A group of three or more steps danced in a staccato.

work lay in a different direction. She was the vision and the impulse and the goal.

(13) Pavlova's ashes were laid in the Golder's Green cemetery near her home, Ivy House, Hampstead Heath. All the glory of the last great Imperial days stood by. Karsavina was there. Lopokova, Massine.[7]

(14) But also in New York, in Los Angeles, in Paris, Berlin, Rome, San Francisco, wherever there was a Russian Orthodox Church, the dancers gathered, those that knew her and many more that didn't. I went in New York and all the dancers of the city were there. My mother came. She said she wished to, that she owed her a debt of many hours of joy. We stood. The Russians held lighted candles; the choir chanted with a high tonal insistency that wore down like rain on rock. The priest passed in and out of his painted, holy screens. A friend leaned to me. "They are singing," she whispered. "Receive the soul of Anna. Cherish our Anna. Bless and protect Anna." But I put my handkerchief to my mouth and heard the drums and the beating of feet and the cries she gave as she leaped. At the conclusion of the service Fokine, as senior friend, colleague, and Russian, received our condolences. He knew very few of us. We walked up silently, strangers, and shook his hand. His wife, Vera Fokina, in black from head to foot with sweeping veils, stood beside him.

(15) We went out into the day. Wherever Pavlova had passed, hearts changed, flames sprang in the grass, and girls ran out to a strange, wild, ancient dedication.

STUDY QUESTIONS

1. By what principle, if any, does Miss de Mille organize the details in this sketch? What does each paragraph contribute to the total picture?
2. How do the knowledge and point of view of the author govern the kind of sketch here given? Is any picture provided of Pavlova as a person? Would information about her ideas and attitudes be relevant in this essay?
3. What method of development is employed in each of the following paragraphs: 2, 5, 14? What basic metaphor underlies the development of

[7] Famous ballet dancers.

paragraphs 3, 4, and 5? What is gained by setting paragraph 9 up as a separate unit? Should it be added to paragraph 8? What is achieved by the brief last paragraph?

4. Select examples of parallelism in sentence structure from paragraphs 2, 3, and 5. Does the variety of sentence length in paragraph 5 fit the flow of meaning in that paragraph?

5. The emotional quality of Miss de Mille's experience is conveyed partly by highly connotative words. Select examples of such words. What is the force of the word *burn* in paragraph 1?

WRITING ASSIGNMENTS

1. Write a sketch of a person you have known intimately in the past (a relative or a close personal friend).

2. Write a description of a fictional character which greatly impressed you.

3. Write a word-portrait of yourself.

4. Write a sketch of someone you do not know intimately but of whom you have distinct impressions (a teacher, a public figure, a campus or town "character").

5. Write a research paper on an historical person.

New Mexico*

D. H. LAWRENCE (1885–1930), *English novelist and poet, was born in Nottinghamshire, the son of a coal miner. After a short period of school-mastering, he shifted to literature with the publication of his first novel,* The White Peacock, *in 1911. In 1912, he ran away with Frieda, wife of Professor Weekley of Nottingham University College, with whom he lived for the rest of his life except for some periods of separation. World fame came with the publication of* Sons and Lovers *in 1913. After the first World War, which was hard for him because of the German origin of his wife, he traveled about the world and continued to write novels and travel books, several of which, because of his treatment of sex, brought him into conflict with the police and with censorship boards.*

(1) Superficially, the world has become small and known. Poor little globe of earth, the tourists trot round you as easily as they trot round the Bois [1] or round Central Park. There is no mystery left, we've been there, we've seen it, we know all about it. We've done the globe, and the globe is done.

(2) This is quite true, superficially. On the superficies, horizontally, we've been everywhere and done everything, we know all about it. Yet the more we know, superficially, the less we penetrate, vertically. It's all very well skimming across the surface of the ocean, and saying you know all about the sea. There still remain the terrifying under-deeps, of which we have utterly no experience.

(3) The same is true of land travel. We skim along, we get there, we see it all, we've done it all. And as a rule, we never once go through

* From *Phoenix: The Posthumous Papers of D. H. Lawrence.* Copyright 1936 by Frieda Lawrence. Reprinted by permission of The Viking Press, Inc., New York. Written December 1928.
[1] A famous large park in Paris.

the curious film which railroads, ships, motor-cars, and hotels stretch over the surface of the whole earth. Peking is just the same as New York, with a few different things to look at; rather more Chinese about, etc. Poor creatures that we are, we crave for experience, yet we are like flies that crawl on the pure and transparent mucous-paper in which the world like a bon-bon is wrapped so carefully that we can never get at it, though we see it there all the time as we move about it, apparently in contact, yet actually as far removed as if it were the moon.

(4) As a matter of fact, our great-grandfathers, who never went any-where, in actuality had more experience of the world than we have, who have seen everything. When they listened to a lecture with lantern-slides, they really held their breath before the unknown, as they sat in the village school-room. We, bowling along in a rickshaw in Ceylon, say to ourselves: "It's very much what you'd expect." We really know it all.

(5) We are mistaken. The know-it-all state of mind is just the result of being outside the mucous-paper wrapping of civilization. Underneath is everything we don't know and are afraid of knowing.

(6) I realized this with shattering force when I went to New Mexico.

(7) New Mexico, one of the United States, part of the U.S.A. New Mexico, the picturesque reservation and playground of the eastern states, very romantic, old Spanish, Red Indian, desert mesas, pueblos, cowboys, penitentes,[2] all that film-stuff. Very nice, the great South-West, put on a sombrero and knot a red kerchief round your neck, to go out in the great free spaces!

(8) That is New Mexico wrapped in the absolutely hygienic and shiny mucous-paper of our trite civilization. That is the New Mexico known to most of the Americans who know it at all. But break through the shiny sterilized wrapping, and actually *touch* the country, and you will never be the same again.

(9) I think New Mexico was the greatest experience from the out-

[2] Penitents. Members of a New Mexican Christian sect which emphasizes extreme penances.

side world that I have ever had. It certainly changed me for ever.
Curious as it may sound, it was New Mexico that liberated me from the
present era of civilization, the great era of material and mechanical
development. Months spent in holy Kandy, in Ceylon, the holy of
holies of southern Buddhism, had not touched the great psyche of
materialism and idealism which dominated me. And years, even in the
exquisite beauty of Sicily, right among the old Greek paganism that
still lives there, had not shattered the essential Christianity on which
my character was established. Australia was a sort of dream or trance,
like being under a spell, the self remaining unchanged, so long as the
trance did not last too long. Tahiti, in a mere glimpse, repelled me:
and so did California, after a stay of a few weeks. There seemed a
strange brutality in the spirit of the western coast and I felt: O, let
me get away!

(10) But the moment I saw the brilliant, proud morning shine
high up over the deserts of Santa Fe, something stood still in my soul,
and I started to attend. There was a certain magnificence in the high-up
day, a certain eagle-like royalty, so different from the equally pure,
equally pristine and lovely morning of Australia, which is so soft, so
utterly pure in its softness, and betrayed by green parrots flying. But
in the lovely morning of Australia one went into a dream. In the magnificent fierce morning of New Mexico one sprang awake, a new part
of the soul woke up suddenly and the old world gave way to a new.

(11) There are all kinds of beauty in the world, thank God, though
ugliness is homogeneous. How lovely is Sicily, with Calabria across the
sea like an opal, and Etna with her snow in a world above and beyond! How lovely is Tuscany, with little red tulips wild among the
corn: or bluebells at dusk in England, or mimosa in clouds of pure
yellow among the grey-green dun foliage of Australia, under a soft,
blue, unbreathed sky! But for a *greatness* of beauty I have never experienced anything like New Mexico. All those mornings when I
went with a hoe along the ditch to the Cañon, at the ranch, and stood,
in the fierce, proud silence of the Rockies, on their foothills, to look
far over the desert to the blue mountains away in Arizona, blue as
chalcedony, with the sage-brush desert sweeping grey-blue in between,

dotted with tiny cube-crystals of houses, the vast amphitheatre of lofty, indomitable desert, sweeping round to the ponderous Sangre de Cristo mountains on the east, and coming up flush at the pine-dotted foot-hills of the Rockies! What splendour! Only the tawny eagle could really sail out into the splendour of it all. Leo Stein [3] once wrote to me: It is the most aesthetically-satisfying landscape I know. To me it was much more than that. It had a splendid silent terror, and a vast far-and-wide magnificence which made it way beyond mere aesthetic appreciation. Never is the light more pure and overweening than there, arching with a royalty almost cruel over the hollow, uptilted world. For it is curious that the land which has produced modern political democracy at its highest pitch should give one the greatest sense of overweening, terrible proudness and mercilessness: but so beautiful, God! so beautiful! Those that have spent morning after morning alone there pitched among the pines above the great proud world of desert will know, almost unbearably how beautiful it is, how clear and unquestioned is the might of the day. Just day itself is tremendous there. It is so easy to understand that the Aztecs gave hearts of men to the sun. For the sun is not merely hot or scorching, not at all. It is of a brilliant and unchallangeable purity and haughty serenity which would make one sacrifice the heart to it. Ah, yes, in New Mexico the heart is sacrificed to the sun, and the human being is left stark, heartless, but undauntedly religious.

(12) And that was the second revelation out there. I had looked over all the world for something that would strike *me* as religious. The simple piety of some English people, the semi-pagan mystery of some Catholics in southern Italy, the intensity of some Bavarian peasants, the semi-ecstasy of Buddhists or Brahmins: all this had seemed religious all right, as far as the parties concerned were involved, but it didn't involve me. I looked on at their religiousness from the outside. For it is still harder to feel religion at will than to love at will.

(13) I had seen what I felt was a hint of wild religion in the so-called devil dances of a group of naked villagers from the far-remote jungle in Ceylon, dancing at midnight under the torches, glittering wet with sweat on their dark bodies as if they had been gilded, at the

[3] Well-known art critic, brother of Gertrude Stein.

celebration of the Pera-hera,[4] in Kandy, given to the Prince of Wales. And the utter dark absorption of these naked men, as they danced with their knees wide apart, suddenly affected me with a *sense* of religion. I *felt* religion for a moment. For religion is an experience, an uncontrollable sensual experience, even more so than love: I use sensual to mean an experience deep down in the senses, inexplicable and inscrutable.

(14) But this experience was fleeting, gone in the curious turmoil of the Pera-hera, and I had no permanent feeling of religion till I came to New Mexico and penetrated into the old human race-experience there. It is curious that it should be in America, of all places, that a European should really experience religion, after touching the old Mediterranean and the East. It is curious that one should get a sense of living religion from the Red Indians, having failed to get it from Hindus or Sicilian Catholics or Cingalese.[5]

(15) Let me make a reservation. I don't stand up to praise the Red Indian as he reveals himself in contact with white civilization. From that angle, I am forced to admit that he *may* be thoroughly objectionable. Even my small experience knows it. But also I know he *may* be thoroughly nice, even in his dealings with white men. It's a question of individuals, a good deal, on both sides.

(16) But in this article, I don't want to deal with the everyday or superficial aspect of New Mexico, outside the mucous-paper wrapping, I *want* to go beneath the surface. But therefore the American Indian in his behaviour as an American citizen doesn't really concern me. What concerns me is what he is—or what he seems to me to be, in his ancient, ancient race-self and religious-self.

(17) For the Red Indian seems to me much older than Greeks or Hindus or any Europeans or even Egyptians. The Red Indian, as a civilized and truly religious man, civilized beyond taboo and totem, as he is in the south, is religious in perhaps the oldest sense, and deepest, of the word. That is to say, he is a remnant of the most deeply religious race still living. So it seems to me.

---

[4] The annual August festival held in honor of the eye-tooth of Buddha, a relic housed in a temple in Kandy.

[5] The principal race of Ceylon. The more normal spelling is *Singhalese*.

(18) But again let me protect myself. The Indian who sells you baskets on Albuquerque station or who slinks around Taos plaza may be an utter waster and an indescribably low dog. Personally he may be even less religious than a New York sneak thief. He may have broken with his tribe, or his tribe itself may have collapsed finally from its old religious integrity, and ceased, really, to exist. Then he is only fit for rapid absorption into white civilization, which must make the best of him.

(19) But while a tribe retains its religion and keeps up its religious practices, and while any member of the tribe shares in those practices, then there is a tribal integrity and a living tradition going back far beyond the birth of Christ, beyond the pyramids, beyond Moses. A vast old religion which once swayed the earth lingers in unbroken practice there in New Mexico, older, perhaps, than anything in the world save Australian aboriginal taboo and totem, and that is not yet religion.

(20) You can feel it, the atmosphere of it, around the pueblos. Not, of course, when the place is crowded with sightseers and motor-cars. But go to Taos pueblo on some brilliant snowy morning and see the white figure on the roof: or come riding through at dusk on some windy evening, when the black skirts of the silent women blow around the white wide boots, and you will feel the old, old roots of human consciousness still reaching down to depths we know nothing of: and of which, only too often, we are jealous. It seems it will not be long before the pueblos are uprooted.

(21) But never shall I forget watching the dancers, the men with the fox-skin swaying down from their buttocks, file out at San Geronimo, and the women with seed rattles following. The long, streaming, glistening black hair of the men. Even in ancient Crete long hair was sacred in a man, as it is still in the Indians. Never shall I forget the utter absorption of the dance, so quiet, so steadily, timelessly rhythmic, and silent, with the ceaseless down-tread, always to the earth's centre, the very reverse of the upflow of Dionysiac or Christian ecstasy. Never shall I forget the deep singing of the men at the drum, swelling and sinking, the deepest sound I have heard in all my life, deeper than thunder, deeper than the sound of the Pacific Ocean, deeper than the

roar of a deep waterfall: the wonderful deep sound of men calling to the unspeakable depths.

(22) Never shall I forget coming into the little pueblo of San Felipe one sunny morning in spring, unexpectedly, when bloom was on the trees in the perfect little pueblo more old, more utterly peaceful and idyllic than anything in Theocritus, and seeing a little casual dance. Not impressive as a spectacle, only, to me, profoundly moving because of the truly terrifying religious absorption of it.

(23) Never shall I forget the Christmas dances at Taos, twilight, snow, the darkness coming over the great wintry mountains and the lonely pueblo, then suddenly, again, like dark calling to dark, the deep Indian cluster-singing around the drum, wild and awful, suddenly rousing on the last dusk as the procession starts. And then the bonfires leaping suddenly in pure spurts of high flame, columns of sudden flame forming an alley for the procession.

(24) Never shall I forget the kiva of birch-trees, away in the Apache country, in Arizona this time, the tepees and flickering fires, the neigh-ing of horses unseen under the huge dark night, and the Apaches all abroad, in their silent moccasined feet: and in the kiva, beyond a little fire, the old man reciting, reciting in the unknown Apache speech, in the strange wild Indian voice that re-echoes away back to before the Flood, reciting apparently the traditions and legends of the tribes, going on and on, while the young men, the *braves* of today, wandered in, listened, and wandered away again, overcome with the power and majesty of that utterly old tribal voice, yet uneasy with their half-adherence to the modern civilization, the two things in contact. And one of these *braves* shoved his face under my hat, in the night, and stared with his glittering eyes close to mine. He'd have killed me then and there, had he dared. He didn't dare: and I knew it: and he knew it.

(25) Never shall I forget the Indian races, when the young men, even the boys, run naked, smeared with white earth and stuck with bits of eagle fluff for the swiftness of the heavens, and the old men brush them with eagle feathers, to give them power. And they run in the strange hurling fashion of the primitive world, hurled forward, not making speed deliberately. And the race is not for victory. It is not

a contest. There is no competition. It is a great cumulative effort. The tribe this day is adding up its male energy and exerting it to the utmost —for what? To get power, to get strength: to come, by sheer cumulative, hurling effort of the bodies of men, into contact with the great cosmic source of vitality which gives strength, power, energy to the men who can grasp it, energy for the zeal of attainment.

(26) It was a vast old religion, greater than anything we know: more starkly and nakedly religious. There is no God, no conception of a god. All is god. But it is not the pantheism we are accustomed to, which expresses itself as "God is everywhere, God is in everything." In the oldest religion, everything was alive, not supernaturally but naturally alive. There were only deeper and deeper streams of life, vibrations of life more and more vast. So rocks were alive, but a mountain had a deeper, vaster life than a rock, and it was much harder for a man to bring his spirit, or his energy, into contact with the life of the mountain, and so draw strength from the mountain, as from a great standing well of life, than it was to come into contact with the rock. And he had to put forth a great religious effort. For the whole life-effort of man was to get his life into contact with the elemental life of the cosmos, mountain-life, cloud-life, thunder-life, air-life, earth-life, sun-life. To come into immediate *felt* contact, and so derive energy, power, and a dark sort of joy. This effort into sheer naked contact, *without an intermediary or mediator*, is the root meaning of religion, and at the sacred races the runners hurled themselves in a terrible cumulative effort, through the air, to come at last into naked contact with the very life of the air, which is the life of the clouds, and so of the rain.

(27) It was a vast and pure religion, without idols or images, even mental ones. It is the oldest religion, a cosmic religion the same for all peoples, not broken up into specific gods or saviours or systems. It is the religion which precedes the god-concept, and is therefore greater and deeper than any god-religion.

(28) And it lingers still, for a little while, in New Mexico: but long enough to have been a revelation to me. And the Indian, however objectionable he may be on occasion, has still some of the strange beauty and pathos of the religion that brought him forth and is now

shedding him away into oblivion. When Trinidad, the Indian boy, and I planted corn at the ranch, my soul paused to see his brown hands softly moving the earth over the maize in pure ritual. He was back in his old religious self, and the ages stood still. Ten minutes later he was making a fool of himself with the horses. Horses were never part of the Indian's religious life, never would be. He hasn't a tithe of the feeling for them that he has for a bear, for example. So horses don't like Indians.

(29) But there it is: the newest democracy ousting the oldest religion! And once the oldest religion is ousted, one feels the democracy and all its paraphernalia will collapse, and the oldest religion, which comes down to us from man's pre-war days, will start again. The skyscraper will scatter on the winds like thistledown, and the genuine America, the America of New Mexico, will start on its course again. This is an interregnum.

STUDY QUESTIONS

1. What part of this essay constitutes the introduction? What specific functions does the introduction serve?

2. List the reasons why New Mexico appealed so strongly to Lawrence.

3. How does Lawrence qualify his conclusions? Why does he do so, do you think?

4. Lawrence points out a basic ironic contrast in this essay. What is it? In what way is it ironic?

5. What use does Lawrence make of contrast to develop his ideas throughout this essay?

6. Notice Lawrence's use of the fly image beginning in paragraph 3. What makes this image appropriate?

7. Why does Lawrence capitalize *God* the first time he uses the term, in paragraph 26, but not the second and third times?

8. Note Lawrence's use of repetition. How does it enable him to gain effectiveness?

9. Study the description in paragraph 11. What part of speech carries the heaviest burden of the description? Do pictorial verbs create the same effect as adjectives? If not, what is the difference? Illustrate from paragraphs 10 and 11.

10. What use is made of alliteration in paragraph 23?

11. Note the places where the author uses exclamation marks. What function do these exclamatory phrases and sentences serve? How do they fit in with the author's central purpose?

12. Why does Lawrence italicize so much? Is the use of italics usually a good practice? What justification can you find for it in this essay?

13. What shortcoming of modern man does Lawrence discuss in his first five paragraphs? On the basis of your personal experience, can you testify to the truth of his observations? If what Lawrence says is true, must one travel halfway around the earth to discover it, as he did? If not, what other ways are there to learn what he learned in New Mexico?

WRITING ASSIGNMENTS

1. Write a description of your college campus, unifying your details around a single dominant impression.

2. Write an analysis of urban life as it can be deduced from the downtown section of any large city or small town. Choose a central thesis and then develop it largely by means of descriptive details.

3. Write an essay in which you use as your thesis the last sentence in paragraph 3 of Lawrence's essay.

4. Write a descriptive account of natural scenery, or of a typical human scene, which has deeply moved you.

5. Write a research paper on the religion of an American Indian tribe.

The American Student as I See Him *

GILBERT HIGHET (1906–   ) is a professor of Greek and Latin at Columbia University. Born in Glasgow, Scotland, he attended Glasgow University and Oxford University. After teaching at Oxford, in St. John's College, he came to the United States in 1937. From 1941 to 1946 he served in the war. His writing includes textbooks on classical subjects, translations of several German works, translations of various poems in The Oxford Book of Greek Verse, The Classical Tradition (1949), an extensive survey of the influence of Greek and Roman literature upon the literature of modern Europe and America, and The Art of Teaching (1950).

(1) The American scholar I have long known and long respected. The American student I met first as an ambitious but depressed graduate working in the hard Scottish medical schools; then as an exotic graft on Oxford's gnarled trunk (like Vergil's tree, "admiring strange new leaves and fruit unlike her own"); and finally in several of the great universities of his own country. I like studying him, and he, by now inured to the fads of his preceptors, supports with surprising affability the endless process of being studied.

(2) As far as I can judge, he is unlike any other student in the whole world. For one thing, he often works three or four hours a day at some job which is at least extra-curricular, if not extra-mural. My friends at St. Andrews and Glasgow were often poor—much poorer than the freshmen whom I see cheerfully filing clippings or toting luncheon trays—but in term-time they never worked at anything outside their studies. The vast mythology of Scottish education is full of

* From The American Scholar, Autumn, 1941. Copyright 1941 by The American Scholar. Reprinted by permission of the author and The American Scholar.

stories about the crofter's son who lived all term in half a room on a barrel of oatmeal and a barrel of herrings brought from home, and then walked a hundred miles back to Inverquharity with the gold medal. And that ideal still persists. Occasionally British and French undergraduates do a little tutoring, and a dozen or two are bookshifters in the libraries or demonstrators in the labs; but they don't *work*. James Joyce's miserable Stephen Dedalus in Dublin, drinking watery tea and eating fried bread while he fingered his parents' pawn tickets, would have been far better for a decent meal earned by honest work.

(3) But it is not, or seldom, done. The feeling is that it would interfere with real work and equally real play: that it would keep the undergraduate from having his full share in the life of the university. And there is some truth in this. To spend three or four hours a day on something wholly unacademic nearly always narrows the student's interest in his academic work. He is apt to feel that it too can be done in the same way: two lectures, four hours at his job, four hours' study, and then stop. This therefore is one of the reasons why so few undergraduates in the universities here aspire to honors, compete for prizes, carry their interest in their courses further than the term paper. In France and Britain, on the other hand, it is common for lecturers to get notes from their undergraduate hearers questioning some statement, seeking a reference, asking for extended treatment of some difficulty. A not very intelligent pupil of my own at Oxford handed me a verse translation of six idylls of Theocritus, which he had made in his spare time during the two winter terms; in Jules Romains's *Les Hommes de Bonne Volonté* [1] a student at the École Normale Supérieure translates and annotates the choric odes of Sophocles, just for fun; and, at all the British universities, essay and poem competitions are nearly always burdensome to mark, there are so many competitors. But they would not have the energy, or even the interest, to do all that, if they had to manage a laundry agency for four hours a day.

(4) The American student himself feels this; for when he becomes

[1] *Men of Good Will.*

a graduate student, a radical change comes over him—a change far greater than the corresponding change in other countries. He will doggedly set himself to read and classify every Elizabethan sonnet, or memorize every decision arising out of the Snite Act; [2] he will plunge into labyrinthine bibliographies, from whose depths he can be heard faintly crying, as if he battled with unseen monsters, and from which he emerges through the gate of ivory, pale but up-lifted, like Aeneas from the world of the dead; [3] and when you and I make jokes to him, he will copy them and write "laughter" in the margin. It is scarcely too much to say that he then feels himself for the first time to be a whole-time student; and the only thing to be regretted about this metamorphosis is that it often keeps him from being a whole-time member of the university, that he is so often debarred by it from games and societies and other junior academic activities. He feels, not without a certain justice, that he is paying for the comparative diffuseness of his undergraduate days.

(5) There is another way of putting this. No European country thinks that education is, or ought to be, wholly democratic. Not even the United States does, in the last resort—for, in awarding fellowships and scholarships, its universities base their distribution not on *need* but on *achievement*. The principle of competition, thus tacitly acknowledged, is carried much further in Europe. In France the A.B. examination is a national contest, whose winners are rewarded not only with the civic tributes which the French know so well how to dispense, but with prizes, money, trips to Cambodia and certainty of a favorable start in their careers. The bad side of this is obvious— suicides are not at all uncommon among disappointed or overworked candidates, and a man's whole life can be darkened by a sense of his own inescapable inferiority, publicly and competitively demonstrated. But it makes the students read, and read hard. All scholarships in Britain (except a very few assigned to localities or family names) are awarded on the basis of a long and difficult competitive examination. And there are very many more scholarships there than there are in

[2] A fictitious act.
[3] In the *Aeneid*, Book VI.

this country: scholarships are endowed and awarded by cities, counties, prep schools, "public" schools,[4] colleges, universities, alumni societies, guilds and national associations. Besides those, there are hundreds upon hundreds of rich scholarships dependent on the wills of long-dead benefactors. I went through one university on money left by a thread manufacturer who died about 1850, and through another on the rentals of farms bequeathed for the purpose by a Court official of King [Charles the Second].[5] It would not be too much to say that the rich man who, in the United States, gives $50,000 for cancer research, gives £10,000 in Britain to support "a student who desires to enter the medical profession, said student to be selected by an examination on the fundamentals of. . . ." The University of Oxford is thought to be full of the leisure class. Yet in 1937 60 per cent of its students were wholly or partially supported by scholarships; and all those scholarships had to be won by keen and difficult competition.[6] From a certain Scots university there is one, and only one, scholarship which will take you to Oxford; and it is competed for by every student who wants it: pre-lawyers, chemists, historians, economists, mathematicians, philologists, they all sit there glowering at one another in the same examination room, and furiously laboring at the twelve three-hour papers on which their future depends. It is a painful ordeal; but it makes you study! Not only in France but in Britain too, enormous emphasis is laid on the exact position of a student in his class. Those who simply collect their grades and their clubs and leave are little regarded; must, practically speaking, have jobs waiting for them; find the higher careers closed. Those who try for honors find themselves arranged into a natural hierarchy, which, *ceteris paribus*, represents their comparative chances of getting a good position when they graduate.

(6) The American student, if I know him, would not care for this system. He would, I think, feel that it too highly rewarded the "grind"

---

[4] Consult the dictionary under "public school."

[5] The references here are to (a) the scholarship in Glasgow left by one of the Coats family, the biggest thread manufacturers in Scotland, and (b) the Snell Exhibition from Glasgow University to Balliol College, Oxford, left by John Snell (1629–1679).

[6] Since this article was written in 1941, it is out of date in a few particulars: for instance, Mr. Highet reports that there are now many more than 60 percent of the students at Oxford living on scholarships.

and undervalued the character-building and social qualities of college life; he would conclude it was unfair to boys who happened to attend schools which gave them less careful preparation for academic competition; ultimately he would think that, by subjecting him to a constant implied pressure, it deprived him of a good deal of his liberty. And yet, it seems to me that it would do him good, and improve the service of schools and universities to individuals and to the state.

(7) Take only one broad consideration. The development of government all over the world, in the democracies as well as in the despotisms, is towards a more numerous, more elaborate, and more highly trained bureaucracy. For good or bad, every national government now interests itself in the lives of its citizens far more closely than at any time since the Byzantine empire. Therefore it is necessary, year by year, for it to command a great supply of diverse and well-trained officials, mostly specialists of one kind or another. In the despotisms these officials are produced by the Party machine, selected and trained by a system which is at least methodically similar to education. In the democracies they are at present produced and trained by no system, except in a few fields like jurisprudence and public health. In Great Britain the diplomatic service, the higher branches of the civil service, and certain other administrative departments are recruited by rigorous competitive examinations for which, in practice, candidates prepare throughout the universities and even during their last years at school.[7] That system is thought to work well, although it is limited in extent. But many educators feel that the bureaucracies, both local and national, ought to be wholly staffed by men and women trained *on purpose*, and that in the democracies the schools and universities ought to be the organizations which produce and train them. Many a large store will not engage salesmen and saleswomen unless they are college graduates with noticeably good records; it is ludicrous that states and colleges should be less careful about choosing their executives. If we are to have a mandarinate, let us be as sensible as the Chinese in selecting our mandarins. If we want intelligent officials let us train them and discipline them and sift them by competitive examination and reward them with good, appropriate jobs, instead of letting our universities

[7] Consult the dictionary under "school."

annually pour out a huge undifferentiated mass of graduates, from which only luck or exceptional perseverance will direct the right man to the right place in the social machine.

(8) However, at present that is not done; and the American student, except in a few eccentric universities, estimates his achievement by time spent, which is quantitative, rather than by competitive achievement, which is qualitative. And yet he is at heart emulous. If it is presented civilly and winningly to him, he will welcome authority. He would welcome it still more if it were organized: if he felt that in school and at college its consistent purpose was to make him fit for a career which depended not entirely on his own whim, but on a long series of tests of his abilities and a constructive estimate of his character and capacity.

(9) Another unique attribute characterizes the American student: his huge numbers. Can four real universities exist in one city? Can it be possible that in one state fifty or sixty thousand youths and maidens are capable of the activity required to absorb a university education? Are the inhabitants of California (whose very name derives from a romance describing the Earthly Paradise) so talented that they can every year produce a myriad of university graduates? And what educators could be at once so inspiring and so industrious as to teach, effectively, this enormous horde? Or, finally, can the vast multitudes of adolescents in the United States all be so much more talented than their coevals in Canada, in France, in Sweden?

(10) The paradox, of course, conceals a dichotomy. To put it bluntly and generally, the American student who is not preparing for a profession does not often go to the university in pursuit of higher education. He goes to complete the education which his school left incomplete. He has been badly schooled. It is not his fault, and not wholly the fault of the school. But it is a pity. It sometimes strikes me with a sense of pathos to read the grave works on education, ranging all the way from Mortimer Adler's *How to Read a Book* to the bulletins of the Carnegie Institute for Educational Research, which treat the American school system in total detachment from all others,

as if it could learn nothing from Europe, and teach Europe nothing—
still less other continents. Mr. Adler, in his efforts to teach his patients
how to read books, makes one or two cursory references to the situation
in Europe, and throughout the rest of his prescription treats the
American student as a chimera bombinating [8] in the void. But of
course he finds it difficult to read Locke or Dante when he gets to
college. He has seldom been compelled to read anything difficult in
school. And a comparison, however invidious, would demonstrate that.
I went to a perfectly ordinary school in Scotland, P.S. 93 as it were.
In my last three years (ages 15–18) we were forced to read and understand *Hamlet, Macbeth, Henry IV*, Chaucer's *Prologue* and *Knight's
Tale, Polyeucte*,[9] *Le Cid*,[9] *Le Misanthrope*,[10] *Eugénie Grandet*,[11] *Seven
Against Thebes*,[12] *The Persians*,[12] *Iliad* XVI and XVIII, *Aeneid* II, IV,
and VI, Livy IX and several other books. And we read them. (Dickens
and Scott and Thackeray and so on, we had read long before.) We
had to, under that stringent discipline. We could write a character
of Macduff or Célimène,[13] we could reproduce the various explanations
and emendations of the "dram of eale" in *Hamlet*, we could compare
the shields of Achilles and Aeneas, we could write little essays on
Balzac's idea of realism. They were not very good; but they proved
that we had read the books. And we were not alone. In Edinburgh they
were doing the same. Bristol Grammar School was doing even more.
Sheffield and Manchester and London and Newcastle were doing
at least as much. French schools are still more arduous, although
they concentrate more closely on the classics of their own tongue; and
so, in a more limited way, were Scandinavian and Dutch schools,
and even German schools before the despotism.

(11) Now why does the average American student need to learn
how to read a book? Why does he approach *Hamlet* or *Crime and
Punishment* with a mixture of awe and bravado, and usually look up
from it with such puzzled delight and half-understood emotion? Mani-

---

[8] Booming.
[9] Plays by Pierre Corneille, 17th century French dramatist.
[10] Play by Molière, 17th century French dramatist.
[11] Novel by Honoré de Balzac, 19th century French writer.
[12] Plays by Aeschylus, ancient Greek dramatist.
[13] A coquette in *Le Misanthrope*.

festly because he has been ill taught at school. And, so far, that is nobody's fault: certainly not his; but there are two main reasons for the
fact.

(12) For one thing, the system of mass-education has nowhere else
been applied to a population so huge and so various. Only a nation
so gallant and so confident as the United States would have dreamt
of administering approximately the same education to the children
of long-settled western Europeans, recent central European immi-
grants, and many millions of emancipated Negroes, of whom Bigger
Thomas [14] with his revolt and his tragedy may well be partially sym-
bolic. Whenever I ask my pupils about their schooling they invariably
say, if they went to public school, that they were held back by the
size of the classes or by lazy and recalcitrant classmates. One of the
best students I have ever had praised the history master at his public
school most highly, but added that he was forced to devote himself
almost wholly to the upper one third of his class. In one of his more
frankly autobiographical essays Mr. James Thurber describes a tough
school in Columbus, Ohio, as it was a generation ago; and even if we
allow for humorous exaggeration there is still the ring of truth in the
sentence about his enormous Negro protector, Floyd: "I was one of
the ten or fifteen male pupils in Sullivant School who always, or almost
always, knew their lessons, and I believe Floyd admired the mental
prowess of a youngster who knew how many continents there were
and whether or not the sun was inhabited." And the problem is
complicated by the almost inevitable rigidity of the school system.
It is true that many high schools have recently endeavored to work
out special courses of study for pupils who are more intelligent than
the average; but such readjustments are not yet common, are nearly
everywhere tentative, and often meet with opposition. It is a task of
almost inconceivable difficulty to raise the educational standards of
an entire population; for at least two thirds of the boys and girls now
leaving American schools are much more highly educated than their
parents were. This difficulty does not exist in western European countries, and it fills me with admiration to see the courage and tenacity
with which it is being faced here. But, in education more than in

[14] Principal character in Richard Wright's novel *Native Son* (1940).

other things, each generation stands on the shoulders of its predecessor, and in another decade or so a great part of this difficulty will have been removed.

(13) The other reason is the comparatively lax discipline of schools in the United States. High school pupils spend appreciably less time in school here than they do in Britain, and much less than they do in France. In school they spend less time on actual study, because of the surprising amount of attention paid to extra-curricular activities. They spend far less time on preparation at home. And there is much less *drive* behind their learning than there is in western European schools. In the last two years at an ordinary British city school, corresponding to a good high school here, the ordinary pupil averages at least five and a half hours of actual classroom work in school and three hours' preparation at home, with a minimum of six hours' preparation at week ends. The working hours of two good provincial lycées in France, where friends of mine taught during the early '30s, are literally almost double those of an American high school. Any extra-curricular occupation, like producing the school magazine, or football practice, or rehearsing in the school orchestra, takes place outside working hours. And there is a constant disciplinary pressure to keep the pupils at work, to keep them actively attentive, to pull up the laggards and push on the leaders. Attendances are rigidly kept: an incident such as that reported in the New York papers in 1940, when a squad of policemen and truant officers "combed" the cinemas on two different mornings and rounded up nearly two thousand school children A.W.O.L, is frankly inconceivable. If anything like it occurred in Europe it would be instantly followed by the discharge or demotion of dozens of school teachers. It may not be unfair to suggest that some of the laxity observable in American schools is due to the much higher proportion of women acting as teachers. Adolescent boys cannot be properly disciplined by women, and adolescent girls only with much difficulty. But there are other reasons, which are too well known or too controversial to be discussed here. The fact remains. The American high school student has a far better time, but he does far less work than his European counterpart.

(14) Accordingly the American student, when he reaches college,

is not so well prepared as the average European freshman. He has not read so much, and he does not know how to read and write so well. He does not buy nearly so many books for his own enjoyment, if indeed he buys any at all. One distinction seems to me particularly significant. English and French undergraduates are apt to publish little magazines in which they practice fine writing: the first sonnet, the first political manifesto, chapters from the first autobiographical novel and so on. The American student hardly ever produces an imitation literary review. Instead, he produces an imitation of a daily newspaper, or occasionally an imitation of a comic weekly. Almost every distinguished contemporary French and British writer wrote his first publishable work when he was an undergraduate; almost no distinguished American writer wrote anything at college which in any way prefigured his later work.

(15) If I have not misunderstood the fairly widespread movement towards establishing "junior colleges" and the frequently emphasized distinction between the first biennium of college work and the second, they are based on this same fact: that some fairly intensive work is required to make up the deficiencies of the schools. Viewed in this light, the multitudinousness of the American student becomes (although still a little bewildering) intelligible and sympathetic.

(16) The third quality which forces itself on the observer of the American student is his freedom. He will, without great heart-searching, move from one university to another—a thing almost never done in France or Britain, and in Germany chiefly by very earnest undergraduates in search of a particular kind of specialized teaching or even of a particular professor. He will give up college altogether with a facility which still amazes me, although the dean's office usually knows exactly what proportion of the student body can be expected to drop out annually. He will in college drop subjects on which he spent four years in school; and he will take eccentric subjects or anomalous combinations of subjects with complete nonchalance. He is infinitely less cut to pattern (even allowing for his numbers) than the European student. In an English university it is often possible to tell what particular

college an undergraduate attends, and even what school he came from, after five minutes' general conversation; but seldom in the United States.

(17) This has its good side and its bad. It makes the American student far more self-reliant—one of my chief difficulties in Oxford was handling the timid, sheltered, pampered boy who might prove to be brilliant and might almost equally well be defeated and crushed; such difficulties hardly ever present themselves here. But, on the other hand, it makes him rather irresponsible, and even restless and discontented. Far too much is left to his own choice, at a time when he is scarcely capable of making a choice. Thanks to the kindly laxity initiated by President Eliot, he is free to take astronomy 17, comparative religion 1, government 33, Spanish drama in translation 21 and hygiene 2A (hygiene 2A is compulsory). A semester of that would, at best, produce a healthy cross between Sir Isaac Newton and the Duke of Plaza-Toro.[15] It is no wonder that the mixture sometimes fails to act, and discourages him that gives and him that takes. The opposite extreme is seen in the English "public" schools, where a schoolboy good at history will be tutored from the age of fifteen till the age of eighteen to win a history scholarship at a good college [16] specializing in history, will spend three or four years reading history for a first class in the final examinations, and then take history at his examination for entrance to the home civil service. (Usually, he will spend most of his time on the same period of history—e.g. medieval history, with special emphasis on the 12th century.) Both extremes are dangerous. The British extreme is often as narrowing as the other is bewildering: it needs, as an offset, the manifold external interests which only a great university and experienced tutors can give. But it has one merit in itself: it sets a premium on unremitting hard work and the long view. The other extreme broadens the student's mind; but it often broadens it without deepening it.

(18) Thus it is that the American student in his last two years at school does not often know what he is going to be, and still less often knows what he will learn in his university; and in the first two years at

[15] A destitute Spanish grandee in *The Gondoliers*, a light opera by Gilbert and Sullivan.

[16] For the use of this term in England, consult your dictionary.

the university (if he is not firmly steered by his parents into a profession) seldom knows how he will spend his junior and senior years, and how they will dovetail into his future. From one point of view, this shows a genuine, disinterested love of learning, a magnificent belief in the virtues of the university; but from another it means waste of good effort, waste of priceless time, waste of irreplaceable enthusiasm. The task of the university is to cast such a light on a man's youth as will illuminate him through his life, and yet to keep the light unblurred by the shadows of the temporary and the inessential. This task is always supremely difficult, but its difficulty is here enhanced by the inadequacy of the liaison between schools and universities and the lack of emphasis on the essentials of education. The schools have more than enough to do. They cannot tackle this job. It is for the American universities to look, like the wise man, before and after: to induce the student to surrender most of his freedom of choice for a more stable set of patterns in education. Wherever such compulsory patterns have been introduced he needs little persuasion to accept them; at Columbia he looks back on the arduous humanities course with feelings of pleasure and gratitude, not unmingled with surprise. He is a good fellow, the American student: he is energetic and ambitious; but he lacks direction, as the young do everywhere. "For," says Thomas Burton, "as he that plays for nothing will not heed his game; no more will voluntary employment so thoroughly affect a student, except he be very intent of himself." And, in these bad days, few of us are very intent of ourselves.

STUDY QUESTIONS

1. What are the three principal characteristics of the American student as Mr. Highet sees him? How is each introduced?

2. How does the first paragraph in this essay introduce the subject? Does it suggest the author's attitude toward his subject? Does it anticipate the principal method of development?

3. How does the concluding paragraph close the writer's discussion? How much of it is a recapitulation of points previously made? Are any new ideas introduced? Does it include any specific pleas for change upon the basis of the preceding arguments?

4. What difficulties are inherent in the kind of argument employed in

this essay, that is, argument based on comparison and contrast? How does Mr. Highet attempt to surmount those difficulties? What other kinds of argument does he use?

5. What specific means does Mr. Highet employ to avoid being dogmatic in his judgments of the American student? In view of the fact that his own education was not American, can one invalidate his arguments with the charge of prejudice?

6. What effect does Mr. Highet achieve by his use of the following words: *exotic* (1), *mythology* (2), *fingered* (2), *labyrinthine* (4), *glowering* (4), *on purpose* (7), *horde* (9), *bombinating in the void* (10), *tackle* (18)?

7. How would you characterize Mr. Highet's feeling toward the American student? Select specific evidence to substantiate your answer.

8. Can you think of any additional arguments either for or against Mr. Highet's position?

9. Of what relevance are Mr. Highet's arguments to you as a student?

WRITING ASSIGNMENTS

1. On the basis of your own experience, support or refute Mr. Highet in an essay of agreement or disagreement.

2. Write an essay supporting or opposing the practice of working at extra-curricular jobs while in college.

3. Write an analysis of the social function of a public school system.

4. Analyze the education you have received thus far and evaluate its accomplishments and its deficiencies.

5. Write a fully developed account of what you would consider a good educational program.

6. Write a research paper on the origin and/or history of elective courses in education.

Bread and Hyacinths *

WILLIAM H. CORNOG (1909–) is a graduate of the University of Pennsylvania. He has taught English at Northwestern University, and since 1943 has been president of Central High School in Philadelphia. He has been associated with various educational committees and important projects. In 1952 he obtained a leave from Central High School to serve as executive director of the School and College Study of Admission with Advanced Standing, a project financed by the Ford Foundation Fund for the Advancement of Education.

(1) I am, in this disputation, the devil's advocate, appointed to find flaws in a righteous argument. The argument is that secondary education must give pupils considerable occupational training, must give them salable skills. Many educators in this country have come to believe that this is a major responsibility of secondary schools. Those who have arrived at this position in their thinking have left a lot of other educators behind—among them, me. I am not merely a devil's advocate, then; I am a true heretic. My waywardness or backwardness may arise from ignorance of the true way—in which case I hope to return to Philadelphia a convert. On the other hand, it may result from a personal conviction that those out in the vanguard of vocational education are chasing will-o'-the-wisps.

(2) To speak more generally for a moment, I have not joined the great hegira from the Mecca of learning and cultivation into the desert of life adjustment. Lacking the state of grace of the theocrats of pedagogical seminaries, I am skeptical of righteous arguments and plausible

* From School and Society, July 8, 1950. Reprinted by permission of William H. Cornog and School and Society. This essay originally was given as a speech at the Vocational Conference at the University of Michigan on May 13, 1950.

30

testaments of educational salvation. Are we preparing our pupils for a voyage of adventure and danger or for a ferryboat run? If life is a ferry-boat run from breakfast to job to lunch to job to home to television set to bed and so to breakfast, then the friendly social philosophers who preach life adjustment are the wisest men among us and we had better all huddle around their cracker barrel. But if life is to be a moral and spiritual adventure and if living is to include the fine art of being a human being, we had better find some stars to steer by and some humane values to live by. It is one thing to know one's way around a provincial inland waterway, to learn the shoals and channels and be-come a skillful navigator of a narrow routine. It is quite another matter and a more important accomplishment to get one's "fix" in time and history and one's relation to one's fellowmen in broadest perspective, in terms of humanity and the world at large, in terms of man's art, literature, science, and philosophy. Is it more important for pupils to learn these things than to learn an occupation? My answer is that it is vastly more important. If it is so much more important, how much time in our secondary schools must be spent on this type of general education? My personal opinion is that so much time needs to be spent on it that there is very little time left for specialized education at what we now think of as the secondary-school level. I believe that specialized occupational training must be delayed to post-high-school years and can be delayed without injury to persons or to society at large. I be-lieve that there is time enough for specialized training after high school. There is general agreement that the next great advance in American education will be the rapid expansion of junior colleges and technical institutes. If there is a world for our youth to inherit, there will be time enough in that world, before they can get jobs, to learn their jobs.

(3) Any consideration of the responsibilities of education at any level in America must begin with a basic consideration of the total responsibility of our educational system. As a stick-in-the-mud classicist, I begin classically with the construction of a syllogism defining the relationship of democracy and education which I regard as extremely pertinent when one is taking up a knife to divide the school pie and trying to decide the size of the segment he shall mark "occupational training." This is the construction I make:

1. The democratic faith rests upon the postulation of primary, fundamental equality and assumes: (a) that *all* men are equally capable of and equally responsible for participating in the complex process of self-government; and (b) that public education—all education—will uphold that faith by imparting a common fund of knowledge and precept, a common sense of political obligation, and a common ability in intelligent judgment and election.

2. The democratic faith further holds that every man has the indisputable right to develop as an individual to the limit of his capacity and aspiration and is, therefore, entitled to an education which will enable him to live as richly in mind and spirit as his natural endowment will allow him to live.

3. Therefore, education in a democracy has the twofold objective of training a man to such social and political competency as will enable him to preserve life and liberty and to such philosophic balance and flexibility of mind as will serve him well in his pursuit of happiness.

(4) If that syllogism, both in its premises and in its conclusion, sounds idealistic, do not blame me. The assumptions made by the democratic faith are the most daring made by the mind of political man. Washington and Jefferson and their friends just wrote the general plan and won us an opportunity to work it out. We have preserved that opportunity to continue working it out through a Civil War and two World Wars, but democracy seems as difficult to follow as a political and economic creed as the Sermon on the Mount is as a moral one. I do not think that we shall settle the issue today, educationally, and the reason is that we educators have been committed from our cradles to the most outreaching idealism in religion, politics, and education that men have dared to conceive.

(5) Let us take, then, what we in America call the realistic approach. We are, we tell the world, a practical people.

(6) Examining the total responsibility of education as expressed in my syllogism we know that we cannot produce good men and good citizens with a snap of the fingers. We are training a generation of future citizens who will live and work in the society which we in our time have been trying to preserve and to advance. We cannot predict with much accuracy the conditions under which these boys and girls will live and work. We hope that they will live in freedom and by the principles upon which our country has been founded and by

which it has flourished. We see for them certainly a shortening of the working day and increased leisure—every technological advance seems to indicate that. We see also for them a foreshortening of their working years—at both ends of the span. Their useful employment will be longer delayed in their youth and sooner ended in their age, and medical science tells us that they will live longer. Some of the youngest of them today possibly will live, barring a world catastrophe, to a time when men shall have at their command such resources of energy as will make our coal, gas, oil, water, and derived electric power seem as puny as the horse and the ox seem to us. For what occupations shall we train them?

(7) Let us take our present high-school pupils. If I hold that we in the secondary schools have only a limited responsibility for the occupational training of our boys and girls, by what is that responsibility limited? It is limited by the great and growing responsibility of education in citizenship—which is far more than an education in history, or political science, or economics, or civics, and which will have to include not merely an understanding of our native ideology and mores but an understanding of the customs and thought processes of the other great nations of the world. The social and moral complexities of modern life demand a kind of broad and comprehensive education that will give men tools of continuous and life-long learning. The high school has a huge task in teaching even the rudiments of these tools. Our responsibility for job training is also limited by the increasing diversification and increasing specialization of occupations and trades. Can any secondary school hope to be all things to all men? Do we have unlimited facilities in our schools for the multiplicity of occupations to be trained for? How well can we train for how many? Can we ever keep pace with our technology and our expanding economy? Do we have the teachers and do they have the versatility, and can they have it? Or is there to be vocational predestination so that we can accurately predict that this specialized occupational training is *the* one for this pupil? Or shall we set up broad all-purpose occupational training? Can we compete in efficiency and economy with on-the-job training? Should we not give our pupils that which they cannot readily get or cannot get at all on the job—namely, general education? I see

little evidence of work as work becoming more attractive, though it may be somewhat casually argued that the more proficient worker is a happier worker. I see some opportunity for the schools to make leisure more endurable and useful. I see great opportunity for the schools to use what little time television allows them to train young people to that social and political competency by which their lives and their liberties may be preserved. I have never believed that the disciplines necessary to intelligent citizenship and a full life were the province of the academic curriculum alone. I have never condoned the practice of dumping the so-called low-ability groups into the commercial and industrial courses. I do not believe in developing a helot class of the hand-skilled and politically inept. I believe that we have a *limited* responsibility to train even the academically minded in some useful and employable skill, and I like the school-work program when it is not preached as a breathless new Evangel, but I believe that we have a major and overwhelming responsibility to train all pupils in the knowledge and the skill it takes to remain a free man. A free man is not one who prizes a job before all else. A free man is not one who seeks security above all else. If you would expand the occupational training in the high schools to give a greater measure of job security to our graduates—and to do it, some part of general education must go— you may end by giving them secure and quick employment in a country no longer free. I am frankly jealous of those years of adolescence and I believe that every day is precious. There is so much to be learned and so little time. It is more important to produce a thinker than a worker. An erring hand on a typewriter or a lathe is inconsequential compared with an erring hand on a voting-machine lever.

(8) You are well aware of the struggle now being waged for the minds of men. One ideology seeks to preserve man's independence of mind, speech, and action; the other seeks not merely to control men's minds but virtually to abolish them as functioning parts of a social order. One philosophy cherishes the intellect and reason and believes in the liberalizing force of a liberal, a general, education. The other philosophy believes in the subordination of intellect to instinct, believes in the excellence of conformity, "correct" attitudes, and habits of nonthinking co-operation and adjustment. This struggle to

preserve or to destroy the mind of man goes on in a seemingly innocuous way in education, too. Those who presume to teach only social attitudes and salable skills exalt adjustment and security and neglect the moral and rational as well as emotional springs of behavior. Those who exalt conformity and seek to produce the well-adjusted child and, I take it, the readily employable man have forgotten that progress most frequently comes by way of people who have the greatest reluctance to adjust and who have the least concern with security of employment. 1096375

(9) I am very skeptical, indeed, of the pretenses made by some educational theorists that they can teach significant lessons by mimicking in the schoolroom "real-life situations," as the loose pedagogical phrase goes. I do not believe that we can teach children to run the mazes of future problems by white-rat trial-and-error methods. Unless their reason be trained, unless they learn to think for themselves, they will be lost and without help if the maze of tomorrow does not quite resemble the maze of today. Learning by doing is an excellent principle, if one can be sure that the things done teach not merely their own doing, but the doing of things which will have to be done in the child's adult life. The only way a child can relate his present doings to his future is by an act of imagination, by the abstraction of the principle of the action, because only the principle of the action can endure through the manifold vicissitudes of life. For example, unless the principles of brotherhood and democracy be learned, the exercise of benevolent emotions and the use of pious pedagogical devices to create democracy in the classroom will break before the onslaught of the hypocrisy, greed, prejudice, and corruption of the adult world. The principles of right conduct and right thinking rest upon the postulation of the will to act and the ability to think. The will to act must receive its support from more powerful sources and sanctions than the habituation of childhood reflexes to patterned democratic stimuli. The will to act for the right must have its moral roots in religion or religious sentiment or some deep wellspring of the culture. Such wellsprings must be tasted by the intellect and the imagination, must be taken internally and not by baptismal rites of immersion in democratic "situations." To train men to act for the common good as men

by giving them deep-breathing exercises of living together as children is but half training, for if you can teach them intuitive democracy now, someone else can come along later and, by the same methods, teach them intuitive totalitarianism. The right choice of action must be and remain a rational and a moral choice and must arise from deliberation, an intellectual process, a process of critical discrimination of values. The responsibility to teach boys and girls to think, to discriminate among values, and to take a stand for the right as they see it—that responsibility is so great and so burdensome that any responsibility for occupational training in the high schools must be limited, indeed.

(10) What should be the curriculum of America's high schools? What should it be their major and almost all-consuming obligation to teach? I think that the dictators have given us the answer. When a dictator takes over a country he seizes the military and police powers first and suspends courts of law and justice. His immediate next step is to seize the schools and to burn books. What books does he burn? He does not burn the technical books, the "useful" books. He burns the books of art and of pure science; he burns the religious books and the works of poets and philosophers. He burns them in his own country first, and then he burns and destroys repositories of the spirit of man wherever he goes. He believes that by levelling the monuments to man's humanity—libraries, churches, schools, and universities—he can place the minds of men in chains.

(11) Believe me when I say that totalitarianism has shown what democracy's high schools must teach. We shall teach whatever dictatorship abhors; we shall teach whatever the dictator most fears; we shall teach that by which he is destroyed. We shall teach the humane studies which exalt the humanity of man. We shall teach the liberating knowledges which free and exalt his mind. We shall teach whatever confirms faith in the dignity of the common man and the preciousness of every soul. We shall teach such moral and spiritual values as will humanize and liberalize the minds of men. When we have done these things as well as we can, we shall then take time to teach the neutral and useful skills associated with bread-winning. We have a way of life to win first, and if we do not win it, black and bitter

will be the bread we shall eat then. There is a proverb which has been ascribed both to an anonymous Greek poet and to the prophet Mohammed, which runs: "If thou hast, of all the world's goods, but two loaves of bread remaining, sell one and buy hyacinths to feed thy soul." I am for letting some of the bread go and buying the hyacinth of liberty.

STUDY QUESTIONS

1. At what point does Mr. Cornog state the purpose of his article?

2. How systematically does Mr. Cornog review the arguments of his opponents, the advocates of vocational education? Does he state any of their arguments directly? Any indirectly, by implication? What bearing would Mr. Cornog's immediate audience have had on this matter?

3. What is Mr. Cornog's tone toward his opponents? Cite evidence from the text to support your answer.

4. What is the function of paragraph 5?

5. Analyze carefully the structure of paragraph 7. What is its topic sentence? How is it developed? What effect is gained by the series of interrogatory sentences? Would Mr. Cornog's meaning be altered if those questions were rephrased as positive assertions? Which sentences in this paragraph are assertions of principles? Which are illustrations of those assertions? What is the value of the illustrations?

6. What effect is gained by the use of repetition of structure in the last paragraph? What is the value of such repetition in a public address?

7. Make a list of the metaphorical expressions Mr. Cornog uses. From what cultural area do most of his metaphors come? Is that dominant imagery merely a reflection of the author's bent of mind, or does it have a special relevance to his subject? How does metaphor tie his opening paragraphs to his conclusion?

8. What connotations are carried by the following words and phrases: *righteous* (1), *desert* (2), *theocrats of pedagogical seminaries* (2), *dumping* (7), *breathless* (7), *presume* (8)? What do those connotations contribute to Mr. Cornog's argument? What do they reveal about his attitude?

9. In the sentence in paragraph 11 beginning "We have a way of life . . ." what effect is gained by the inverted word order of the second independent clause? Would normal word order do as well?

10. Mr. Cornog's argument rests on a number of basic premises, often stated in this article in conditional clauses. Make a list of these premises or hypotheses. Are any of them debatable?

11. Does Mr. Cornog's argument suggest any possibility of a compromise between his position and that of the vocational educators? Document your answer with evidence from the text.

12. How does your own high school education fit into the general picture drawn by Mr. Cornog? Does the issue he discusses have any relevance for you as a college student?

WRITING ASSIGNMENTS

1. On the basis of your own experience, write an essay attacking or defending Mr. Cornog's position.

2. Write an analysis of the role played by vocational education in the high school you attended.

3. Write an analysis of the extent to which you think college training should be vocational.

4. Write an essay elaborating upon Mr. Cornog's statement, "I believe that we have a major and overwhelming responsibility to train all pupils in the knowledge and the skill it takes to remain a free man."

5. Write a research paper on education in a totalitarian country: Soviet Russia, Germany under Hitler, Italy under Mussolini, etc.

The Humble Female*

AGNES ROGERS (1893–   ) *is an associate editor of* The Reader's Digest. *She has contributed articles and light verse to* Harper's Magazine, The New Yorker, McCall's, The American Scholar, *and other periodicals. In collaboration with her husband, Frederick Lewis Allen, Editor of* Harper's, *she has published* The American Procession (1933), Metropolis (1934), *and* I Remember Distinctly (1947). *On her own she has written* Flight (1935), Why Not Enjoy Life (1937), Abraham Lincoln, A Pictorial Biography (1939), Vassar Women (1940), From Man to Machine (1941), *and* Women are Here to Stay (1949).

I

(1) Not so long ago I was meeting my young friend Margaret for lunch. "Do you mind stopping at the bank first?" she asked. "I have to send some money to my boss. He's in Washington, and he telephoned this morning that he's short of cash. It won't take a minute."

(2) It wouldn't have taken a minute, either, if when we got to the bank we'd happened on the bright and capable Miss Dixon first. But she wasn't sitting at one of those desks out in the open. That is where the men sit. A very handsome young one was at the desk we stopped at. He rose courteously as we approached and listened with mounting bewilderment while Margaret, with admirable clarity, stated the nature of her errand.

(3) He didn't get it the first time and, after her second try, shook his head sadly. "Oh, we couldn't very well do that," he said.

(4) "But Mr. Kent has an account here—has had for years,"

* From *Harper's Magazine*, March 1950. Copyright 1950 by Harper & Brothers. Reprinted by permission of the author and Harper & Brothers.

Margaret explained, "and besides, here is a check made out to him for the exact amount."

(5) The handsome young man looked around helplessly, then his eye brightened as a girl came briskly by. "Oh, Miss Dixon," he called, "have you got a moment? Will you take care of these ladies?"

(6) Miss Dixon understood the problem immediately. "Of course," she said, "it's very simple," and led us to a window where there was another man, elderly this time, and not very glad to see us. Miss Dixon explained the situation carefully and then, step by step, told him what to do. Even so he had to be prompted by Margaret several times after Miss Dixon had left us. Margaret is a quick study.

(7) We laughed about it a bit at lunch and said that what that bank needed was more Miss Dixons, or to make Miss Dixon president. We agreed that the latter seemed unlikely (both of us having read in *Time* that while women hold 60 per cent of all bank jobs, they hold only 10 per cent of bank executive jobs). Just why Miss Dixon will in all probability never be president of this bank it is hard to say. Very likely the officers of this large New York bank have never seriously considered the possibility of a woman president. (There are some women bank presidents, but most of them are in small towns. Mrs. Georgia Clark, for instance, the Treasurer of the United States, was formerly the president of a bank in Richland, Kansas, population 200.) It may well be that the directors, the borrowers, the depositors would not care to see a woman in charge in this traditionally masculine field.

(8) But it may also be that Miss Dixon herself would shy violently away from such an idea. She'd much rather be right where she is than president.

(9) I well remember a conversation I had with a friend with whom I had been working in a wartime government agency which was about to dissolve. She had had a position of real responsibility and had executed her manifold duties with apparent ease and vigorous good sense. We were talking about what we would be doing next. "You know," she said, "it sounds absurd, and I'm ashamed to admit it, but the kind of job I really want is to be that invaluable assistant to a man who is doing something I believe in. I'd work like a nailer,[1]

[1] Work hard.

and I'd be so tactful that he wouldn't know how much he depended on me, but I want him to make the final decisions." She paused a minute and then said reflectively, "I think it's the kind of job most women really want." I may confess that her words gave me a real shock, but I believe that she uttered a profound truth. I believe that a great many women have an essentially low opinion of their own powers, that they are possessed by a feeling of humility that is at the same time touching and infuriating.

(10) In the rash of recapitulations of the half century just ended that has been appearing in periodicals and broadcast over the air, hardly a commentator has failed to mention the emancipation of women as one of the most striking phenomena of the period. And, indeed, the political, economic, and social changes in the status of women during the past fifty years represent—in theory, at least—an accumulation of freedoms and opportunities that *should* add up to a brave new world hardly dreamed of by the early feminists. I hardly need to enumerate them: all the way from the right to vote and to hold public office, the right to enter practically any field of work, and the broader opportunity for higher education, down to the right to drink and smoke in public, restrictions and taboos have disappeared right and left.

(11) The astonishing thing is that, with all these gains, the great majority of women regard themselves so slightly and put so low an estimate on their individual worth as members of society as a whole.

(12) There seems little doubt that this is true. Everyone I know who has done much volunteer work with women declares that for each one who will head up a committee or take charge of a drive, there are dozens who shrink from a position of responsibility. "Let me lick the stamps," they beg. Devoted and hard-working, they are so humble that they do not honestly think they are capable of making decisions or directing other people.

(13) For the sake of argument, I'll admit that perhaps many of this type may be found among the older women who grew up before the era of their liberation, and who still think along the old lines: that woman's work is the execution of small details, necessary but unremarkable, while someone else—a man—directs the enterprise. These

are the women who have always worked in the Ladies' Aid or the Women's Auxiliary and never dreamed of being on the Vestry (although everybody in town knows that without their support the church would fade away).

(14) Well, what about the younger women? What about the girls ending college and contemplating the next step? Are they for the most part confident, self-assured? Do they give the impression that the world is their oyster?

(15) During the past few years I've had the opportunity of talking to the heads of vocational bureaus in several women's colleges, and it has been my good fortune, too, to discuss jobs with a fair number of the girls themselves. These girls have struck me as highly intelligent, mature, and capable—so much more knowledgeable and generally attractive than my own college generation was at the same age that I am awed by them. But I am also struck by how often these most excellent young women lack the confident ambition that their equipment would seem to warrant. Modesty is a pleasing quality, but their approach is often more humble than modest, and their reasons for wanting a job are strangely nebulous. "All my friends are working," or "I'd like to live in New York," or "I have to do something" recur over and over. Obviously all girls emerging from college aren't in this category. The surprising thing is that so many are.

(16) Nobody expects the recent graduate to have a long-range program planned in detail. Lots of people don't know exactly what they want to do. They have to feel their way around and see how they can fit into our complex industrial pattern. I do think, however, that the girl who announces that she would like a research job, and apparently hasn't thought of anything beyond that, is setting her sights pretty low. The safe and anonymous spot where you work hard and someone else signs his name and takes the final praise or blame may be all very well, but the positive note, not to mention the pioneer note, is certainly lacking. I have noticed, too, when girls discuss a change of jobs, how seldom they seem to have explored the possibility of making something more of the old job before giving it up. Instead of looking around to see what needs to be done in the office where they are working, and how it could be done, they complain about lack of

opportunity and advancement—forgetting that advancement usually comes to those who can see beyond their noses.

(17) As far as these girls are concerned, one must not forget that their generation has taken quite a beating. Children of the Great Depression, they faced up to World War II at a highly impressionable age. It is little wonder that their generation—girls and men alike— views the chances of another depression or another war with a special dismay, and wants to hold on to and cherish whatever it can of the normal, the stable, the safe, rather than to reach out for the uncertain. The concept of security has been dinned into us as the chief desideratum for some years now, and it's not surprising that young people have been persuaded by this most unsiren-like song.

(18) A *Fortune* survey of the class of '49 (which numbers some 150,000 men) from some 1,200 colleges reveals that in general "Forty-nine is taking no chances . . . what they don't want is risk. Bulling about the future, the state of the economy, and their place in it, they seem, to a stranger from another generation, somehow curiously old before their time. Above everything else, security has become the great goal."

II

(19) The preoccupation with security is not, then, a quality of mind that is confined to women. Men want it too. But it's the women I'm talking about, and I cannot believe that this is the whole explanation of their humility. Let's return to those great gains made for and by women in the past fifty years. How much has been real and how much illusory? One field where the results are comparatively easy to estimate is in "gainful occupations." How much has the picture changed since the days when nursing and teaching were almost the only polite occupations in which women could engage?

(20) Numerically speaking, the change is enormous. More than eighteen million women—about 30 per cent of the nation's labor force —are in paid employment (a significant term if ever there was one, implying that the active housekeeper's daily routine is of no economic value!). The figure has been rising for a long time, and there seems

to be no reason to suppose that it will presently begin to slide down-hill. Moreover, the fields open to women appear to include practically everything. Ten years ago the census report showed women employed in all but nine of the 451 job classifications. Even in the professions, there are very few graduate schools left that refuse admission to women students. The Harvard Medical School, for example, held out against their admission for many years, and capitulated after World War II. The war demonstrated women's ability to learn highly technical skills with an ease that surprised everybody. And the idea of women working outside the home is now so socially acceptable that the daughters of even prosperous families look for a job as a matter of course, when they leave school or college—unless they are getting married at once or taking graduate courses.

(21) So far so good; but on closer examination, the available data are less impressive. There is no question as to the complete acceptance of the feminine secretary in the business world. How many times have you heard a man boast about his secretary? A good many, I'll warrant. "She's the real brains of this outfit" or "She knows more about this business than I do" are familiar accolades. Nobody has any doubts about the place of the good secretary in the industrial scene. She's indispensable, that's all. In this essentially secondary, ministering role, she has won a secure place for herself. But when one examines the higher echelons, women are much less numerous than one might expect. There's no biological reason why women can't be presidents, vice presidents, editors-in-chief. Too many of them are filling these positions for that old argument to hold water. Josephine Roche, Elizabeth Arden, Edna Woolman Chase, Carmel Snow, Dorothy Shaver,[2] to mention only a few conspicuously successful executives, have conclusively proved that women can get to the top. It is quite possible to make an imposing list of women in high executive jobs. The wonder is that such lists are still compiled, that a successful business woman

[2] Josphine Roche is a prominent industrialist and lecturer, who served as Assistant Secretary of the U.S. Treasury after her defeat in the campaign for the Governorship of Colorado in 1934. Elizabeth Arden is the founder and sole owner of the large cosmetics firm bearing her name. Edna Woolman Chase, mother of Ilka Chase, is the editor-in-chief of *Vogue*. Carmel Snow is the editor of *Harper's Bazaar*. Dorothy Shaver is the president of Lord and Taylor, the New York department store.

should be news. And in the lower brackets, where most of the working women are found, they do not yet get equal pay with men for the same kind of work. In the professions and the arts (with the exception of writing and acting) women's performance cannot compare with men's in terms of per capita distinction.

(22) It is impossible to say whether this is the fault of women themselves or of the way business and the professions are rigged. I suspect that both are responsible and that it makes for a vicious circle.

(23) Politically the situation seems to be much the same. When women got the vote in 1920, there were those who predicted that in a short time women would be holding office all over the place. Nothing of the sort happened. In a speech given early in 1948 to the Women's Bureau Conference, Miss C. Mildred Thompson, Dean of Vassar College, said, "There are, of course, today notable women in high political offices, and it has been the custom in the last few years for the Administration to appoint one woman on each of several important public commissions. But notice, please, that it is generally *one* woman, not five or six among a dozen members. This continued failure to assume full positions of power remains a problem. It is a surprise and a source of disappointment to many women—and to some men—that in these thirty years almost since women attained the franchise, so few women hold public office high or low, and so few even have stood for election to office."

(24) Again I rather imagine that the fact that women have not risen more noticeably to "full positions of power" in the political world is not wholly their fault. In the smoke-filled rooms as around the directors' boards there are still a great many men who would not be entirely at ease if there were women present, and the problems of a woman in authority over men are infinitely greater than when the situation is reversed.

(25) So when we reflect on these two great gains—the freedom to choose one's occupation and the right to vote and to hold public office —we see that women have still a long way to go before they realize completely the dreams and aspirations of the early champions of women's rights.

(26) The last thing I would advocate would be a return to the

militant tactics of some of the early feminists. Their battles were fought and won with an aggressiveness that would today be as out-of-date as it would be unlovely. Let us not forget the doors they opened; the woman of 1950 doesn't have to push her way in, she does have to make herself welcome. Only by the exercise of her own individual talents and powers in full co-operation with others can she make the contribution to society that the times need. Part of Mrs. Roosevelt's extraordinary influence is due to the very fact that she is a woman and talks a woman's language. Senator Margaret Chase Smith's ability as a politician is certainly in no way hampered by the fact that she is a very attractive person.

(27) And what about the housewives? Freedom from domestic drudgery is something that is talked about a good deal, particularly by the manufacturers of household machinery, and there is no question but that labor-saving devices and processed foods have vastly simplified the techniques of cooking and cleaning and washing clothes. But there are two sides to this medal. Servants have largely disappeared from the homes of all but the wealthy, small children still need constant attention, and the business of housekeeping takes more time, no matter how many mechanical aids you have, than the advertisements suggest. Moreover, even if some time has been saved, the disappearance of fine needlework and other domestic crafts has cut off a number of outlets for creative energy that our grandmothers enjoyed and took pride in. (We're trying to re-open small creative avenues with our talk about hobbies, but such occupations used to be part of daily home living.) In short, in simplifying the work of the house, we have shorn the position of housekeeper of much of the dignity and prestige it once had. Women are not as proud of the title of good housekeeper as they were when housekeeping was an executive job, with servants to direct, household arts and crafts to supervise and execute, and when mother and father were nearly absolute authority. (Those were the days before the phrase, "Mother knows best," was the big joke it is today. She used to think she *did* know best, poor soul, before that was beaten out of her.)

(28) It must be admitted, too, that women get very little to bolster their morale from reading about themselves. And there's a lot to read

—usually under the general heading, "What's the Matter with Women?" You don't find people writing on "What's the Matter with Men?" They write about the shortcomings of American husbands or business men or politicians or farmers, but they don't take the entire sex as a target. But with women, it's always open season—and they are lumped together as if all women were alike. They are scolded for being clinging and possessive mothers and demanding wives; they are sighed over by the older feminists, men and women, for not making the most of their great opportunities; they are criticized for leaving home, and they are urged to get out of their homes. At the same time, they are exhorted to protect and elevate public morals and manners, to work for the good of the community, to keep alive the sacred flame of the arts, and to be the pillars of the church. Moreover, as keepers of the family purse, they are cajoled and bullied by the advertiser with all the artful cunning he can muster—which is considerable. It is small wonder if some, confronted by this formidable list of obligations, feel that they are failing.

(29) But in addition to these, perhaps the strongest reason for a humble attitude on the part of many women is quite simply the desire to be liked by men. The old notion that men love only those women who look up to them with passive admiration has been given a new lease on life by certain present-day psychiatrists who are saying firmly that society is sick because women are sick; and that the reason women are sick is that they have been trying too hard to compete with men, that they have special emotional stresses and strains that are resolved only by strict devotion to the role of wife and mother. This attitude is reflected—as Mirra Komarovsky pointed out in the November *Harper's*—in a movement in educational circles to change the college curriculum for girls on the grounds that it was mistakenly patterned after that of the men's colleges and that girls should be taught quite different things—things like preparation for marriage, bringing up children, household economics. (As if they and they alone were responsible for family life!)

(30) This seems to me to be getting back to the battle of the sexes that I thought we'd got over. I cannot see that much is going to be gained by all this emphasis on women as females, and I can see a great

deal lost. For in the great historic movement of the past century toward human liberty and equality, the changing status of women has been only one aspect of the general revolution. Women did not win what rights they now possess through their own efforts alone. Nor will they be able to adapt themselves fully to their changed status of today and tomorrow without the understanding aid of men; and everything that separates men and women into different categories instead of strengthening their community of interests is a brake on civilized progress.

III

(31) Is there anything to be done to help women disabuse themselves of their humility? I think there are several things. The first is to understand the interweaving pressures and the changes that have come about, some rapidly, some slowly, and to bring our own social thinking up to date to conform with the real conditions of today's living. We are burdened with a number of outworn ideas and concepts that are costly anachronisms and cloud the scene. In spite of these, many women have adjusted to their changed status with marked success. They are not humble-minded, and we don't have to worry about them. It's the others, who haven't adjusted so well, whom we're considering. Each individual must, of course, in the long run, do her own adjusting, but it isn't quite fair to put the whole burden on her, for it's everybody's business.

(32) Before I move on to specific ideas that I think we should discard, let me point out a factor in women's lives today that is comparatively new and much more important than many of us realize— the lack of continuity. When families were larger, and the period of child-bearing consequently longer, the married woman passed from the duties of mother to the duties of grandmother with only a small break in time. And the duties and pleasures of grandmother were very real. Now, with a period of work outside the home before marriage, and usually up to the time children begin to come, you have a very different picture. The young mother is faced with a complete change of occupation, with demanding duties, until her children are fourteen

or fifteen, and then, when she is in her forties, these duties are done, and she has to make another radical change and find some rewarding occupation if she doesn't want to face a series of empty days and a general feeling of uselessness. Grandmothers are pretty well intimidated these days and are told to keep out of the way—unless, of course, a crisis arises. Indeed, the problems of the older woman are serious enough to rate a whole new literature.

(33) In short, it's more complicated to be a woman. More complicated than it used to be? More complicated than to be a man? Both.

(34) And now as to the ideas I believe it's time to abandon. First, I'd like women to think of themselves first as people and then as women. I'd like men to do the same, but that's probably asking too much, right at the start. I am, I will confess, tired of the automatic laugh the word "wife" produces in some circles of male society. It's like "Brooklyn," and seems to have succeeded "mother-in-law."

(35) Our intense preoccupation with youth is another concept that has got out of hand. Granted that youth is—or can be—highly attractive, and that Browning was certainly stretching things in that "best is yet to be" line,[3] still the aspect of youth that is most often presented to us—in mass media at any rate—is physical charm or the eccentricities of the teen-agers, rather than the tireless vigor, the confident idealism, the fearless adventuring spirit that are the classic attributes of youth.

(36) The older man has been getting a break lately: Hardly a critic failed to remark gratefully on the novelty of the middle-aged planter's winning the young Army nurse in "South Pacific," and the intense and widespread interest in the recent marriages of Vice President Barkley and Mayor O'Dwyer would seem to show that glamour-beyond-fifty for men is a concept that the public is prepared to accept. But that a mature woman might have some charm of her own is still dismissed as absurd, if not downright unwholesome. If by any chance such a creature appears in popular fiction, she is up to no good, and is a cause of acute discomfort and misery to her family. This pressure

---

[3] Rabbi Ben Ezra, in Browning's poem of the same name, remarks,
"Grow old along with me!
The best is yet to be,
The last of life, for which the first was made:"

to remain young, or to attempt to preserve an illusion of youth, shows up even among scientists; in a recent issue of the *Journal of Social Psychology*, Ralph R. Norman comments on the fact that ten times as many women as men fail to list their age in the Directory of the American Psychological Association, and attributes this concealment to (1) the glorification of youth in our culture; (2) the premium placed by society on marriage and motherhood; (3) a potential competition with men for jobs, where the older woman is at a double disadvantage, on the score of age as well as sex.

(37) That marriage per se is the ultimate in happy security is another concept that we'd better jettison. One might suppose that the fairy-story ending, ". . . and so they were married and lived happily ever after," belonged to the literature of the nursery, or of the Victorian era, but a glance at any issue of any woman's magazine shows that this is not so. Page after page is illustrated with close-ups of melting girls and ardent youths clasped in fond embraces, and although the final goal—matrimony—is not reached until you get to the back of the book, there it is, the solution to all problems. It seems hardly necessary to point out that marriage is not an end in itself, that like every other worth-while thing it has to be worked at, that the wedding is the starting point, not the finish line, that divorce is unhappily on the increase, or that single women have been known to have full, happy, even distinguished lives. One can only wonder at the persistence of the myth that marriage automatically ensures a safe and desirable existence.

(38) The mechanics of daily living—the way she spends the hours —is something that every woman has to decide for herself, but the married woman who wants to work outside the limits of the domestic routine has to consider the needs and desires of the family group. It must be remembered that the mother of young children who undertakes a full-time job outside the home must have an abundance of energy; and also that the cost of competent care for the children in her absence comes high. It can be done, it has been done successfully, but it takes a lot of doing.

(39) The married woman who works is not flouting convention, but whereas it is accepted that the man is the breadwinner and no

nonsense, the wife who through necessity or choice (or both) sets out to augment the family income will have a much easier time if her husband regards her efforts as having equal importance to his own, even if the financial return is less. And our thinking should somehow be adjusted to the fact that if the woman happens to make more money than her husband it is not a real "problem" in their relationship.

(40) I cannot emphasize strongly enough my point that I am not urging an active career in the outside world for *all* women. I am only hoping that women who do undertake such ventures will set their sights a little higher, will not shrink from responsibility, will occasionally take the daring chance, essay the high venture, and will realize that opportunities are not always plainly so labeled. Sometimes you have to make them yourself. That there are still dead ends for women in various fields, I admit, but these ends can be moved back if we push hard.

(41) Nor am I suggesting that the housewife rush out immediately and organize a drive for slum clearance or undertake an investigation of the state of affairs in the nearest mental hospital, or take up the lute and Sanskrit. I do believe that in many communities, however, there could be a healthier distribution of civic energy if more attention were paid to individuals as such and if it were not assumed that men hold the executive jobs and women do what they are told. At the very least, in social gatherings, it would be refreshing to hear more women join in the talk about politics or foreign affairs without the shield of a quotation from Edward Murrow [4] or "my son in Washington."

(42) I've tried to suggest some of the causes that contribute to the humility of women who have no business being humble: but they are offered as explanations, not as excuses. What this country—in its new, if unsought, position of world leadership—needs is a vigorous and fearless society in which men and women work and live together in mutual respect and good will. There's too much to be done to allow those who have gifts and advantages the luxury of sinking into the back seat, however comfortable it may be.

---

[4] Radio reporter and news commentator who gained special prominence with his broadcasts from London during World War II.

STUDY QUESTIONS

1. Is the title of this essay appropriate to Miss Rogers' subject? In general what criteria determine a good title? Does this title satisfy these criteria?

2. Miss Rogers introduces her essay with an anecdote. What other kind of introduction might have been used? Write out an example of a different kind of introduction to this essay.

3. Miss Rogers devotes Sections I and II of her essay to a discussion of the apparent unjustified humility of women outside the home. How does she account for that humility? What is the basis of her division of this discussion into two parts?

4. What important turn does Miss Rogers' argument take in Section III? Why does this section come last in the essay?

5. To make her point, Miss Rogers uses illustrative narratives, allusions to historical and contemporary fact and persons, quotations from and references to authorities, and statistics. What do they contribute to the effectiveness of her essay? To what extent is the use of material of this sort justified in expository essays? Is it possible to use too much of such material? How does one determine how much is enough?

6. Study the opening sentences in the following paragraphs: 8, 13, 14, 21, 24, 27, 29, 31, 34. How do they connect their paragraphs with the preceding discussion? How do they serve to arouse or hold the reader's interest?

7. Normally, except in occasional dialogue, the best contemporary writers write in an easy informal style of diction and syntax—in what might be called good informal English. Does Miss Rogers write on this level? Select some words and phrases which you think are typical of her level of diction.

8. What does Miss Rogers mean to imply by the phrase *Victorian era* in paragraph 37?

9. Notice Miss Rogers' use of the first person singular pronoun. What effect is gained by the use of this point of view? Rewrite paragraphs 16 and 17, using an impersonal point of view.

10. How would you characterize the tone of this essay? Do you think it is appropriate to Miss Rogers' subject? Explain your answer.

11. Analyze Miss Rogers' argument closely for strengths and weaknesses. Is her presentation dogmatic? Is she in any sense biased? Is she a qualified authority on her subject? Are all her points equally strong? If

not, which are strongest? Can you think of any further arguments she might have used?

WRITING ASSIGNMENTS

1. On the basis of your own experience write an essay on your reaction to Miss Rogers' essay.

2. Write an analysis of female attitudes on your campus as evidence for or against Miss Rogers' thesis.

3. Write an argument for or against the idea and/or the practice of a married woman's pursuing a career.

4. Assuming that the social role of women changes in the ways Miss Rogers suggests, draw an imaginary sketch of the woman of tomorrow.

5. Write a research paper on the Feminist Movement in the United States.

Bibliotherapy*

IRWIN EDMAN (1896–   ) *is a professor of philosophy at Columbia University who has held many visiting professorships and lectureships elsewhere. His literary productions have been very extensive, including numerous contributions to magazines and newspapers, a dozen books written on his own, and several more which he co-authored or edited. Among his more popular works are* Philosopher's Holiday (1938), Philosopher's Quest (1947), *and* Under Whatever Sky (1951), *a collection of short pieces from Mr. Edman's column in* The American Scholar.

(1) The brisk little man came into my office and said he wanted to study philosophy because he needed it in his profession. In a small South American country (though he himself is a European), he had been practicing what seemed to be a vague, free-wheeling psychiatry. He had discovered, he told me blandly, that many of his patients could best be cured by prescribing the proper books. Apparently quite by accident he had discovered that certain of the books that were most healing were philosophical books, about which, he said, he had hitherto concerned himself very little. He therefore had come to this country for a year to try to discover what curative volumes were in vogue in the philosophic world. He had decided hereafter to confine himself almost completely to bibliotherapy as a form of healing.

(2) The term, I confess, was quite new to me, but it was not without charm. It suddenly made me realize that perhaps the academic degree of Doctor of Philosophy was less of a quack accolade than I had supposed. For years now, I suddenly realized, I had been practicing bibliotherapy. And I suddenly realized how good an excuse there was

* From *Under Whatever Sky* by Irwin Edman. Copyright 1951 by Irwin Edman. Reprinted by permission of The Viking Press, Inc., New York.

for selling books at drugstores, though perhaps they ought to be placed behind the drug counter and not given out without a doctor's explicit prescription.

(3) It chills me now to the marrow as I turn the advertising pages of the Sunday book review and see with how little restriction bibliotherapy is practiced by writers and publishers, and by reviewers, too. "This book," the phrase runs, "is strongly recommended." But for whom? by whom? for what disease of the spirit? These long historical novels, for instance: opiates many of them are truly. But is it fair to allow them to be bought by the strained and the neurotic? They might get into the habit of reading such things always. I will scarcely even mention the serious dangers of the unguarded circulation of detective and mystery stories. The state controls other drugs, while it lets these go freely on sale. And there are among books subtler opiates and stimulants than either historical novels or detective stories: works on metaphysics and morals, for instance.

(4) It would be a fine thing, I am sure, if one could go to one's doctor to have the proper books recommended for one's health. But it is my experience that my own doctor is always asking *me* what to read. I foresee a new type of medical education in which, instead of the usual first-year course in anatomy, there will be classes in the anatomy of criticism, and the last-year students touring the wards will look not at their patients' chests, but at their intelligence quotients and at the books by their bedsides.

(5) Before my visitor left I had decided it might be a very good thing if the medical schools were hardly distinguishable from liberal arts colleges. I smiled a little at my visitor who spoke of bibliotherapy, but the greatest advances in medicine have always been achieved over the stupid opposition of reactionaries. Before my bibliotherapist left, I found myself prescribing some good books for him, and for his future patients.

STUDY QUESTIONS

1. This essay originally appeared as a column in a magazine. How has this fact influenced the author's organization and style?

2. In paragraph 3, Mr. Edman inverts the normal order of the clause in "opiates many of them are truly." Inasmuch as the meaning of most sentences in English is determined by adherence to a relatively rigid word order, sentence inversion is sparingly used by English prose writers. In this instance, is Mr. Edman justified? Explain your answer.

3. What is the effect of Mr. Edman's use of the following words: *freewheeling* (1), *accolade* (2), *opiates* (3), and *reactionaries* (5)?

4. How would you define *bibliotherapy*?

5. What objections can be raised to bibliotherapy as a serious idea?

WRITING ASSIGNMENTS

1. With Mr. Edman's essay in mind, write an essay, either formal or familiar, on the comic book menace.

2. Write a comparative analysis of the relative advantages of elective and prescribed reading.

3. Write an essay of personal experience, recounting, either seriously or humorously, the therapeutic values you have found in your reading.

4. Write an imaginative account of Mr. Edman's idea viewed quite literally and carried to absurdity.

5. Write a research paper on public censorship of books, past and/or present.

What Is Good English? *

ALBERT MARCKWARDT (1903–   ), *a professor of English at the University of Michigan, is a specialist in linguistics and the English language. He has written numerous books on the grammar and history of English and is a director of the* Linguistic Atlas of America, *which is mapping the characteristics of the area vocabularies of the United States and Canada.*

(1) Editorials are written about every phase of it. Teachers are deluged with letters asking them to referee disputes over it. Even our statesmen have manifested a consistent interest in the problem—both Benjamin Franklin and Theodore Roosevelt tried to reform our spelling. As far as the schools are concerned, everyone generally agrees upon one point: Good English should be successfully taught. But when it comes to deciding what is not Good English, there are almost as many points of view as there are persons to hold them.

(2) In all this diversity, two diametrically opposed attitudes may be discerned. At one extreme are those who look to the conventional rules of grammar, to dictionaries, to lists of frequently mispronounced words as absolute authorities. This attitude of dependence upon authority, since it implies a belief that a language may arrive at and maintain a relatively static condition—that it may be kept pure—is usually spoken of as *purism*. Little more need be said about this point of view for most of us are quite familiar with it. We have all met it somewhere, in the schools or out.

(3) During the last twenty-five years, however, there have been

* From *Talks*, January 1938, Vol. 3, No. 1, published by the Columbia Broadcasting System. Reprinted by permission of the author. This essay was originally broadcast over the radio.

indications of a change of attitude toward the question of Good English and its teaching, both in the schools and among the most competent linguists in the country. There has been formulated what may be called for want of a more accurate term a "liberal" attitude toward language, which is directly in opposition to many of the tenets and practices of the purists. As in the case of any liberal movement, this one has been accompanied by much misunderstanding as to its aims and methods. There are abroad sinister rumors that "anything you hear is right," and dire forebodings of future generations whose verbs and nouns will not agree.

(4) It is most important, I believe, to the general success of the English language program in our schools, to clear away some of the erroneous conceptions which have sprung up in connection with linguistic liberalism. This may best be accomplished by pointing out, first of all, how and why this change in attitude came about; second, by defining the standards of Good English which the liberal grammarians uphold; and finally, by pointing out certain ideas and attitudes which they do not put forward. The limitations of space necessitate my treating only one aspect of this broad question, namely grammar in its more restricted sense; although what I have to say may be applied in most cases to problems of pronunciation and vocabulary as well.

(5) To explain the rise of the liberal attitude toward a standard of Good English, we must examine briefly the history of the rules which are to be found in the school grammars of today. These rules, for the most part, originated with certain English grammarians of the eighteenth century—notably William Ward, Robert Lowth, and James Buchanan. These men were not as interested in reflecting and codifying the actual spoken English of their time as in setting up an ideal language for their own and future generations to strive to master. This ideal language was based in part upon the rules of Latin grammar —for the eighteenth century was an age which revered the classics— and in part upon what seemed to be a rational arrangement for a language—for the eighteenth century was also an age of reason.

(6) In the two hundred years which have elapsed since the formulation of these rules, the study of language has progressed remarkably, and we have learned much concerning this aspect of human be-

havior. The early nineteenth century was marked by a tremendous growth in our knowledge of the history of both ancient and modern languages.

(7) The grammarians of the eighteenth century assumed that language was static, that it might reach and be kept at a state of perfection. In the nineteenth century we learned to apply the evolutionary concept to language as well as to botany and zoology. We came to see that language is not stationary, that it is in a state of continuous development, that standards which may hold good for one century are not necessarily applicable to another.

(8) Along with our increased knowledge of the history of the English language and the conception of language as an evolving organism, came the realization that many of the rules of so-called correct English did not reflect actual speech habits; that they set up standards which were not only absent from spoken English but, more than this, were virtually foreign to the genius of the language.

(9) In 1927, the late Professor S. A. Leonard, together with Professor H. Y. Moffat, began to study this problem. They selected from typical school text-books then in use 102 expressions condemned as incorrect; they submitted these to a jury composed of twenty-six eminent linguists and a similar number of authors, editors, business executives, teachers of English and of speech—about 225 all told. This jury was asked to rate the 102 condemned expressions as acceptable, questionable, or illiterate. It is possible to give only a few of the results of the survey here, but it was found that more than 40 of the 102 expressions usually condemned in the school texts were considered acceptable by over 75 percent of the linguists, and many others were held by them to be matters of divided usage.

(10) Among the expressions condemned by the text-books and accepted by the jury were: "This is a man I used to know," "That will be all right," "You had better stop that foolishness." The first of these omits the relative pronoun; the second used the term "all right" to which some grammars object; in the third the locution "had better" is at times condemned by text-books as a colloquialism. All of them are obviously in current use today.

(11) It is interesting to read what an eminent British linguist, Pro-

fessor J. H. G. Grattan, has said on this same subject. He writes, "The attitude of the American schools is, so far as the English language is concerned, ultraconservative. Eighteenth century ideas of correctness are not yet dead in the United States. Indeed, by American standards, many idiomatic usages long sanctioned in Great Britain are still bad grammar."

(12) When it became apparent that the rules of many of the school grammars prescribed something that was not idiomatic English, the question immediately arose: If the rules of the grammars cannot be held to constitute a valid standard of good English, what standard can be set up in its place? This is, it will be recalled, the second of the three questions which were raised before.

(13) The liberal grammarians answer in the following manner: The history of most modern languages shows that from generation to generation, and from century to century, there has been in existence an accepted or received standard form of that language—English, French, or whatever it may be; and that that standard form has been based upon the speech of the class and section of the country which was politically, economically, and culturally dominant at the time.

(14) London English, just one of many English dialects, became the standard speech of England chiefly because the city of London rose to a position of prime importance in the affairs of the English-speaking people. The same was true of the language of the Ile de France and of the Kingdom of Castile. If this is generally the case, why should we not consider as the standard of present-day English that speech which is in actual use by the large group who is carrying on the affairs of the English speaking people? An attitude of this kind is usually spoken of as a doctrine of usage.

(15) In connection with such a doctrine or standard, one problem arises. Suppose the usage of this dominant group is not wholly in agreement on all points? Suppose some of its members occasionally use a split infinitive while others do not? What then is to be our guiding principle?

(16) Here again we may have recourse to our knowledge of the history of our language. Since it is possible to examine with some accuracy the forms of the English language during the last thousand

years, such a study will indicate that certain inflectional and syntactical traits have been constantly expanding and developing, while others have been disappearing. If it is possible from an examination of what has gone on in the past to make a reasonable prediction as to what will come about in the future—and we assume this with most of the studies we undertake—then, in the case of a divided usage, let us choose that form or construction which seems to be in accord with the developing tendencies or patterns of the English language.

(17) To return to the problem of a split infinitive. Since a careful examination of the English of the last five hundred years shows such a construction to have been in constant use, and to have arisen from a desire to speak English naturally and clearly, the least we can do is to allow it equal rank with the alternative construction; to favor it when it seems better to perform the function of communicating the idea involved; and to rule it out when it does not express the thought as clearly.

(18) Unfortunately a number of misconceptions have arisen in connection with such a proposed standard of usage. Uninformed people frequently ask if such a doctrine means that any sort of English that may be heard on the street is Good English. If an expression is used, no matter where or by whom, must it then necessarily be correct? The answer is no. The doctrine of usage does not legalize the language of the gutter, for the language of the gutter is not the English which is apt to prevail as Standard Spoken English. It is perfectly true that upon occasion certain expressions and certain modes of pronunciation have spread from one social class to another, frequently from a higher to a lower, and at times from a lower to a higher. The broad *a* sound in such words as *past* and *half*, now considered to be ultrarefined by many speakers, is a case in point; for in the late eighteenth and early nineteenth centuries it was, as a dictionary of the time puts it, "the sound used by the vulgar but not the polite and learned world." But these occasional cross currents do not justify an acceptance of wholly uncultivated speech as a norm. By virtue of the historical principles upon which the liberal grammarians proceed, they are still committed to the speech of the people who direct the affairs of the community as a standard. On the other hand, since the English speaking countries are

democratic in character, the limitation of the speech standard to the narrowest top layer of the social order is also precluded.

(19) The second aspect of the doctrine of usage which frequently troubles people to whom the idea is somewhat new is the fear that the lack of strict and ironclad rules will lead to eventual disintegration. Again history shows such fears to be unfounded. It has been pointed out that rules for the speaking of correct English date chiefly from the beginning of the eighteenth century. They have existed only two hundred years of the fifteen hundred since the Angles and Saxons first came to the British Isles. Accordingly when English is considered in the light of its millennium of existence as a separate language, one is inclined to feel that the rules have had relatively little effect in either hindering or accelerating the main trends of development.

(20) Moreover, we can never be too sure as to just what is meant by disintegration of a language, which innovations are bad and which are good. As one eminent linguist has written, "To the conservative grammarian all change is decay. Although he knows well that an old house often has to be torn down in part or as a whole in order that it may be rebuilt to suit modern conditions, he never sees the constructive forces at work in the destruction of old grammatical forms. He is fond of mourning over the loss of the subjunctive and the present slovenly use of the indicative. He hasn't the slightest insight into the fine constructive work of the last centuries in rebuilding the subjunctive."

(21) At present the greatest need confronting those who are entrusted with the teaching of our language in the schools is for new text-books which describe accurately the language of those now carrying on the affairs of the English speaking people, particularly grammars which will record the forms and syntax of present day American English. A most significant beginning in this direction has already been made by the National Council of Teachers of English who, in November 1932, sponsored the publication of *Current English Usage*. This volume is in reality a continuation of the survey mentioned above, begun by Professors Leonard and Moffat, a survey which has for its purpose a codification of the usages of present day English, and which proceeds upon the theory that it is the principal function of the gram-

marian to describe the language as it exists rather than to prescribe a state of perfection for it.

(22) I can close in no more appropriate manner than to quote from Miss Ruth Mary Weeks' introduction to this forward looking work. She writes, "Language is a living thing and the greatest law of life and growth is change. Dictionaries, grammars, books of rhetoric are not eternal statutes handed down from heaven like the tables of Mosaic law. They are history, not dogma; description, not command—description of the changing speech habits of the mass of men.

(23) "As our speech changes, so do dictionaries and grammars change; so must they change if we are to prepare our students to speak the language of their own time, or to secure from the better speech of our own day reinforcement of our teaching."

STUDY QUESTIONS

1. Mr. Marckwardt devotes the first four paragraphs of his talk to introducing his subject. Determine the relationships among the four. Could they be incorporated within one paragraph? Is there any one sentence within those paragraphs which states the central idea of the whole discussion?

2. In paragraph 4, Mr. Marckwardt states the threefold division of his exposition. Which paragraphs constitute his discussion of each division?

3. Can you justify the fact that most of the paragraphs in this essay are short? Are there any points at which paragraphs could be combined into larger units? At what points might the author have elaborated had he written a more extended discussion?

4. What is the tone of the last sentence in paragraph 3? What specific words are instrumental in conveying this tone? Is this tone maintained throughout the essay? If not, why not?

5. What is the function of the quotations in this essay? How can an appropriate quotation strengthen an argument?

6. What *kind* of arguments do the "liberal" linguists use in support of their views?

7. What specific arguments do you think purists might use in answer to the "liberal" linguists?

8. Do you think the attitudes of Marckwardt would make it any easier for the layman to speak Good English? What has the fact of linguistic

change to do with Good English? What bearing do the views of "liberal" linguists have on your own attempts to learn the art of writing Good English?

WRITING ASSIGNMENTS

1. Write an account of how you were taught English in primary and secondary schools.

2. Write a familiar essay on the pleasures of reading a dictionary.

3. On the basis entirely of your own experience and thinking, write an analysis of the social importance of language.

4. On the basis of research, write an essay presenting the position of the linguistic purists.

5. Write an essay on the jargon of a specific group (journalists, sports writers, radio advertisers, political speakers, campus politicians, railroad men, etc.).

What Is the Bible? *

MARY ELLEN CHASE (1887–   ) is a professor of English at Smith College. Her writings are many and varied, including book reviews, stories, essays, textbooks, critical studies, and novels. Her best known works are Mary Peters (1934), Dawn in Lyonesse (1938), Windswept (1941), and The Bible and the Common Reader (1944), the first chapter of which is printed here. Of particular interest to college students is the fact that she worked her way through college by writing stories for juveniles.

(1) In the derivation of our word, Bible, lies its definition. It comes from the Greek word, biblion [1] which in its plural biblia signifies "little books." The Bible is actually a collection of little books, of every sort and description, written over a long period of time, the very earliest dating, in part at least, as far back as 1200 B.C. or perhaps even earlier; the latest as late as 150 A.D. In its rich and manifold nature it might be called a library of Hebrew literature; in its slow production over a period of many centuries it might be termed a survey of that literature to be understood as we understand a survey of English literature, in which we become familiar with types of English prose and poetry from Anglo-Saxon times to the twentieth century.

(2) The Bible, in the form in which most of us wisely read it, the King James, or Authorized Version, has been called by John Livingston Lowes [2] "the noblest monument of English prose." It is as well

---

* From The Bible and Common Reader by Mary Ellen Chase. Copyright 1944 by Mary Ellen Chase. Reprinted by permission of The Macmillan Company, New York.

[1] Biblos was the name given to the inner bark of the papyrus; and the word biblion meant a papyrus roll, upon which the Bible was originally copied. (Miss Chase's note.)

[2] American scholar and educator, for many years professor of English at Harvard.

65

the richest monument, for within its covers are to be found all types of literature, both in prose and in poetry. Here are ancient songs, written by unknown hands before the year 1000 B.C., preserved in old collections, now lost, or tenaciously bequeathed by word of mouth to succeeding generations, songs of war and of triumph, such as the famous martial song of Deborah in the 5th chapter of Judges; or in the 10th chapter of the book called by his name the dramatic command of Joshua to the sun and the moon that they should stand still upon Gibeon and in the valley of Ajalon until the Amorites should be destroyed; or in Exodus 15 the triumphant song of Miriam, the sister of Moses, who with her women sang "with timbrels and with dances" over the destruction of Pharaoh and his hosts in the Red Sea; the revengeful song of Lamech, boasting to his terrified wives, Adah and Zillah, in the 4th chapter of Genesis; the little song to the well in the 21st chapter of Numbers, a song which the children of Israel sang in the wilderness of the desert when they thirsted for water and which is today in similar form sung by roaming Arabian tribes. Here are riddles, old perhaps as the famous riddle of the Sphinx,[3] such as the riddle in Judges 14 propounded by Samson at his wedding feast about the honey in the carcass of the lion which he had killed with his bare hands; here are fables, exemplified in Judges 9 by Jotham's fable of the talking trees, the olive, the fig tree, the grape vine, and the bramble, and, like all fables, containing in its words a teaching for its time; here are oracles (for the great men of ancient Israel sometimes spoke in oracles as well as did the gods of ancient Greece), the beautiful oracles in Numbers 23 of Balaam, who went astride his wise and talkative ass to confound Balak, king of Moab.

(3) These, which are among the oldest pieces of Hebrew literature, existed as folk material long before they were incorporated into the biblical narratives to give added richness to the narratives themselves. And what narratives! For the story-tellers of the Bible have never been

[3] According to ancient legend, the Sphinx, stationed on the road to Thebes, put to death all passers-by who could not solve this riddle: "What is it that, though it has one voice, is four-footed, and two-footed, and three-footed?" Oedipus guessed the answer correctly as man, who crawls on four legs as an infant, walks on two in his prime, and supports himself with a cane when old. Thereupon the Sphinx killed herself.

surpassed, if equalled, by those of any later age or race, who time and time again have gone to them as to models of the art of narration. The Old Testament teems with stories: legends such as those in Genesis of the creation and of the flood, sagas like the Jacob-Joseph saga in Genesis 27-50, hero tales like those of Gideon, Jephthah, and Samson in the book of Judges, romances like much of the story of David, tragedies like the dark, ironic story of Saul, realistic stories like those many sordid incidents in King David's tempestuous and ill-governed household or in the cruel, designing lives of Ahab and Jezebel. There are short stories in the Bible, the idyllic love story of Ruth and the humorous, ironic story of Jonah sulking under his withering gourd. And there is a novel in the book of Esther, which in plot design and irony of incident has never been surpassed.

(4) The story-tellers of the Bible, both in the Old Testament and the New, understood men and women of all sorts and in all conditions. There is literally no type of person whom they have neglected. All are here: the wise and the foolish, the rich and the poor, the faithful and the treacherous, the designing and the generous, the pitiful and the prosperous, the innocent and the guilty, the spendthrift and the miser, the players of practical jokes and their discomfited victims, the sorry, the tired, the old, the exasperated young, misled and impetuous girls, young men who lusted and young men who loved, friends who counted no cost for friendship, bad-mannered children and children well brought up, a little boy who had a headache in a hay-field, a little servant girl who wanted so much her master's health that she dared to give him good, if unpalatable, advice. Once one discovers such persons as these, still alive after many centuries, they become not only fascinating in themselves but typical of persons whom we know today, just as Mr. Micawber and Fagin are typical of the easy-going and the cruel, or as Robin Hood and Captain Blood [4] typify two different attitudes toward daring and adventure, or as Don Quixote and Parson Adams [5] are typical of men who, although they exist in this world, actually live in a kinder, better, more glorified one.

(5) These stories of men and women, old and young, although they

[4] Principal character in Rafael Sabatini's novel *Captain Blood*.
[5] Important character in Henry Fielding's novel *Joseph Andrews* (1742).

occupy a large portion of the Bible, are only one of its many literary forms. There is poetry in the Bible. In addition to the ancient songs already spoken of, there are lyrical love songs, odes, laments, hymns of all kinds, both secular and religious, dramatic monologues, and, above all else, the exalted poetry of the prophets and of the book of Job. And the poets who wrote this biblical poetry, some of them known by name, others unknown, were as distinct and individual in their method of writing and in their ways of thought as were the familiar English poets. Indeed many of them in their manner of expression and in their attitude toward life bear a striking resemblance to other poets whom we know far better than we know the poets of the Bible. Amos, for example, is like Milton in his sonorous, ringing lines; Hosea sounds the sad and minor notes of A. E. Housman; Second-Isaiah is like Shelley in his ecstasy; certain of the Psalmists are like William Blake, or Thomas Traherne, or John Donne.

(6) There is at least one great drama in the Bible, that contained in the book of Revelation, with its majestic and awful stage settings, its celestial actors, its solemn acts and scenes. And there are a score of tragedies which, if placed in dramatic form, would rival *Othello* or *Hamlet* on Broadway.

(7) There are great biographers among the biblical writers: Baruch, who wrote the biography of the prophet Jeremiah and whose first copy of it was cut in pieces by King Jehoiakim's pen-knife and thrown into the open fire on a cold December day; the unknown, vivid biographer of David, who rivalled Boswell in frankness and detail; the naive, almost childish chronicler, also unknown, who wrote in awed accents of King Solomon's magnificence, how he drank from cups of gold, how he spoke in proverbs, and how "he spake of trees"; and, in the New Testament, the biographers of Jesus, especially St. Luke, whose Gospel, to many readers, is more sensitive, more revealing, and more beautiful, than those of the other three writers. And the earliest autobiography of which we have record in ancient literature is that found in Nehemiah's thrilling account of how he left his service as cup-bearer to King Artaxerxes to return to Jerusalem and to rebuild the broken-down walls and gates of his fathers' city.

(8) The best letters ever written are in the Bible, and St. Paul is

the author of them, a more vivid letter writer than even Horace Wal-
pole or Lord Chesterfield largely because he had far more important
things than they to say. St. Paul is never dull. Whether he writes for a
room to be made ready for him, or thanks his friends for presents, or
gives his opinions on marriage or on the behaviour of women in church,
or describes his utter dejection or his astounding faith, or is concerned
over the collection of money or the virtue of charity, or rises to im-
passioned heights over the corruptible and the incorruptible, the terrestrial and the celestial, he is always vibrant with life, and his language
in its force and vigour, clarity and beauty, can never be forgotten.

(9) There are countless proverbs in the Bible, many contained in
the book bearing their name, others scattered elsewhere, maxims and
aphorisms, some of great antiquity, some of other origin than Jewish.
Proverbs, as all know, are one of the most ancient and perennial forms
of literature, reflecting the sagacity and common sense of practical men
of all ages in their attempts to get on reasonably well in life. They are,
in other words, the records of long and sometimes hazardous experience
expressed in short sentences. Here in the Bible we have them at their
best and, often unconscious of their origin, quote them over and over
again as Sancho Panza, in his exasperation, quoted ancient Spanish
proverbs to Don Quixote.

(10) There are two philosophers in the Bible, both of whom give to
us in mingled prose and poetry their questions and their conclusions
concerning the meaning of life and the ways of God with men. They
are the unknown authors of the books of Ecclesiastes and of Job, the
one a skeptic, the other a tortured man of faith. Because they dealt,
each in his own way, with man's great quest, his search for Reality in
life, because they recognized the problems of evil and of pain, and
because, like other thoughtful and honest men, they found no sure
and certain answers to their questions, the books which they wrote,
disparate though they are in both literary and philosophical value, are
surely among the most deathless of all the books of the Bible.

(11) The Bible, then, is a collection, a library of various books,
reflecting and illuminating the long life of a small, yet a great people.
If it were only that, its value would be imperishable. But it is more.
It is, indeed, in its most perfect of translations, the noblest monument

of our English prose; and its words and phrases, images and similes have become part and parcel of our common English speech. Think for a moment how in the course of a single day spent in the homely, necessary details of living, we clarify and illuminate our talk with one another by the often unconscious use of its language. An unwelcome neighbour becomes "gall and wormwood" or "a thorn in the flesh"; a hated task, "a millstone about the neck"; we escape from one thing or another "by the skin of our teeth"; we earn our bread "by the sweat of our faces"; like Martha we become "careful and troubled about many things"; we "strain at gnats and swallow camels"; tired at night, we say that "our spirit is willing but our flesh is weak"; in moments of anger we remember that "a soft answer turneth away wrath"; intrusions upon our sleep are "the pestilence that walketh in darkness"; we warn our children to be "diligent in business" so that they may not "stand before mean men," or prophesy that if "they sow the wind, they shall reap the whirlwind," or puzzle them by knowledge "brought by a bird"; we recall that "the tongue is a little member but boasteth great things"; our pay-days mean "corn in Egypt"; words fitly spoken are "like apples of gold in pictures of silver"; the price of our generous friends is still "far above rubies," they are, in fact, "shining lights" or "the salt of the earth"; we pray that our sons may be brought safely homeward "to the haven where they would be"; we "heap coals of fire" on the heads of recalcitrant children or of harassed wives or husbands; having no servants, we are ourselves "hewers of wood and drawers of water"; we long for the time when men "shall beat their swords into ploughshares and their spears into pruning-hooks"; and, after an irritating session with ration books, we are forced to remember that "better a dinner of herbs where love is than a stalled ox and hatred therewith."

(12) The language of the Bible, now simple and direct in its homely vigour, now sonorous and stately in its richness, has placed its indelible stamp upon our best writers from Bacon to Lincoln and even to the present day. Without it there would be no *Paradise Lost*, no *Samson Agonistes*,[6] no *Pilgrim's Progress*; no William Blake, or Whittier, or T. S. Eliot as we know them; no Emerson or Thoreau, no negro Spirituals, no Address at Gettysburg. Without it the words of Burke and

[6] A poetic tragedy by John Milton.

Washington, Patrick Henry and Winston Churchill would miss alike their eloquence and their meaning. Without a knowledge of it the best of our literature remains obscure, and many of the characteristic features and qualities of our spoken language are threatened with extinction.

(13) The Bible belongs among the noblest and most indispensable of our humanistic and literary traditions. No liberal education is truly liberal without it. Yet in the last fifty years our colleges have, for the most part, abandoned its study as literature, and our schools, for reasons not sufficiently valid, have ceased to teach, or, in many cases, even to read it to their young people. Students of English literature take for granted that a knowledge of the *Iliad*, the *Odyssey*, the *Aeneid*, and the *Divine Comedy* ⁷ are necessary not only for the graduate schools but for cultured and civilized life, as, indeed, they are; but most of them remain in comfortable and colossal ignorance of a book which antedates Dante and, in large part, Vergil by many centuries, some of which was written before Homer, and all of which has contributed more to the humanistic civilization of the Western World than have the so-called "Classics."

(14) To all English-speaking peoples the Bible is a national as well as a noble monument, for much of their history is securely rooted and anchored within it. In 17th century England it nurtured the Puritan revolt and paved the way for the Bill of Rights. In 17th and 18th century America it supplied not only the names of our ancestors but the stout precepts by which they lived. They walked by its guidance; their rough places were made plain by their trust in its compassionate promises. It was a lamp to their feet and a light to their path, a pillar of cloud by day and of fire by night. It was the source of the convictions that shaped the building of this country, of the faith that endured the first New England winters and later opened up the Great West. It laid the foundations of our educational system, built our earliest colleges, and dictated the training within our homes. In the words alike of Jefferson and Patrick Henry, John Quincy Adams and Franklin it made better and more useful citizens to their country by reminding a man

---

⁷ The great poetic work by the Italian poet Dante, describing the Christian Inferno, Purgatory, and Paradise.

of his individual responsibility, his own dignity, and his equality with his fellow-man. The Bible is, indeed, so imbedded in our American heritage that not to recognize its place there becomes a kind of national apostasy, and not to know and understand it, in these days when we give all for its principles of human worth and human freedom, an act unworthy of us as a people.

(15) And, lastly, the Bible in its slow, patient evolution is the noblest record in any language of the hearts and the minds of men. Those who wrote it and those of whom it was written thought and wondered over the eternal questions of life and death, of man's lot upon this earth, and of his ultimate destiny. Amos on the Tekoan hills, the Great Isaiah by the waters of Shiloah and the Second Isaiah by those of Babylon, Job in the dust with his sententious friends, "physicians of no value" to him, St. John on the island of Patmos, Daniel by the river Ulai—these were men of dreams and of visions who struggled with the questions that beset us all. Consumed like Dante "by the Love that moves the sun and the other stars," they were intent upon the possible reaches of man's spirit even in a dry and thirsty land. In the midst of desolation and suffering, of oppression and greed, they saw hope; in war, the ways of peace; in the perennial processes of nature, the treasures of the snow, the former and the latter rain, the waste places of the deep, the singing of the morning stars, they saw the mysterious ways of God with men. Because of their vision, deep calleth unto deep in their pages; and the unanalyzed perception of the meaning and value of threescore years and ten is woven into the very texture of their speech. In their two-fold recognition of wisdom, that moral and ethical code by which a just man lives his life and that intangible and spiritual Power, set up from everlasting and possessed by God in the beginning of His way, only by the understanding of which man achieves his triumph, they encompassed all the affairs, small and great, of one's sojourn on this earth.

(16) "I myself also am a mortal man, like to all. . . . And when I was born, I drew in the common air, and fell upon the earth, which is of like nature, and the first voice I uttered was crying, as all others do. . . . For all men have one entrance into life, and the like going out. Wherefore I prayed, and understanding was given me; I called

upon God, and the spirit of wisdom came to me. I preferred her before sceptres and thrones, and esteemed riches nothing in comparison to her. . . . I loved her above health and beauty, and chose to have her instead of light; for the light that cometh from her never goeth out. All good things together came to me with her, and innumerable riches in her hands. For she is a treasure unto men that never faileth; which they that use become the friends of God." [8]

STUDY QUESTIONS

1. What arguments does Miss Chase make for the importance of the Bible in education? How is each argument introduced?

2. Although this essay is called "What Is the Bible?" and although the greater part of it is descriptive, yet Miss Chase has a serious purpose beyond merely describing the Bible. What is that purpose? In this essay, how is description effective in furthering that purpose?

3. How specifically does Miss Chase demonstrate the infinite richness and variety of the Bible?

4. How is paragraph 2 developed? How does the sentence structure reinforce that development? What other paragraphs are developed in the same way?

5. Analyze thoroughly the structure and function of the first sentence in paragraph 11. Does its structure have any special relevance to its function?

6. Miss Chase employs several expressions from the Bible not specifically identified as such. With the aid of a concordance of the Bible, see how many of them you can detect. Why is her procedure especially justified in this essay?

7. How does the etymology of the word *Bible* help us to understand it? The argument from etymology can sometimes be misleading and false, resulting in what is known as the "etymological fallacy." At other times, it may make a point effectively or serve to introduce an essay of definition. How does it serve to introduce this essay?

8. What inference can you draw from the word *wisely* in the first sentence of paragraph 2? In a good standard dictionary look up the difference between the words *inference* and *implication*. How could the question you are answering here be rephrased to use the word *imply* or *implication* instead of *infer* or *inference*?

[8] These words are taken from the seventh chapter of the Wisdom of Solomon from the *Apocrypha*. (Miss Chase's note.)

9. Miss Chase begins four of her paragraphs with the phrase *there are* or *there is*. Why is this phrase often considered weak? Can you justify Miss Chase's use of the phrase?

10. One of the tests of effective writing of this sort is the extent to which the writer can arouse the reader's interest. Does this essay make you want to read or study the Bible? How does Miss Chase present allusions so as to arouse a maximum of interest?

11. What is the relevance of the concluding quotation in this essay?

WRITING ASSIGNMENTS

1. Read one of the Old Testament narratives to which Miss Chase alludes and write an evaluation of its lasting significance for man.

2. Read some of the letters of St. Paul and write a sketch of St. Paul as a person.

3. Read Ecclesiastes and write an essay in which you analyze the view of life therein portrayed and give your judgment of its validity.

4. Write an essay in which you compare Miss Chase's account of the Bible with your previous impressions of it. Before writing this paper, reread one of the portions of the Bible in which your interest was aroused by Miss Chase's account.

5. Write a research paper on the social, historical, and cultural background of one of the episodes or books of the Old Testament.

Copernicus and the Planets *

HERBERT DINGLE (1890–   ), *British physicist and historian of science, was educated at Plymouth Technical School and the Imperial College of Science, London. At present, he is professor of the history and philosophy of science at University College, University of London. He has written many scientific articles and books. Among the latter are* Relativity for All (1922), Science and Human Experience (1931), Through Science to Philosophy (1937), *and* Science and Literary Criticism (1949).

(1) The work with which I am going to deal is the outstanding example in history of the tremendous consequences that can follow a very slight change in our way of looking at things. The Copernican revolution, as it is sometimes called, is the supreme symbol of the passage from the medieval to the modern world, from an outlook which now seems like that of fairyland to the matter-of-fact outlook of the present day; yet it involved no great discovery, no new idea, and caused no abrupt change in the philosophy even of its originator. Its whole importance lies in what it made possible. We will try to see how this happened, but first let us take a brief glance at Copernicus himself.

(2) Copernicus was one of those universal geniuses of whom former times afford several examples, but who in our complex modern life can scarcely any longer appear. Churchman, statesman, scholar, lawyer, artist, poet, physician, economist, mathematician, astronomer—he was all these things, but his ruling passion—if passion is the right word for so mild and gentle a thinker—was mathematical astronomy. He was born in 1473 at Torún in Poland. After a prolonged education, first

* From *The History of Science. Origins and Results of the Scientific Revolution,* A *Symposium,* 1951. Reprinted by permission of The Free Press, Glencoe, Illinois. This essay was originally broadcast over BBC.

in the University of Cracow and then at Bologna and Rome, he returned in 1506, at the age of 33 years, to take up duties as Canon of
Frauenburg Cathedral, and there until his death in 1543 he pursued
his various activities as occasion demanded, but with the perfection
of his astronomical system always at the back of his mind.

(3) What was that system? As you know, the people of his time
thought of the Earth as fixed at the centre of a universe of spheres
which revolved with perfect regularity round it. The heavenly bodies
—Sun, Moon, stars and planets—were attached to the spheres and
showed by their movements how the spheres moved, but in a very
indirect way. A particular planet (Mars, for instance) showed only the
resultant movement of many spheres, each with its own radius, axis
and rate of revolution. It therefore appeared to move very irregularly,
but since the spheres themselves were invisible it gave the only available
clue to their number and character. The problem of astronomy was
thus to discover what combination of uniformly moving spheres could
produce the movements seen, and this problem, applied to all the
bodies in the sky, had engaged the attention of astronomers for 1400
years.

(4) Now this view of things was not the result of guesswork or
stupid prejudice. In the time of the early Greeks there was no such
universally accepted scheme, and even the first element of it—the
fixed central position of the Earth—was a matter for enquiry and discussion. Certainly appearances suggested that the Earth was fixed and
stationary, but some thinkers—notably Aristarchus of Samos in the
third century B.C.—held that the Earth not only rotated about an
axis but also moved in an orbit round the Sun, and that the appearances
of movements in the sky were simply consequences of these movements of the Earth. However, in the second century A.D., Ptolemy of
Alexandria made a judicial enquiry into the whole matter. He seriously
considered the possibility of the Earth's movement, but rejected it on
grounds which to him appeared final and which, with the knowledge
he had, were certainly reasonable. Thereafter the principle of the
geocentric universe was generally accepted, and the system grew more
and more elaborate as more and more spheres were added to account

for the irregularities which the movements of the heavenly bodies went on revealing.

(5) It was the extreme complexity into which the system had grown by the end of the fifteenth century that offended the mathematical mind of Copernicus. By that time more than eighty spheres were found necessary "to save appearances," as the phrase went—i.e. to account for the observed movements—and, even so, the movements were not completely explained. It seemed to Copernicus unlikely that God, who could do all things perfectly, would make such an ugly universe, and he accordingly turned back to the long discredited idea that the Earth moved, to see if, by thus relieving the spheres of some movements, he could account for the rest by a simpler system. He soon saw that this was possible, and for some thirty years, in season and out, he worked unceasingly to devise a new universe, pencilling his ideas on scraps of paper, the margins of books, and even on walls, until he had completed a scheme which not only explained all that Ptolemy's scheme had done, but did so more exactly and with only thirty-four spheres. He told the whole story in a great work—*De Revolutionibus Orbium Caelestium* ("On the Revolutions of the Heavenly Spheres" —not heavenly *bodies*, but heavenly *spheres*)—of which we are told the earliest copy was brought to him as he lay on his death-bed.

(6) It is often said that Copernicus was afraid to publish his work during his lifetime from fear of persecution, but there is no evidence for this. He did in fact circulate a short account of it in manuscript form in his *Commentariolus* [1] many years before his death, and in 1540 he allowed his pupil Rheticus to print a preliminary statement of the system. Moreover, his work was well known to the Pope and others high in the Councils of the Roman Church, and greatly admired. What actually deterred Copernicus was fear of ridicule. At that time it seemed so obvious that the Earth was at rest that anyone who asserted the contrary would certainly become the object of foolish jokes, and this he was too sensitive and retiring to risk. He accordingly told his ideas only to those who could appreciate the reasons for them.

(7) Why was it, then, that a century after his death his work be-

[1] A *Brief Treatise.*

came the centre of one of the most violent intellectual controversies that the world has known? The reason was that, though apparently simple and harmless, it in fact gave the death-blow to the whole medieval system of thought, for it touched that system at its most vital spot. It is hard for us to realise today, when so many quite dissimilar departments of knowledge surround us on all sides, that medieval thought was essentially a unity. The subjects we know as astronomy, physics, chemistry, theology, psychology, physiology, and so on, were then all fused together in a single system. Above the outermost sphere of astronomy was the heaven of theology, pictured in the same diagram. The stars were not remote globes of gas; they affected men's temperaments and to some extent controlled their destinies. The planets had affinities with the earthly metals. Human bodies represented the universe on a smaller scale. For instance, as you learned in the opening chapter of this book, everything that we call "matter" was supposed by medieval thinkers to be made up of four elements—earth, water, air, fire—mixed in various degrees; in liquids, for example, water predominated, and in solids, earth. Similarly, human temperaments were made up of four so-called "humours" mixed in various degrees, and according as one or another predominated so you were phlegmatic, choleric, sanguine or melancholy. Thus the humours were to what we should call the mental world what the elements were to the material world, and the parallel was so close that you may remember that Shakespeare makes Antony say of Brutus: "The elements . . . so mixed in him that nature might stand up . . . and say to all the world 'This was a man.' " [2] Nothing, in fact, that concerned men's lives here or hereafter was unrelated to the whole scheme of things. Upset the astronomical machinery, then, and you destroy the whole body of thought.

(8) Now at first sight Copernicus had done nothing to upset the astronomical machinery in any essential point. True, he put the Sun and not the Earth at the centre and made it the standard of rest, but the main organisation, the spheres of heaven which controlled the stars and planets, were still there performing their eternally uniform motions, and by its greater simplicity the Copernican view seemed to

[2] *Julius Caesar*, V.v.73.

establish still more firmly a philosophy that ultimately saw the whole universe as an expression of God's wisdom. But in fact it did nothing of the kind. On the contrary, it destroyed the whole system of belief.

(9) To see how this was so, let us ask ourselves why the spheres were ever supposed to exist. They were not seen or directly observed in any way; why, then, were they believed to be there? If you imagine the Earth to be at rest and watch the sky for a few hours, you will have no difficulty in answering this question. You will see a host of stars, all moving in circles round a single axis at precisely the same rate of about one revolution a day. You cannot then believe that each one moves independently of the others, and that their motions just happen to have this relation to one another. No one but a lunatic would doubt that he was looking at the revolution of a single sphere with all the stars attached to it. And if the stars had a sphere, then the Sun, Moon and planets, whose movements were almost the same, would also be moved by the same kind of mechanism. The existence of the spheres having thus been established and accepted implicitly for century after century, men no longer thought of the reasons which demanded them, but took them for granted as facts of experience; and Copernicus himself, despite his long years of meditation on the fundamental problems of astronomy, never dreamed of doubting their existence.

(10) But actually, you see, he had destroyed the whole basis of it. In his system the movements of the stars which were so closely related to one another were taken away from them and given to the Earth. But, that being so, why assume that the stars were attached to a sphere? The appearance would be the same if there were no sphere and even if the stars were at various distances, provided that those distances were very great. There was no reason, in fact, why space should not extend outwards without limit, with stars scattered at random all the way. And if the stars had no sphere, why should the planets have them? These thoughts were bound to arise sooner or later, and arise they did. In the century after the death of Copernicus, Bruno taught the doctrine of an infinite universe, without centre, in which the innumerable stars were Suns; Kepler discarded the circular motions which the spheres demanded and described the orbits of the planets as ellipses; Galileo with his telescope saw the Milky Way as a realisation of Bruno's vision

and discovered satellites of Jupiter which would have had to move through Jupiter's sphere if it had had one. In short, the spheres became thoroughly discredited, and with them went the whole edifice of medieval thought.

(11) We can hardly imagine today the effect of such a change on the minds of thoughtful men in the sixteenth century. It is scarcely possible that anything like it can ever occur again because, as I have said, our knowledge is now so divided into separate departments that whatever fundamental change may occur in one will leave most of the rest almost untouched. But the Copernican revolution upset everything—the whole medieval system of thought. With the spheres went a localised heaven for the souls of the blessed, the distinction between celestial and sublunar matter and motion became meaningless, the whole place of man in the cosmic scheme became uncertain.

(12) Take astrology—the belief that the details of men's temperaments and careers were appreciably affected by the movements of the heavenly bodies. This had fallen, by the middle of the seventeenth century, from the recognised science it had been to the superstition it is today, although, of course, it was still widely practised by the unenlightened. Can you see why? Here are the lines on which the argument for astrology would run. It was irreverent to suppose that God had created useless bodies, and therefore, with man as the centre of creation, it followed that the planets had a human significance—an influence on man—which we might reasonably try to discover. But once the Earth is seen to be but a minor planet of a minor star in an infinite host of stars, and man anything but the centre of creation, the whole argument falls to the ground. Why should the planets in such a system influence the affairs of men? They might have other much more important work to do, of which we knew nothing. It is small wonder, then, that, when the overwhelming implications of the Copernican view became realised, it was resisted by all the means thought appropriate at the time. It inevitably appeared at first as purely destructive, and destructive of everything worth preserving. We can see it today in another light. To us it is not only the end of one intellectual age but the necessary preparation for another—the scientific age in which we are now thoroughly immersed. Copernicus himself

was in no sense the originator of modern science. He was thoroughly medieval in outlook, and had he been able to foresee what his work was to do we may well believe that he would have shrunk in the utmost horror from the responsibility which he would have felt. But what he did was to make it possible for the new scientific philosophy to emerge.

(13) In brief, what happened was this. Between Ptolemy and Copernicus no question arose in men's minds concerning the meaning of motion. It was obvious: if a body was changing its position with respect to the Earth it was moving; otherwise it was at rest. But after Copernicus, whatever view you took, you had to consider the possibility that motion meant something else—namely, change of position with respect to the Sun. You made your choice and argued against the other view, but at least you thereby acknowledged that it stood in need of defeat by argument and was not a manifest absurdity. It was just this state of affairs that made it possible for Galileo, at the beginning of the seventeenth century, to propound his doctrine of "local motion," which became the foundation of science. According to this doctrine, if you had any number of bodies, all moving at different constant speeds, you could take any one you liked to be at rest. It was idle to ask which body was *really* stationary, because it was entirely a matter of convenience.

(14) A simple example may give us some idea of the simplification thus introduced into the study of motion. When you are in a train moving smoothly at 60 miles an hour, everything happens just as though you were sitting in your room at home. You can read and write in comfort and throw a ball into the air and catch it as it comes down. Hence, said Galileo in effect, you may take the train to be at rest, and if you walk along the corridor at an ordinary pace you may say quite truly that you are walking at the rate of 6 ft. a second—that is, ordinary walking pace, about 4 miles an hour. Before Copernicus, however, such a statement would not have been held to be true; in one second you would really have walked 94 ft., not six. That is to say, your speed would have been reckoned as your walking speed (6 ft. per second) plus the train's speed (88 ft. per second). The calculation in this case is not difficult, but when you take into account many bodies moving in different directions at different speeds, not all uniform, the complications that would result if you had to reduce them all to the standard

of the Earth would have made it impossible to discover any laws of motion at all.

(15) Newton took advantage of the liberty which this idea provided, as you will read in a later chapter. When he was considering the motion of the planets he took the Sun to be at rest, as Copernicus held, but when he was considering the fall of an apple to the ground he took the Earth to be at rest, as the anti-Copernicans held. He was then able to show that the same general law of gravitation held for the planets as for the apple, and to build on Galileo's principle the general laws of motion on which almost all subsequent science rests. The story has no end as yet because we cannot even guess what further developments of science will bring. But whatever it may be, we know, from the very nature of science itself, that it will necessarily grow out of what has gone before. So when you hear in the future of the new knowledge that is coming to light, and perhaps take part in discovering it, remember that it has all become possible because of the ideas of a man who thought he was simplifying the established scheme of the world, and who changed the course of the world's thought for ever.

STUDY QUESTIONS

1. To what audience do you think this discussion is addressed? How does the type of audience affect Mr. Dingle's style and tone? Select words, phrases, and clauses which illustrate his style and tone.

2. What is the Copernican theory? What does Mr. Dingle include in his essay besides an explanation of what the theory is? Write a long thesis sentence or a paragraph in which you summarize the ground covered by Mr. Dingle. What does paragraph 2 contribute to the essay?

3. In preparing this essay Mr. Dingle had to formulate his explanations for a literate but unspecialized audience. Does Mr. Dingle succeed in explaining all technical concepts? Were there any points at which you failed to understand him? Select examples of explanations which you think Mr. Dingle would not have found it necessary to make for a more learned audience.

4. Mr. Dingle devotes paragraph 4 to a very brief comment on ancient and medieval astronomy. Why is that historical background necessary to his purposes?

5. What are the consequences of Copernicus' theory as Mr. Dingle gives them?

6. What is a rhetorical question? Find examples in this essay and study their appropriateness.

7. What is the difference between a loose and a periodic sentence? Select five periodic sentences from this essay. What is their stylistic effect, in terms of tone, emphasis, euphony, and rhythm?

8. What is the difference between a simple, a compound, and a complex sentence? Select examples of each from this essay. Which type is most frequently used by Mr. Dingle? Why?

9. Would you say that the author's diction and style are formal or informal? Document your answer with evidence from the text. Select several adjectives which will further characterize the diction and style.

10. What attitude does Mr. Dingle assume toward the "errors" of the past? Why is this attitude especially satisfactory? Why does he take this attitude? Why is it possible for him to do so?

WRITING ASSIGNMENTS

1. Write an account of how an attitude of yours was changed by the educational process of learning a new fact or discovering a new area of knowledge.

2. Write a research paper on another famous scientist whose work has profoundly influenced human life (Harvey, Newton, Pasteur, Einstein, etc.).

3. Write a similar paper on a famous political figure, musician, inventor, or literary figure.

4. Write an analysis of the influence on modern life of an invention such as gunpowder, printing press, steam engine, combustion engine, telephone, radio, television, etc.

5. Write an imaginative picture of how future discoveries will change the life of the future.

The Shape of Ancient Seas *

RACHEL CARSON (1907–   ), *an aquatic biologist, is the editor-in-chief of the U.S. Fish and Wildlife Service of the Department of the Interior. Formerly she taught at the Johns Hopkins Summer School and the University of Maryland. As a result of her articles in various magazines, including* Collier's, The Yale Review, *and* Science Digest, *she was given the George Westinghouse Foundation Award for 1950, bestowed for outstanding magazine writing on science. The enthusiastic reception given* The Sea Around Us (1951) *led to the republication of* Under the Sea Wind, *which had first appeared in 1941. Both books then made nonfiction best seller lists simultaneously, a rare occurrence in the book trade. In recognition of her achievement, Miss Carson was awarded a Guggenheim Fellowship in 1951.*

> Till the slow sea rise and the sheer cliff crumble,
> Till terrace and meadow the deep gulfs drink.
>   SWINBURNE

(1) We live in an age of rising seas. Along all the coasts of the United States a continuing rise of sea level has been perceptible on the tide gauges of the Coast and Geodetic Survey since 1930. For the thousand-mile stretch from Massachusetts to Florida, and on the coast of the Gulf of Mexico, the rise amounted to about a third of a foot between 1930 and 1948. The water is also rising (but more slowly) along the Pacific shores. These records of the tide gauges do not include the transient advances and retreats of the water caused by winds and storms, but signify a steady, continuing advance of the sea upon the land.

84

(2) This evidence of a rising sea is an interesting and even an exciting thing because it is rare that, in the short span of human life, we can actually observe and measure the progress of one of the great earth rhythms. What is happening is nothing new. Over the long span of geologic time, the ocean waters have come in over North America many times and have again retreated into their basins. For the boundary between sea and land is the most fleeting and transitory feature of the earth, and the sea is forever repeating its encroachments upon the continents. It rises and falls like a great tide, sometimes engulfing half a continent in its flood, reluctant in its ebb, moving in a rhythm mysterious and infinitely deliberate.

(3) Now once again the ocean is overfull. It is spilling over the rims of its basins. It fills the shallow seas that border the continents, like the Barents, Bering, and China seas. Here and there it has advanced into the interior and lies in such inland seas as Hudson Bay, the St. Lawrence embayment, the Baltic, and the Sunda Sea. On the Atlantic coast of the United States the mouths of many rivers, like the Hudson and the Susquehanna, have been drowned by the advancing flood; the old submerged channels are hidden under bays like the Chesapeake and the Delaware.

(4) The advance noted so clearly on the tide gauges may be part of a long rise that began thousands of years ago—perhaps when the glaciers of the most recent Ice Age began to melt. But it is only within recent decades that there have been instruments to measure it in any part of the world. Even now the gauges are few and scattered, considering the world as a whole. Because of the scarcity of world records, it is not known whether the rise observed in the United States since 1930 is being duplicated on all other continents.

(5) Where and when the ocean will halt its present advance and begin again its slow retreat into its basin, no one can say. If the rise over the continent of North America should amount to a hundred feet (and there is more than enough water now frozen in land ice to provide such a rise) most of the Atlantic seaboard, with its cities and towns, would be submerged. The surf would break against the foothills of the Appalachians. The coastal plain of the Gulf of Mexico would lie under water; the lower part of the Mississippi Valley would be submerged.

(6) If, however, the rise should be as much as 600 feet, large areas in the eastern half of the continent would disappear under the waters. The Appalachians would become a chain of mountainous islands. The Gulf of Mexico would creep north, finally meeting in mid-continent with the flood that had entered from the Atlantic into the Great Lakes, through the valley of the St. Lawrence. Much of northern Canada would be covered by water from the Arctic Ocean and Hudson Bay.

(7) All this would seem to us extraordinary and catastrophic, but the truth is that North America and most other continents have known even more extensive invasions by the sea than the one we have just imagined. Probably the greatest submergence in the history of the earth took place in the Cretaceous period, about 100 million years ago. Then the ocean waters advanced upon North America from the north, south, and east, finally forming an inland sea about 1000 miles wide that extended from the Arctic to the Gulf of Mexico, and then spread eastward to cover the coastal plain from the Gulf to New Jersey. At the height of the Cretaceous flood about half of North America was submerged. All over the world the seas rose. They covered most of the British Isles, except for scattered outcroppings of ancient rocks. In southern Europe only the old, rocky highlands stood above the sea, which intruded in long bays and gulfs even into the central highlands of the continent. The ocean moved into Africa and laid down deposits of sandstones; later weathering of these rocks provided the desert sands of the Sahara. From a drowned Sweden, an inland sea flowed across Russia, covered the Caspian Sea, and extended to the Himalayas. Parts of India were submerged, and of Australia, Japan, and Siberia. On the South American continent, the area where later the Andes were to rise was covered by sea.

(8) With variations of extent and detail, these events have been repeated again and again. The very ancient Ordovician seas, some 400 million years ago, submerged more than half of North America, leaving only a few large islands marking the borderlands of the continent, and a scattering of smaller ones rising out of the inland sea. The marine transgressions of Devonian and Silurian time were almost as extensive. But each time the pattern of invasion was a little different, and it is

doubtful that there is any part of the continent that at some time has not lain at the bottom of one of these shallow seas.

(9) You do not have to travel to find the sea, for the traces of its ancient stands are everywhere about. Though you may be a thousand miles inland, you can easily find reminders that will reconstruct for the eye and ear of the mind the processions of its ghostly waves and the roar of its surf, far back in time. So, on a mountain top in Pennsylvania, I have sat on rocks of whitened limestone, fashioned of the shells of billions upon billions of minute sea creatures. Once they had lived and died in an arm of the ocean that overlay this place, and their limy remains had settled to the bottom. There, after eons of time, they had become compacted into rock and the sea had receded; after yet more eons the rock had been uplifted by bucklings of the earth's crust and now it formed the backbone of a long mountain range.

(10) Far in the interior of the Florida Everglades I have wondered at the feeling of the sea that came to me—wondered until I realized that here were the same flatness, the same immense spaces, the same dominance of the sky and its moving, changing clouds; wondered until I remembered that the hard rocky floor on which I stood, its flatness interrupted by upthrust masses of jagged coral rock, had been only recently constructed by the busy architects of the coral reefs under a warm sea. Now the rock is thinly covered with grass and water; but everywhere is the feeling that the land has formed only the thinnest veneer over the underlying platform of the sea, that at any moment the process might be reversed and the sea reclaim its own.

(11) So in all lands we may sense the former presence of the sea. There are outcroppings of marine limestone in the Himalayas, now at an elevation of 20,000 feet. These rocks are reminders of a warm, clear sea that lay over southern Europe and northern Africa and extended into southwestern Asia. This was some 50 million years ago. Immense numbers of a large protozoan known as nummulites swarmed in this sea and each, in death, contributed to the building of a thick layer of nummulitic limestone. Eons later, the ancient Egyptians were to carve their Sphinx from a mass of this rock; other deposits of the same stone they quarried to obtain material to build their pyramids.

(12) The famous white cliffs of Dover are composed of chalk deposited by the seas of the Cretaceous period, during that great inundation we have spoken of. The chalk extends from Ireland through Denmark and Germany, and forms its thickest beds in south Russia. It consists of shells of those minute sea creatures called foraminifera, the shells being cemented together with a fine-textured deposit of calcium carbonate. In contrast to the foraminiferal ooze that covers large areas of ocean bottom at moderate depths, the chalk seems to be a shallow-water deposit, but it is so pure in texture that the surrounding lands must have been low deserts, from which little material was carried seaward. Grains of wind-borne quartz sand, which frequently occur in the chalk, support this view. At certain levels the chalk contains nodules of flint. Stone Age men mined the flint for weapons and tools and also used this relic of the Cretaceous sea to light their fires.

(13) Many of the natural wonders of the earth owe their existence to the fact that once the sea crept over the land, laid down its deposits of sediments, and then withdrew. There is Mammoth Cave in Kentucky, for example, where one may wander through miles of underground passages and enter rooms with ceilings 250 feet overhead. Caves and passageways have been dissolved by ground water out of an immense thickness of limestone, deposited by a Paleozoic sea. In the same way, the story of Niagara Falls goes back to Silurian time, when a vast embayment of the Arctic Sea crept southward over the continent. Its waters were clear, for the borderlands were low and little sediment or silt was carried into the inland sea. It deposited large beds of the hard rock called dolomite, and in time they formed a long escarpment near the present border between Canada and the United States. Millions of years later, floods of water released from melting glaciers poured over this cliff, cutting away the soft shales that underlay the dolomite, and causing mass after mass of the undercut rock to break away. In this fashion Niagara Falls and its gorge were created.

(14) Some of these inland seas were immense and important features of their world, although all of them were shallow compared with the central basin where, since earliest time, the bulk of the ocean waters have resided. Some may have been as much as 600 feet deep, about the same as the depths over the outer edge of the continental

shelf. No one knows the pattern of their currents, but often they must have carried the warmth of the tropics into far northern lands. During the Cretaceous period, for example, breadfruit, cinnamon, laurel, and fig trees grew in Greenland. When the continents were reduced to groups of islands there must have been few places that possessed a continental type of climate with its harsh extremes of heat and cold; mild oceanic climates must rather have been the rule.

(15) Geologists say that each of the grander divisions of earth history consists of three phases: in the first the continents are high, erosion is active, and the seas are largely confined to their basins; in the second the continents are lowest and the seas have invaded them broadly; in the third the continents have begun once more to rise. According to the late Charles Schuchert, who devoted much of his distinguished career as a geologist to mapping the ancient seas and lands: "Today we are living in the beginning of a new cycle, when the continents are largest, highest, and scenically grandest. The oceans, however, have begun another invasion upon North America."

(16) What brings the ocean out of its deep basins, where it has been contained for eons of time, to invade the lands? Probably there has always been not one alone, but a combination of causes.

(17) The mobility of the earth's crust is inseparably linked with the changing relations of sea and land—the warping upward or downward of that surprisingly plastic substance which forms the outer covering of our earth. The crustal movements affect both land and sea bottom but are most marked near the continental margins. They may involve one or both shores of an ocean, one or all coasts of a continent. They proceed in a slow and mysterious cycle, one phase of which may require millions of years for its completion. Each downward movement of the continental crust is accompanied by a slow flooding of the land by the sea, each upward buckling by the retreat of the water.

(18) But the movements of the earth's crust are not alone responsible for the invading seas. There are other important causes. Certainly one of them is the displacement of ocean water by land sediments. Every grain of sand or silt carried out by the rivers and deposited at sea displaces a corresponding amount of water. Disintegration of the land and the seaward freighting of its substance have gone on without

interruption since the beginning of geologic time. It might be thought that the sea level would have been rising continuously, but the matter is not so simple. As they lose substance the continents tend to rise higher, like a ship relieved of part of its cargo. The ocean floor, to which the sediments are transferred, sags under its load. The exact combination of all these conditions that will result in a rising ocean level is a very complex matter, not easily recognized or predicted.

(19) Then there is the growth of the great submarine volcanoes, which build up immense lava cones on the floor of the ocean. Some geologists believe these may have an important effect on the changing level of the sea. The bulk of some of these volcanoes is impressive. Bermuda is one of the smallest, but its volume beneath the surface is about 2500 cubic miles. The Hawaiian chain of volcanic islands extends for nearly 2000 miles across the Pacific and contains several islands of great size; its total displacement of water must be tremendous. Perhaps it is more than coincidence that this chain arose in Cretaceous time, when the greatest flood the world has ever seen advanced upon the continents.

(20) For the past million years, all other causes of marine transgressions have been dwarfed by the dominating role of the glaciers. The Pleistocene period was marked by alternating advances and retreats of a great ice sheet. Four times the ice-caps formed and grew deep over the land, pressing southward into the valleys and over the plains. And four times the ice melted and shrank and withdrew from the lands it had covered. We live now in the last stages of this fourth withdrawal. About half the ice formed in the last Pleistocene glaciation remains in the ice caps of Greenland and Antarctica and the scattered glaciers of certain mountains.

(21) Each time the ice sheet thickened and expanded with the unmelted snows of winter after winter, its growth meant a corresponding lowering of the ocean level. For directly or indirectly, the moisture that falls on the earth's surface as rain or snow has been withdrawn from the reservoir of the sea. Ordinarily, the withdrawal is a temporary one, the water being returned via the normal runoff of rain and melting snow. But in the glacial period the summers were cool, and the snows of any winter did not melt entirely but were carried

over to the succeeding winter, when the new snows found and covered them. So little by little the level of the sea dropped as the glaciers robbed it of its water, and at the climax of each of the major glaciations the ocean all over the world stood at a very low level.

(22) Today, if you look in the right places, you will see the evidences of some of these old stands of the sea. Of course the strand marks left by the extreme low levels are now deeply covered by water and may be discovered only indirectly by sounding. But where, in past ages, the water level stood higher than it does today you can find its traces. In Samoa, at the foot of a cliff wall now 15 feet above the present level of the sea, you can find benches cut in the rocks by waves. You will find the same thing on other Pacific islands, and on St. Helena in the South Atlantic, on islands of the Indian Ocean, in the West Indies, and around the Cape of Good Hope.

(23) Sea caves in cliffs now high above the battering assault and the flung spray of the waves that cut them are eloquent of the changed relation of sea and land. You will find such caves widely scattered over the world. On the west coast of Norway there is a remarkable, wave-cut tunnel. Out of the hard granite of the island of Torghatten, the pounding surf of a flooding interglacial sea cut a passageway through the island, a distance of about 530 feet, and in so doing removed nearly 5 million cubic feet of rock. The tunnel now stands 400 feet above the sea. Its elevation is due in part to the elastic, upward rebound of the crust after the melting of the ice.

(24) During the other half of the cycle, when the seas sank lower and lower as the glaciers grew in thickness, the world's shorelines were undergoing changes even more far-reaching and dramatic. Every river felt the effect of the lowering sea; its waters were speeded in their course to the ocean and given new strength for the deepening and cutting of its channel. Following the downward-moving shorelines, the rivers extended their courses over the drying sands and muds of what only recently had been the sloping sea bottom. Here the rushing torrents—swollen with melting glacier water—picked up great quantities of loose mud and sand and rolled into the sea as a turgid flood.

(25) During one or more of the Pleistocene lowerings of sea level, the floor of the North Sea was drained of its water and for a time

became dry land. The rivers of northern Europe and of the British Isles followed the retreating waters seaward. Eventually the Rhine captured the whole drainage system of the Thames. The Elbe and the Weser became one river. The Seine rolled through what is now the English Channel and cut itself a trough out across the continental shelf—perhaps the same drowned channel now discernible by soundings beyond Lands End.

(26) The greatest of all Pleistocene glaciations came rather late in the period—probably only about 200 thousand years ago, and well within the time of man. The tremendous lowering of sea level must have affected the life of Paleolithic man. Certainly he was able, at more than one period, to walk across a wide bridge at Bering Strait, which became dry land when the level of the ocean dropped below this shallow shelf. There were other land bridges, created in the same way. As the ocean receded from the coast of India, a long submarine bank became a shoal, then finally emerged, and primitive man walked across "Adam's Bridge" [1] to the island of Ceylon.

(27) Many of the settlements of ancient man must have been located on the seacoast or near the great deltas of the rivers, and relics of his civilization may lie in caves long since covered by the rising ocean. Our meager knowledge of Paleolithic man might be increased by searching along these old drowned shorelines. One archeologist has recommended searching shallow portions of the Adriatic Sea, with "submarine boats casting strong electric lights" or even with glass-bottomed boats and artificial light in the hope of discovering the outlines of shell heaps—the kitchen middens of the early men who once lived here. Professor R. A. Daly has pointed out:

The last Glacial stage was the Reindeer Age of French history. Men then lived in the famous caves overlooking the channels of the French rivers, and hunted the reindeer which throve on the cool plains of France south of the ice border. The Late-Glacial rise of general sealevel was necessarily accompanied by a rise of the river waters downstream. Hence the lowest caves are likely to have been partly or wholly drowned . . . There the search for more relics of Paleolithic man should be pursued.

[1] A thirty-mile chain of sandbanks between Ceylon and India, the remainder of an earlier continuous isthmus.

(28) Some of our Stone Age ancestors must have known the rigors of life near the glaciers. While men as well as plants and animals moved southward before the ice, some must have remained within sight and sound of the great frozen wall. To these the world was a place of storm and blizzard, with bitter winds roaring down out of the blue mountain of ice that dominated the horizon and reached upward into gray skies, all filled with the roaring tumult of the advancing glacier, and with the thunder of moving tons of ice breaking away and plunging into the sea.

(29) But those who lived half the earth away, on some sunny coast of the Indian Ocean, walked and hunted on dry land over which the sea, only recently, had rolled deeply. These men knew nothing of the distant glaciers, nor did they understand that they walked and hunted where they did because quantities of ocean water were frozen as ice and snow in a distant land.

(30) In any imaginative reconstruction of the world of the Ice Age, we are plagued by one tantalizing uncertainty: how low did the ocean level fall during the period of greatest spread of the glaciers, when unknown quantities of water were frozen in the ice? Was it only a moderate fall of 200 or 300 feet—a change paralleled many times in geologic history in the ebb and flow of the epicontinental seas? Or was it a dramatic drawing down of the ocean by 2000, even 3000 feet?

(31) Each of these various levels has been suggested as an actual possibility by one or more geologists. Perhaps it is not surprising that there should be such radical disagreement. It has been only about a century since Louis Agassiz gave the world its first understanding of the moving mountains of ice and their dominating effect on the Pleistocene world. Since then, men in all parts of the earth have been patiently accumulating the facts and reconstructing the events of those four successive advances and retreats of the ice. Only the present generation of scientists, led by such daring thinkers as Daly, have understood that each thickening of the ice sheets meant a corresponding lowering of the ocean, and that with each retreat of the melting ice a returning flood of water raised the sea level.

(32) Of this "alternate robbery and restitution" most geologists have taken a conservative view and said that the greatest lowering of the sea level could not have amounted to more than 400 feet, possibly

only half as much. Most of those who argue that the drawing down was much greater base their reasoning upon the submarine canyons, those deep gorges cut in the continental slopes. The deeper canyons lie a mile or more below the present level of the sea. Geologists who maintain that at least the upper parts of the canyons were stream-cut say that the sea level must have fallen enough to permit this during the Pleistocene glaciation.

(33) This question of the farthest retreat of the sea into its basins must await further searchings into the mysteries of the ocean. We seem on the verge of exciting new discoveries. Now oceanographers and geologists have better instruments than ever before to probe the depths of the sea, to sample its rocks and deeply layered sediments, and to read with greater clarity the dim pages of past history.

(34) Meanwhile, the sea ebbs and flows in these grander tides of earth, whose stages are measurable not in hours but in millennia—tides so vast they are invisible and uncomprehended by the senses of man. Their ultimate cause, should it ever be discovered, may be found to be deep within the fiery center of the earth, or it may lie somewhere in the dark spaces of the universe.

STUDY QUESTIONS

1. There are various general ways of organizing expository essays: by working up to a climax (climactic), by steady accumulation of details (additive), by expanding beyond an initial point and then returning to it (circular), by suggestion or association (oblique), etc. What general method of organization is used in this essay? Illustrate your answer.

2. What does Miss Carson gain by using the quotation from Swinburne?

3. How does Miss Carson strive to gain the reader's attention in her opening paragraphs (1–6)?

4. This essay is a popular presentation of scientific information. How does Miss Carson make her facts interesting for a nonspecialist?

5. Miss Carson assumes some knowledge of geography on the part of her readers. If you do not possess sufficient knowledge of this sort, how could you easily remedy this lack?

6. Must one be a geologist or oceanographer to write an essay of this kind?

7. Miss Carson is concerned in this essay with giving her readers not only facts but also an attitude toward these facts. How does the concluding paragraph make explicit this attitude which has been urged implicitly throughout the essay?

8. The first sentence of paragraph 10 is longer than most of Miss Carson's sentences. Is there any special justification for its length and structure?

9. Examine closely the sentence structure of paragraphs 5 and 6. After the introductory sentence of paragraph 5, the basic structure of both paragraphs consists of a conditional statement followed by hypothetical conclusions presented in a series of clauses with basically parallel structure. How does Miss Carson avoid monotony in her use of parallelism in these paragraphs?

10. Define the following words as used in their contexts: *transgressions* (8), *submarine* (19), *dwarfed* (20), *reluctant* (2), *intruded* (7), *invasion* (8), *processions* (9), *turgid* (24), *probe* (33). Upon what exact connotation of each does Miss Carson rely? Are the words appropriate in their contexts?

11. Would you characterize Miss Carson's language generally as richly connotative or largely denotative? Aside from the technical geologic terms, is her diction relatively commonplace or highly literary? How does her choice of language reflect her purpose and govern her accomplishment?

WRITING ASSIGNMENTS

1. Write a personal sketch of the impression a sea has made upon you. If you have never seen a sea, write the same sort of essay about a natural phenomenon which has meant something to you: a river, a mountain, a lake, or the like.

2. Write an account of the value for you of reading Miss Carson's essay.

3. Write a reflective essay on the role which the sea has played in the history of mankind.

4. Write a research paper on the geologic history of a natural phenomenon in your experience.

5. Write a sketch, based on research, on Miss Carson's interest in the sea.

The Snout*

LOREN C. EISELEY (1907–   ) *is a professor of anthropology at the University of Pennsylvania. His principal scholarly interests are problems relating to prehistoric man, interests which have led him on several paleontological and archaelogical expeditions in the western United States and have produced numerous articles for professional journals. The essay printed here, along with several other essays that have appeared in* Harper's Magazine, *is shortly to be included in a book by Mr. Eiseley.*

I

(1) I have long been an admirer of the octopus. The cephalopods are very old, and they have slipped, protean, through many shapes. They are the wisest of the molluscs, and I have always felt it to be just as well for us that they never came ashore, but—there are other things that have.

(2) There is no need to be frightened. It is true some of the creatures are odd, but I find the situation rather heartening than otherwise. It gives one a feeling of confidence to see nature still busy with experiments, still dynamic, and not through nor satisfied because a Devonian fish managed to end as a two-legged character with a straw hat. There are other things brewing and wriggling in the oceanic vat. It pays to know this. It pays to know there is just as much future as there is past. The only thing that doesn't pay is to be sure of man's own part in it.

(3) There are things down there still coming ashore. Never make the mistake of thinking life is now adjusted for eternity. It gets into

* From *Harper's Magazine*, September, 1950. Copyright 1950 by Harper & Brothers. Reprinted by permission of the author and Harper & Brothers.

your head—the certainty, I mean—the human certainty, and then you miss it all—the things on the tide-flats and what they mean, and why, as my wife says, "they ought to be watched."

(4) The trouble is, we don't know what to watch for. I have a friend, one of those Explorers Club people, who drops in now and then between trips to tell me about the size of crocodile jaws in Uganda, or what happened on some back beach in Arnhem Land.[1]

(5) "They fell out of the trees," he said. "Like rain. And into the boat."

(6) "Uh?" I said, noncommittally.

(7) "They did *so*," he protested, "and they were hard to catch."

(8) "Really," I said.

(9) "We were pushing a dugout up one of the tidal creeks in northern Australia and going fast when smacko we jammed this mangrove bush and the things came tumbling down.

(10) "What were they doing sitting up there in bunches? I ask you. It's no place for a fish. Besides that they had a way of sidling off with those pop-eyes trained on you. I never liked it. Somebody ought to keep an eye on them."

(11) "Why?" I asked.

(12) "I don't know why," he said impatiently, running a rough, square hand through his hair and wrinkling his forehead. "I just mean they make you feel that way, is all. A fish belongs in the water. It ought to stay there—just as we live on land in houses. Things ought to know their place and stay in it, but those fish have got a way of sidling off. As though they had mental reservations and weren't keeping any contracts. See what I mean?"

(13) "I see what you mean," I said gravely. "They ought to be watched. My wife thinks so too. About a lot of things."

(14) "She does?" He brightened. "Then that's two of us. I don't know why, but they give you that feeling."

(15) He didn't know why, but I thought that I did.

[1] A northern region in the Northern Territory of Australia.

II

(16) It began as such things always begin—in the ooze of un-noticed swamps, in the darkness of eclipsed moons. It began with a strangled gasping for air.

(17) The pond was a place of reek and corruption, of fetid smells and of oxygen-starved fish breathing through laboring gills. At times the slowly contracting circle of the water left little windrows of min-nows who skittered desperately to escape the sun, but who died, never-theless, in the fat, warm mud. It was a place of low life. In it the human brain began.

(18) There were strange snouts in those waters, strange barbels nuzzling the bottom ooze, and there was time—three hundred million years of it—but mostly, I think, it was the ooze. By day the temperature in the world outside the pond rose to a frightful intensity; at night the sun went down in smoking red. Dust storms marched in incessant pro-gression across a wilderness whose plants were the plants of long ago. Leafless and weird and stiff they lingered by the water, while over vast areas of grassless uplands the winds blew until red stones took on the polish of reflecting mirrors. There was nothing to hold the land in place. Winds howled, dust clouds rolled, and brief erratic torrents choked with silt ran down to the sea. It was a time of dizzying contrasts, a time of change.

(19) On the oily surface of the pond, from time to time a snout thrust upward, took in air with a queer grunting inspiration, and swirled back to the bottom. The pond was doomed, the water was foul, and the oxygen almost gone, but the creature would not die. It could breathe air direct through a little accessory lung, and it could walk. In all that weird and lifeless landscape, it was the only thing that could. It walked rarely and under protest, but that was not surprising. The creature was a fish.

(20) In the passage of days the pond became a puddle, but the Snout survived. There was dew one dark night and a coolness in the empty stream bed. When the sun rose next morning the pond was an empty place of cracked mud, but the Snout did not lie there. He had

gone. Downstream there were other ponds. He breathed air for a few hours and hobbled slowly along on the stumps of heavy fins.

(21) It was an uncanny business if there had been anyone there to see it. It was a journey best not observed in daylight, it was something that needed swamps and shadows and the touch of the night dew. It was a monstrous penetration of a forbidden element, and the Snout kept his face from the light. It was just as well, though, the face should not be mocked. In three hundred million years it would be our own.

(22) There was something fermenting in the brain of the Snout. He was no longer entirely a fish. The ooze had marked him. It takes a swamp and tide-flat zoologist to tell you about life; it is in this domain that the living suffer great extremes, it is here that the water-failures, driven to desperation, make starts in a new element. It is here that strange compromises are made and new senses are born. The Snout was no exception. Though he breathed and walked primarily in order to stay in the water, he was coming ashore.

(23) He was not really a successful fish except that he was managing to stay alive in a noisome, uncomfortable, oxygen-starved environment. In fact the time was coming when the last of his kind, harried by more ferocious and speedier fishes, would slip off the edge of the continental shelf, to seek safety in the sunless abysses of the deep sea. But the Snout was a fresh-water Crossopterygian, to give him his true name, and cumbersome and plodding though he was, something had happened back of his eyes. The ooze had gotten in its work.

(24) It is interesting to consider what sort of creatures we, the remote descendants of the Snout, might be, except for that green quagmire out of which he came. Mammalian insects perhaps we should have been—solid-brained, our neurones wired for mechanical responses, our lives running out with the perfection of beautiful, intricate, and mindless clocks. More likely we should never have existed at all. It was the Snout and the ooze that did it; with perhaps there also among rotting fish heads and blue, night-burning bog lights, the careful finger of God. It was not much. It was two bubbles, two thin-walled little balloons at the end of the Snout's small brain. The cerebral hemispheres had appeared.

(25) Among all the experiments in that dripping, ooze-filled world, one was vital: the brain had to be fed. The nerve tissues are insatiable devourers of oxygen. If they do not get it, life is gone. In stagnant swamp waters, only the development of a highly efficient blood supply to the brain can prevent disaster. And among those gasping, dying creatures, whose small brains winked out forever in the long Silurian drought, the Snout and his brethren survived.

(26) Over the exterior surface of the Snout's tiny brain ran the myriad blood vessels that served it; through the greatly enlarged choroid plexuses other vessels pumped oxygen into the spinal fluid. The brain was a thin-walled tube fed from both surfaces. It could only exist as a thing of thin walls permeated with oxygen. To thicken, to lay down solid masses of nervous tissue such as exist among the fishes in oxygenated waters was to invite disaster. The Snout lived on a bubble, two bubbles in his brain.

(27) It was not that his thinking was deep; it was only that it had to be thin. The little bubbles of the hemispheres helped to spread the area upon which higher correlation centers could be built, and yet preserve those areas from the disastrous thickenings which meant oxygen death to the swamp dweller.

(28) There is a mystery about those thickenings which culminate in the so-called solid brain. It is the brain of insects, of the modern fishes, of some reptiles, and all birds. Always it marks the appearance of elaborate patterns of instinct and the end of thought. A road has been taken which, anatomically, is well-nigh irretraceable; it does not lead in the direction of a high order of consciousness.

(29) Wherever, instead, the thin sheets of gray matter expand upward into the enormous hemispheres of the human brain, laughter or, it may be, sorrow enters in. Out of the choked Devonian waters emerged sight and sound and the music that rolls invisible through the composer's brain. They are there still in the ooze along the tideline, though no one notices. The world is fixed, we say: fish in the sea, birds in the air. But in the mangrove swamps by the Niger, fish climb trees and ogle uneasy naturalists who try unsuccessfully to chase them back to the water. There are things still coming ashore.

III

(30) The door to the past is a strange door. It swings open and things pass through it, but they pass in one direction only. No man can return across that threshold, though he can look down still and see the green light waver in the water weeds.

(31) There are two ways to seek the doorway: in the swamps of the inland waterways and along the tide flats of the estuaries where rivers come to the sea. By those two pathways life came ashore. It was not the magnificent march through the breakers and up the cliffs that we fondly imagine. It was a stealthy advance made in suffocation and terror, amidst the leaching bite of chemical discomfort. It was made by the failures of the sea.

(32) Some creatures have slipped through the invisible chemical barrier between salt and fresh water, into the tidal rivers, and later come ashore; some have crept upward from the salt. In all cases, however, the first adventure into the dreaded atmosphere seems to have been largely determined by the inexorable crowding of enemies and by the retreat further and further into marginal situations where the oxygen supply was depleted. Finally, in the ruthless selection of the swamp margins, or in the scramble for food on the tide flats, the land becomes home.

(33) Not the least interesting feature of some of the tide-flat emergents is their definite antipathy for the full tide. It obstructs their food-collecting on the mud banks and brings their enemies. Only extremes of fright will drive them into the water for any period.

(34) I think it was the great nineteenth-century paleontologist Cope who first clearly enunciated what he called the "law of the unspecialized," the contention that it was not from the most highly organized and dominant forms of a given geological era that the master type of a succeeding period evolved, but that instead the dominant forms tended to arise from more lowly and generalized animals which were capable of making new adaptations, and which were not narrowly restricted to a given environment.

(35) There is considerable truth to this observation, but, for all that, the idea is not simple. Who is to say without foreknowledge of

the future which animal is specialized and which is not? We have only
to consider our remote ancestor, the Snout, to see the intricacies into
which the law of the unspecialized may lead us.

(36) If we had been making zoological observations in the Paleozoic
Age, with no knowledge of the strange realms life was to penetrate in
the future, we would probably have regarded the Snout as specialized.
We would have seen his air-bladder lung, his stubby, sluggish fins, and
his odd ability to wriggle overland as specialized adaptations to a pe-
culiarly restricted environmental niche in stagnant continental waters.
We would have thought in water terms and we would have dismissed
the Snout as an interesting failure off the main line of progressive evolution, escaping from his enemies and surviving successfully only in
the dreary and marginal surroundings scorned by the swift-finned
teleost fishes who were destined to dominate the seas and all quick
waters.

(37) Yet it was this poor specialization—this bog-trapped failure—
whose descendants, in three great movements, were to dominate the
earth. It is only now, looking backward, that we dare to regard him as
"generalized." The Snout was the first vertebrate to pop completely
through the water membrane into a new dimension. His very specializa-
tions and failures, in a water sense, had pre-adapted him for a world he
scarcely knew existed.

(38) The day of the Snout was over three hundred million years
ago. Not long since I read a book in which a prominent scientist spoke
cheerfully of some ten billion years of future time remaining to us. He
pointed out happily the things that man might do throughout that
period. Fish in the sea, I thought again, birds in the air. The climb all
far behind us, the species fixed and sure. No wonder my explorer friend
had had a momentary qualm when he met the mud skippers with their
mental reservations and lack of promises. There is something wrong
with our world view. It is still Ptolemaic, though the sun is no longer
believed to revolve around the earth.

(39) We teach the past, we see farther backward into time than any
race before us, but we stop at the present, or, at best, we project far
into the future idealized versions of ourselves. All that long way behind
us we see, perhaps inevitably, through human eyes alone. We see our-

selves as the culmination and the end, and if we do indeed consider our passing, we think that sunlight will go with us and the earth be dark. We are the end. For us continents rose and fell, for us the waters and the air were mastered, for us the great living web has pulsated and grown more intricate.

(40) To deny this, a man once told me, is to deny God. This puzzled me. I went back along the pathway to the marsh. I went, not in the past, not by the bones of dead things, not down the lost roadway of the Snout. I went instead in daylight, in the Now, to see if the door was still there, and to see what things passed through.

(41) I found that the same experiments were brewing, that up out of that ancient well fins still were scrambling toward the sunlight. They were small things, and which of them presaged the future I could not say. I saw only that they were many and that they had solved the oxygen death in many marvelous ways, not always ours.

(42) I found that there were modern fishes who breathed air, not through a lung but through their stomachs or through strange chambers where their gills should be, or breathing as the Snout once breathed. I found that some crawled in the fields at nightfall pursuing insects, or slept on the grass by pond sides and drowned, if kept under water, as men themselves might drown.

(43) Of all these fishes the mud skipper *Periophthalmus* is perhaps the strangest. He climbs trees with his fins and pursues insects; he pulls worms like a robin on the tide flats; he sees as land things see, and above all he dodges and evades with a curious pop-eyed insolence more suggestive of the land than of the sea. Of a different tribe and a different time he is, nevertheless, oddly reminiscent of the Snout.

(44) But not the same. There lies the hope of life. The old ways are exploited and remain, but new things come, new senses try the unfamiliar air. There are small scuttlings and splashings in the dark, and out of it come the first croaking, illiterate voices of the things to be, just as man once croaked and dreamed darkly in that tiny vesicular forebrain.

(45) Perpetually, now, we search and bicker and disagree. The eternal form eludes us—the shape we conceive as ours. Perhaps the old road through the marsh should tell us. We are one of many ap-

pearances of the thing called Life; we are not its perfect image, for it has no image except Life, and life is multitudinous and emergent in the stream of time.

(46) Yesterday at the zoo I saw a pair of spectral tarsiers, remote relatives of ours, far-wandered from the Eocene. They were cold and ill in a small box, and very soon to die. I think they knew it, for they clung together and found warmth and comfort—ever so little—in their small, disconsolate world.

(47) It caught my throat in passing, for there—a million lives removed from our own—something—the sympathy we conceive is human—flickered bravely in another shape and looked wistfully out of alien and nocturnal eyes. I think that in that moment I ceased to fear the passing of my kind. The things we are and the things we are not will be realized in other shapes. I saw the forms as One and I thought that life must not lose faith in life so long as the last ribbon-like leech lashes in the last stagnant pool on a planet from which mankind has been expunged. And as I thought it, a vision formed across my eyelids and a face was turned to mine. The eyes held a look of promise, and for the first time I saw that visage without shuddering, and with something close to affection. It was the face of the Snout.

STUDY QUESTIONS

1. What is the basis of Mr. Eiseley's organization of his subject? In what other ways might the same material be organized?

2. Note the points at which Mr. Eiseley uses narrative. In each instance, what effect is gained?

3. How is coherence gained in paragraphs 38 and 45?

4. What effect is achieved by the use of parallelism in sentence structure in paragraphs 16, 21, 31, 40, 41, and 42?

5. Find examples of inverted sentence structure in the following paragraphs: 24, 39, and 41. What is the effect of each inversion? Would normal word order have done as well?

6. Study the rhythm and euphony of paragraphs 18, 20, 24, 44, and 47. In each instance, how is the sound effect achieved? Is it appropriate to the meaning it conveys?

7. Much of the appeal of this essay derives from its tone. How would

you characterize it? How important is that tone to the author's purpose? How is it achieved?

8. What is the effect of Mr. Eiseley's use of the following words: *protean* (1), *marched* (18), *winked out* (25), *choked* (29), *lashes* (47)?

9. Several of Mr. Eiseley's statements are vague or imprecise: e.g., "There are other things brewing and wriggling in the oceanic vat" (2), "It began as such things always begin" (16). Find other examples of such vagueness. How may the vagueness be justified?

10. What change in our point of view does Mr. Eiseley suggest we should make? How would a formal argument for such a change differ from this essay in purpose, structure, and language?

11. Do you find Mr. Eiseley's point of view optimistic or pessimistic? Explain your answer.

WRITING ASSIGNMENTS

1. Rewrite Mr. Eiseley's essay as a formal expository report.

2. Write an analysis of the implications for human behavior, both social and individual, of Mr. Eiseley's view of man's future.

3. Write an argument in defense of or in disagreement with the statement in paragraph 40: "To deny this [the homocentric view of the universe], a man once told me, is to deny God."

4. Write an imaginative account of what human life would be like if we had turned out as "mammalian insects" with "our lives running out with the perfection of beautiful, intricate, and mindless clocks."

5. Write a research paper on a species of animal that has disappeared: the dinosaur, the passenger pigeon, the dodo, etc.

Queer Customs, Potsherds, and Skulls *

CLYDE KLUCKHOHN (1905–   ) is a professor of anthropology at Harvard University and director of Harvard's Russian Research Center. His studies of Navaho culture led to the writing of To the Foot of the Rainbow (1927), Beyond the Rainbow (1933), and The Navaho (1946, in collaboration with Dorothia Leighton). Mirror for Man (1949), the first chapter of which is printed here, won the $10,000 Whittlesey House— Science Illustrated Contest for scientific books for the layman.

(1) Anthropology provides a scientific basis for dealing with the crucial dilemma of the world today: how can peoples of different appearance, mutually unintelligible languages, and dissimilar ways of life get along peaceably together? Of course, no branch of knowledge constitutes a cure-all for the ills of mankind. If any statement in this book seems to support such messianic pretensions, put this absurd claim down as a slip of an enthusiast who really knows better. Anthropology is, however, an overlapping study with bridges into the physical, biological, and social sciences and into the humanities.

(2) Because of its breadth, the variety of its methods, and its mediating position, anthropology is sure to play a central role in the integration of the human sciences. A comprehensive science of man, however, must encompass additional skills, interests, and knowledge. Certain aspects of psychology, medicine and human biology, economics, sociology, and human geography must be fused with anthropology in a general science which must likewise embrace the tools of historical

* From The Mirror for Man by Clyde Kluckhohn. Reprinted by permission of McGraw Hill Book Company, Inc. Copyright 1949 by McGraw Hill Book Company, Inc.

and statistical methods and draw data from history and the other humanities.

(3) Present-day anthropology, then, cannot pretend to be the whole study of man, though perhaps it comes closer than any other branch of science. Some of the discoveries that will here be spoken of as anthropological have been made possible only by collaboration with workers in other fields. Yet even the traditional anthropology has a special right to be heard by those who are deeply concerned with the problem of achieving one world. This is because it has been anthropology that has explored the gamut of human variability and can best answer the questions: what common ground is there between human beings of all tribes and nations? What differences exist? what is their source? how deep-going are they?

(4) By the beginning of the twentieth century the scholars who interested themselves in the unusual, dramatic, and puzzling aspects of man's history were known as anthropologists. They were the men who were searching for man's most remote ancestors; for Homer's Troy; for the original home of the American Indian; for the relationship between bright sunlight and skin color; for the origin of the wheel, safety pins, and pottery. They wanted to know "how modern man got this way": why some people are ruled by a king, some by old men, others by warriors, and none by women; why some peoples pass on property in the male line, others in the female, still others equally to heirs of both sexes; why some people fall sick and die when they think they are bewitched, and others laugh at the idea. They sought for the universals in human biology and in human conduct. They proved that men of different continents and regions were physically much more alike than they were different. They discovered many parallels in human customs, some of which could be explained by historical contact. In other words, anthropology had become the science of human similarities and differences.

(5) In one sense anthropology is an old study. The Greek historian, Herodotus, sometimes called the "father of anthropology" as well as the "father of history," described at length the physique and customs of the Scythians, Egyptians, and other "barbarians." Chinese scholars of the Han dynasty wrote monographs upon the Hiung-Nu, a light-

eyed tribe wandering near China's northwestern frontier. The Roman historian, Tacitus, produced his famous study of the Germans. Long before Herodotus, even, the Babylonians of the time of Hammurabi collected in museums objects made by the Sumerians, their predecessors in Mesopotamia.

(6) Although ancients here and there showed that they thought types and manners of men worth talking about, it was the voyages and explorations from the fifteenth century onward that stimulated the study of human variability. The observed contrasts with the tight little medieval world made anthropology necessary. Useful though the writings of this period are (for example, the travelogues of Peter Martyr) they cannot be ranked as scientific documents. Often fanciful, they were written to amuse or for narrowly practical purposes. Careful accounts of firsthand observation were mixed up with embellished and frequently secondhand anecdotes. Neither authors nor observers had any special training for recording or interpreting what they saw. They looked at other peoples and their habits through crude and distorting lenses manufactured of all the prejudices and preconceptions of Christian Europeans.

(7) It was not until the late eighteenth and nineteenth centuries that scientific anthropology began to develop. The discovery of the relationship between Sanskrit, Latin, Greek, and the Germanic languages gave a great impetus to the comparative point of view. The first systematic anthropologists were gifted amateurs—physicians, natural historians, lawyers, businessmen to whom anthropology was a hobby. They applied common sense, the habits they had learned in their professions, and the fashionable scientific doctrines of their day to growing knowledge about "primitive" peoples.

(8) What did they study? They devoted themselves to oddities, to matters which appeared to be so trivial or so specialized that the fields of study which had been established earlier failed to bother with them. The forms of human hair, the variations in skull formation, shades of skin color did not seem very important to anatomists or to practicing physicians. The physical remains of cultures other than the Greco-Roman were beneath the notice of classical scholars. Languages unrelated to Greek and Sanskrit had no interest for the comparative

linguists of the nineteenth century. Primitive rites interested only a few of the curious until the elegant prose and respectable classical scholarship of Sir James Frazer's *Golden Bough* [1] won a wide audience. Not without justification has anthropology been termed "the science of leftovers."

(9) It would be going too far to call the nineteenth-century anthropology "the investigation of oddments by the eccentric." The English Tylor, the American Morgan, the German Bastian, and other leading figures were respected citizens. Nevertheless, we shall understand the growth of the subject better if we admit that many of the first anthropologists were, from the point of view of their contemporaries, eccentrics. They were interested in bizarre things with which the average person had no serious concern and even the ordinary intellectual felt to be inconsequential.

(10) If one does not confuse the results of intellectual activities with the motives leading to these activities, it is useful to ask what sort of people would be curious about these questions. Archaeology and museum anthropology provide an obvious happy hunting ground for those who are driven by that passion for finding and arranging which is common to collectors of everything from stamps to suits of armor. Anthropology has also always had with it the romantics, those who have taken it up because the lure of distant places and exotic people was strong upon them. The lure of the strange and far has a peculiar appeal for those who are dissatisfied with themselves or who do not feel at home in their own society. Consciously or unconsciously, they seek other ways of life where their characteristics are understood and accepted or at any rate, not criticized. Like many historians, the historical anthropologist has an urge to escape from the present by crawling back into the womb of the cultural past. Because the study had something of the romantic aroma about it and because it was not an easy way to make a living, it drew an unusual number of students who had independent means.

(11) The beginnings do not sound very promising, either from the point of view of the students who were attracted to the subject or of

[1] A monumental work on primitive customs and beliefs. It appeared first in 1890 in two volumes. The final version was published in 1911–1915 in twelve volumes.

what they were drawn to study. Nevertheless these very liabilities provided what are the greatest advantages of anthropology as compared with other approaches to the study of human life. Because nineteenth-century anthropologists studied the things they did out of pure interest and not either to earn a living or to reform the world, a tradition of relative objectivity grew up. The philosophers were shackled by the weighty history of their subject and by the vested interests of their profession. Auguste Comte, the founder of sociology, was a philosopher, but he tried to model sociology after the natural sciences. However, many of his followers, who were only slightly disguised philosophers of history, had a bias in favor of reasoning as opposed to observation. Many of the first American sociologists were Christian ministers, more eager to improve the world than to study it with detachment. The field of political science was also tinged with the philosophic point of view and with reforming zeal. The psychologists became so absorbed in brass instruments and the laboratory that they found little time to study man as one really wants to know him—not in the laboratory but in his daily life. Because anthropology was the science of leftovers and because leftovers were many and varied, it avoided the preoccupation with only one aspect of life that stamped, for instance, economics.

(12) The eagerness and energy of the amateurs gradually won a place for their subject as an independent science. A museum of ethnology was established in Hamburg in 1850; the Peabody Museum of Archaeology and Ethnology at Harvard was founded in 1866; the Royal Anthropological Institute in 1873; the Bureau of American Ethnology in 1879. Tylor was made Reader in Anthropology at Oxford in 1884. The first American professor was appointed in 1886. But in the nineteenth century there were not a hundred anthropologists in the whole world.

(13) The total number of anthropological Ph.D.'s granted in the United States prior to 1920 was only 53. Before 1930 only four American universities gave the doctorate in anthropology. Even today there are a bare dozen. Nor has anthropology become in any sense a staple of the undergraduate curriculum. In only two or three secondary schools is instruction regularly given.

(14) The astonishing thing, considering the trifling number of

anthropologists and the minute fraction of the population that has been exposed to formal instruction in the subject is that during the last decade or so the word "anthropology" and some of its terms have come out of hiding in recondite literature to appear with increasing frequency in *The New Yorker, Life, The Saturday Evening Post,* detective stories, and even in moving pictures. It is also symptomatic of a trend that many colleges and universities and some secondary schools have indicated their intention of introducing anthropology in their revised courses of study. Although anthropologists—like psychiatrists and psychologists—are still regarded with a bit of suspicion, present-day society is beginning to feel they have something useful as well as diverting to offer.

(15) In the American Southwest one of the signs of summer is the arrival of many "-ologists" who disrupt the quiet of the countryside. They dig up ruins with all the enthusiasm of small boys hunting for "Indian curios" or of delayed adolescents seeking buried treasure. They pry into the business of peaceful Indians and make a nuisance of themselves generally with a lot of queer-looking gadgets. The kind who dig into ruins are technically called "archaeologists," those who dig into the minds of Indians, "ethnologists" or "social anthropologists," those who measure heads, "physical anthropologists," but all are varieties of the more inclusive breed term "anthropologists."

(16) Now what are they really up to? Is it just sheer curiosity about "ye beastly devices of ye heathen" or do the diggings, questionings, and measurings really have something to do with the world today? Do anthropologists merely produce exotic and amusing facts which have nothing to do with the problems of here and now?

(17) Anthropology is something more than brooding over skulls or hunting for "the missing link," and it has a greater usefulness than providing means to tell one's friends from the apes. Seen from the outside, anthropological activities look, at best, harmlessly amusing, at worst, pretty idiotic. No wonder many a Southwesterner quips, "The Indians are going to start putting a bounty on you fellows." The lay reaction is well summed up by the remark of an army officer. We had met socially and were getting along very well until he asked me how

I made my living. When I told him I was an anthropologist he drew away and said, "Well, you don't have to be crazy to be an anthropologist, but I guess it helps."

(18) An anthropologist is a person who is crazy enough to study his fellow man. The scientific study of ourselves is relatively new. In England in 1936 there were over 600 persons who earned their living as students of one specialized branch (biochemistry) of the science of things, but fewer than 10 were employed as anthropologists. There are less than a dozen jobs for physical anthropologists in the United States today.

(19) Yet nothing is more certain than that men ought to see whether the scientific methods which have given such stupendous results in unlocking the secrets of the physical universe might not help them understand themselves and their neighbors in this rapidly shrinking world. Men build machines that are truly wonderful, only to find themselves next to helpless when it comes to treating the social disorders that often follow the introduction of these machines.

(20) Ways of making a living have changed with such bewildering rapidity that we are all a bit confused most of the time. Our ways of life have altered too—but not symmetrically. Our economic, political, and social institutions have not caught up with our technology. Our religious beliefs and practices and our other idea systems have much in them that is not appropriate to our present way of life and to our scientific knowledge of the physical and biological world. Part of us lives in the "modern" age—another part in medieval or even Greek times.

(21) In the realm of treating social ills we are still living in the age of magic. We often act as if revolutionary and disturbing ideas could be exorcised by a verbal rite—like evil spirits. We hunt for witches to blame for our troubles: Roosevelt, Hitler, Stalin. We resist changing our inner selves even when altered conditions make this clearly necessary. We are aggrieved if other peoples misunderstand us or our motives; but if we try to understand them at all, we insist on doing so only in terms of our own assumptions about life which we take to be infallibly correct. We are still looking for the philosopher's stone—some magic formula (perhaps a mechanical scheme for international

organization) that will make the world orderly and peaceful without other than external adaptations on our part.

(22) We don't know ourselves very well. We talk about a rather vague thing called "human nature." We vehemently assert that it is "human nature" to do this and not to do that. Yet anybody who has lived in the American Southwest, to cite but one instance, knows from ordinary experience that the laws of this mysterious "human nature" do not seem to work out exactly the same way for the Spanish-speaking people of New Mexico, for the English-speaking population, and for the various Indian tribes. This is where the anthropologists come in. It is their task to record the variations and the similarities in human physique, in the things people make, in ways of life. Only when we find out just how men who have had different upbringings, who come from different physical stocks, who speak different languages, who live under different physical conditions, meet their problems, can we be sure as to what all human beings have in common. Only then can we claim scientific knowledge of raw human nature.

(23) It will be a long job. But perhaps before it is too late we will come close to knowing what "human nature" really is—that is, what the reactions are that men inevitably have as human beings, regardless of their particular biological or social heritage. To discover human nature, the scientific adventurers of anthropology have been exploring the byways of time and of space. It is an absorbing task—so absorbing that anthropologists have tended to write only for each other or for scholars in other professions. Most of the literature of anthropology consists of articles in scientific journals and of forbidding monographs. The writing bristles with strange names and unfamiliar terms and is too detailed for the general reader. Some anthropologists may have had an obsession for detail as such. At any rate there are many whole monographs devoted to such subjects as "An Analysis of Three Hairnets from the Pachacamac Area." Even to other students of man the great mass of anthropological endeavor has appeared, as Robert Lynd says, "aloof and preoccupied."

(24) Though some research thus appears to leave the "anthropos" (man) off to one side, still the main trends of anthropological thought have been focused on a few questions of broad human interest, such

as: what has been the course of human evolution, both biologically and culturally? Are there any general principles or "laws" governing this evolution? What necessary connections, if any, exist between the physical type, the speech, and the customs of the peoples of past and present? What generalizations can be made about human beings in groups? How plastic is man? How much can he be molded by training or by the necessity to adapt to environmental pressures? Why are certain personality types more characteristic of some societies than of others?

(25) To most people, however, anthropology still means measuring skulls, treating little pieces of broken pottery with fantastic care, and reporting the outlandish customs of savage tribes. The anthropologist is the grave robber, the collector of Indian arrowheads, the queer fellow who lives with unwashed cannibals. As Sol Tax [2] remarks, the anthropologist has had a function in society "something between that of an Einstein dealing with the mysterious and that of an entertainer." His specimens, his pictures, or his tales may serve for an hour's diversion but are pretty dull stuff compared to the world of grotesque monsters from distant ages which the paleontologist can recreate, the wonders of modern plant and animal life described by the biologist, the excitement of unimaginably far-off universes and cosmic processes roused by the astronomer. Surely anthropology seems the most useless and impractical of all the "-ologies." In a world of rocket ships and international organizations, what can the study of the obscure and primitive offer to the solution of today's problems?

(26) "The longest way round is often the shortest way home." The preoccupation with insignificant nonliterate peoples that is an outstanding feature of anthropological work is the key to its significance today. Anthropology grew out of experience with primitives and the tools of the trade are unusual because they were forged in this peculiar workshop.

(27) Studying primitives enables us to see ourselves better. Ordinarily we are unaware of the special lens through which we look at life. It would hardly be fish who discovered the existence of water. Students who had not gone beyond the horizon of their own society could not be expected to perceive custom which was the stuff of their own think-

[2] Professor of Anthropology at the University of Chicago.

ing. The scientist of human affairs needs to know as much about the eye that sees as the object seen. *Anthropology holds up a great mirror to man and lets him look at himself in his infinite variety.* This, and not the satisfaction of idle curiosity nor romantic quest, is the meaning of the anthropologist's work in nonliterate societies.

(28) Picture the field worker in a remote island of the South Seas or among a tribe of the Amazon jungle. He is usually alone. But he is expected to bring back a report on both the physique and the total round of the people's activities. He is forced to see human life as a whole. He must become a Jack-of-all-trades and acquire enough diverse knowledge to describe such varying things as head shape, health practices, motor habits, agriculture, animal husbandry, music, language, and the way baskets are made.

(29) Since there are no published accounts of the tribe, or only spotty or inadequate ones, he depends more on his eyes and his ears than upon books. Compared with the average sociologist, he is almost illiterate. The time that the sociologist spends in the library, the anthropologist spends in the field. Moreover, his seeing and his listening take on a special character. The ways of life he observes are so unfamiliar that it is next to impossible to interpret them through his own values. He cannot analyze in terms of the things he had decided in advance were important, because everything is out of pattern. It is easier for him to view the scene with detachment and relative objectivity just because it is remote and unfamiliar, because he himself is not emotionally involved. Finally, since the language has to be learned or interpreters found, the anthropologist is compelled to pay more attention to deeds than to words. When he cannot understand what is being said, the only thing he can do is devote himself to the humble but very useful task of noting who lives with whom, who works with whom in what activities, who talks loudly and who talks softly, who wears what when.

(30) A perfectly legitimate question at this point would be: "Well, perhaps anthropologists in working in nonliterate societies did happen to pick up some skills that have given good results when applied to studies of our society. But in the name of everything, why, if you anthropologists are really interested in modern life, do you keep on bothering with these inconsequential little tribes?"

(31) The anthropologist's first answer would be that the life ways of these tribes are part of the human record and that it is his job to see that these things get recorded. Indeed anthropologists have felt this responsibility very keenly. They have felt that they had no time to write general books when each year saw the extinction of aboriginal cultures that had not yet been described. The descriptive character of most anthropological literature and the overpowering mass of detail are to be traced to the anthropologist's obsession with getting down the facts before it is too late.

(32) The traditional scientific attitude is that knowledge is an end in itself. There is much to be said for this point of view. Probably the applications that have been made possible by pure science have been richer and more numerous because scientists did not narrow their interests to fields that promised immediate practical utility. But in these troublous times many scientists are also concerned about the social justification of their work. There is such a thing as scientific dilettantism. It is nice that a few rich museums can afford to pay a few men to spend their lives in the intensive study of medieval armor, but the life careers of some anthropologists do remind one of Aldous Huxley's character who consecrated his existence to writing the history of the three-tined fork. Society cannot afford, in a period like the present, to support many specialists in highly esoteric studies unless they show promise of practical usefulness. Fortunately, the detailed study of primitive peoples falls into the useful category.

(33) I may decide that what is really needed is knowledge of urban communities like Cambridge, Massachusetts. But, in the present situation of social science, a host of practical difficulties confront me. In the first place, to do a comprehensive job, I should need more collaborators than could be paid for under existing arrangements for the support of research on human behavior. Then I should have to ask: in terms of actual human interactions, where does Cambridge leave off and where do Boston, Watertown, and Somerville begin? Many people living in Cambridge grew up in different parts of the United States and in foreign countries. I should always be in danger of attributing to conditions in Cambridge ways of behavior which in fact should be explained as results of upbringing in far-distant places.

Finally, I should be dealing with dozens of different biological stocks and mixtures between them. L. J. Henderson [3] used to say, "When I go into my laboratory and try an experiment in which there are five or six unknowns, I can sometimes solve the problem if I work long enough. But I know better than even to try when there are twenty or more unknowns."

(34) This is not to argue that it is useless to study Cambridge at the present time. Far from it. Certain small problems can be defined and answers of a high degree of validity obtained. Something of scientific and practical benefit could be learned about the workings of the whole community. The issue is not Shall the scientific student of man work in our own society *or* among primitives? It is rather: Does the anthropologist by working in the simpler scene isolate certain crucial factors which can then be investigated more effectively in the complex picture? The right questions to ask and the right techniques for getting the answers to them can best be discovered by work on smaller canvases, that is, in more homogeneous societies that have been by-passed by civilization.

(35) The primitive society is the closest to laboratory conditions the student of man can ever hope to get. Such groups are usually small and can be studied intensively by few people at slight expense. They are ordinarily rather isolated so that the question does not arise as to where one social system begins and another ends. The members of the group have lived their lives within a small area and have been exposed continually to the pressure of the same natural forces. They have had an almost identical education. All of their experiences have much more in common than is the case with members of complex societies. Their ways of life are comparatively stable. Commonly there is a high degree of biological inbreeding so that any member of the society chosen at random has about the same biological inheritance as any other. In short, many factors can be regarded as more or less constant, and the anthropologist is free to study a few variables in detail with real hope of ferreting out the connections between them.

(36) This can be made clearer by an analogy. How much would we know today of human physiology if we had been able to study

[3] Professor of biological chemistry at Harvard until his death in 1942.

the physiological processes only among human beings? The fact that we would have been blocked at every turn is due partly to the humanitarian limitations we place upon using humans as guinea pigs, but it must also be traced to the complexity of the human organism. There are so many variables that it would have been enormously difficult to isolate the decisive ones had we not been able to study physiological processes in simpler settings. A reflex could be speedily isolated in the frog, then studied with more complications in the simpler mammals. Once these complexities had been mastered, it was possible to go successfully to monkeys and apes and then to mankind. This is, of course, the essential method of science: the method of successive steps, the method of going from the known to the unknown, from the simple to the ever more and more complex.

(37) Nonliterate societies represent the end results of many different experiments carried out by nature. Groups that have largely gone their way without being absorbed in the great civilizations of the West and the East show us the variety of solutions which men have worked out for perennial human problems and the variety of meanings that peoples attach to the same and to different cultural forms. Contemplation of this vast tableau gives us perspective and detachment. By analyzing the results of these experiments, the anthropologist also gives us practical information on what works and what doesn't.

(38) A nonanthropologist, Grace de Laguna,[4] has luminously summed up the advantages of a view of ourselves from the anthropological angle:

It is indeed precisely with regard to standards of life and thought that the intimate studies of primitive peoples have cast more light on human nature than all the reflections of sages or the painstaking investigations of laboratory scientists. On the one hand, they have shown concretely and vividly the universal kinship of mankind, abstractly recognized by the Stoics and accepted as an article of Christian faith; on the other hand, they have revealed a wealth of human diversity and a variety of human standards and of modes of feeling and thinking hitherto unimagined. The horrid practices of the savage have shown themselves to the intimate and unprejudiced study of the field ethnologist at once more amazing and

[4] Professor of philosophy at Bryn Mawr College.

more understandable than romance had painted them. The wider sympathy with men and the deeper insight into human nature which these studies have brought have done much to shake our complacent estimate of ourselves and our attainments. We have come to suspect that even our own deepest beliefs and our most cherished convictions may be as much the expression of an unconscious provincialism as are the fantastic superstitions of the savage.

STUDY QUESTIONS

1. What is the significance of the title of this essay? Does it specifically indicate the author's thesis? What was your reaction to the title, before you read the essay?

2. What unit of thought is covered in paragraphs 1–4? Could those paragraphs logically be incorporated into one? If so, what objections could be raised to such a longer paragraph? How are paragraphs 1 and 3 closely tied together?

3. What unit of thought is developed in paragraphs 5–14? What subtopics are treated in this section? How many paragraphs are devoted to each?

4. What turn in Mr. Kluckhohn's thought is indicated by the extra spacing between paragraphs 14 and 15?

5. What is the function of paragraph 16?

6. What unit of thought is developed in paragraphs 15–38?

7. Summarize in one paragraph the value of studying primitive societies.

8. Study the structure of paragraph 4. Is the topic explicitly stated? If so, where? If it is not stated, what is it? What method is used to develop the topic? How many kinds of parallelism in structure are used in this paragraph? Why is the use of parallelism especially suited to the kind of development used here?

9. Would you characterize the diction of this essay as highly connotative or largely denotative? very dramatic or relatively subdued? highly literary or rather commonplace?

10. Why do you think Mr. Kluckhohn selected Cambridge as his example in paragraph 33?

11. Does Mr. Kluckhohn, in so strongly defending his own special field of anthropology, give the impression of being biased in his appraisals of other branches of knowledge? Cf. paragraphs 3, 11, and 32.

WRITING ASSIGNMENTS

1. Write an essay to illustrate the opening sentences of paragraph 22. That is, write on your notions of what constitutes human nature. Even with the handicap of your own ignorance and your lack of experience, you can write an essay in which you can at least organize your own confusions.

2. Write an essay, using as your central thesis any sentence in paragraph 21.

3. Using as your starting point the first sentence of this essay, write an account of some of the *specific* problems which you think can be helped toward solution by the kind of information which anthropology affords.

4. Write a research paper on one of the following: the Folsom Man, the civilization of the Incas, the practice of polygamy.

The Courtship of Animals *

JULIAN HUXLEY (1887–), *prominent English biologist, is the brother of Aldous, represented elsewhere in this collection, and grandson of Thomas Henry Huxley, the famous scientist. In addition to teaching in England, he taught at the Rice Institute in Texas in 1912–1916. He has done important research in biology and has taken an active part in various scientific and cultural societies, including UNESCO. For his work, he has received numerous awards and honorary degrees. He was biological editor of the* Encyclopaedia Britannica, 14th Edition. *His numerous books include* Essays on Popular Science (1926), Man Stands Alone (1927), The Uniqueness of Man (1941), Man in the Modern World (1947), Evolution and Ethics (1947), *and* Heredity East and West (1949).

(1) We men like to see animals courting. It amuses us to see them thus imitating humanity, and throws something at once romantic and familiar into those dumb and hidden lives which they veil so closely from us. "One touch of Nature makes the whole world kin," [1] we murmur, and find a new pleasure in the hackneyed words. They are really not quite apropos, however; for what we in our heart of hearts mean to say is one touch of *human* nature. Man is a vain organism, and likes to stand surrounded by mirrors—magnifying mirrors if it be possible, but at any rate mirrors. And so we read the ideas of our own mind into the animals, and confidently speak of "suitors" and "coy brides to be won" and "jealous rivals" and what not, as if birds or even spiders or newts were miniature human beings, in fancy dress no doubt, but with the thoughts of a twentieth-century inhabitant of London or New York.

* From *Man Stands Alone* by Julian Huxley. Copyright 1926 by Julian Huxley. Reprinted by permission of Harper & Brothers.
[1] Shakespeare, *Troilus and Cressida*, III.iii.175.

(2) Some of the more reflective, perhaps, may wonder how far we are justified in our assumptions as to the motives and meaning of animal courtship; while others, with maybe some biological knowledge behind them, may try to look at it all from the other side of the gulf between man and beast, imagine how our own courtship would look to an external and dispassionate intelligence, wonder whether much of human behaviour had better not be interpreted from the animal side rather than the animal's from ours, and how much we are walled in by our biological heritage.

(3) Animal courtship is an unfashionable topic among biologists at present; and I do not exaggerate when I say that it is also one on which both ignorance and prejudice prevail. My own real interest in the subject began when, one spring in Wales, I observed the beautiful courtship of the redshank, a common shore bird, and when I got back to libraries, could find no ordered account of it, or indeed of bird courtship in general. And now, after some twenty-five years of reading and thinking about the subject, interspersed with a number of pleasant if strenuous holidays in Britain, in Louisiana, in Holland, in Spitsbergen, trying to find out what really does happen with this or that common bird, I can confidently assert that Darwin's theory of sexual selection, though wrong in many details, yet was essentially right: that there is no other explanation for the bulk of the characters concerned with display, whether antics, song, colour, or special plumes or other structures, than that they have been evolved in relation to the mind of the opposite sex; that *mind* has thus been the sieve through which variations in courtship characters must pass if they are to survive.

(4) Down at the base of the animal scale courtship of course does not exist. Jellyfish or sponges or sea-urchins simply shed their reproductive cells into the water and trust to luck for fertilization. It is only when male and female must actually co-operate for fertilization to be effected, that we can expect to find courtship; and even so it will not exist unless there is a fairly elaborate brain and nervous system.

(5) Perhaps the first adumbration of courtship is seen in the nuptial dances of certain marine bristle-worms (Polychaetes), in which at certain seasons of the year and phases of the moon the creatures swim up out of their crannies in the rocks and gather in groups, excited

males wriggling round the females. It is possible that the presence of the dancing males in some way stimulates the females to lay their eggs, upon which the male elements are discharged in milky clouds. Snails too have a primitive courtship, which is complicated by the fact that they are bi-sexual and each in its rôle of male attempts to stimulate the other in its rôle of female.

(6) But the first actions to which the name *courtship*, and not merely perhaps direct stimulus to fertilization, must be given are those of a few crabs and most spiders. Among the crustaceans, the fiddler-crab is characterized by the presence in the male of one enormously enlarged claw, which may weigh almost as much as the rest of the body, and is often brightly coloured. It used to be supposed that with this the males stopped their burrows, or fought other males, or seized and carried off the females. However, the careful studies of Dr. Pearce show that its main function is one of display. In the mating season, when a female comes past, the males throw themselves into a tiptoe attitude, with big claw rigidly held aloft. If the female takes no notice, the male runs again to where she can see him, and again strikes the statuesque pose: if she goes too far, he returns to his burrow. The observer summed up his impressions thus: "One could only say that the males appeared to be displaying their maleness."

(7) There we have the clue to the origins of courtship in a nutshell. Once the brain reaches a certain complexity, it controls behaviour. A crab can react to various situations—a food-situation, a hunger-situation, a fear-situation, a sex-situation; and the statuesque male with his uplifted claw is the sign and symbol of the sex-situation, just as the coming of a man or other large animal among the burrows constitutes an enemy-situation, with resultant scuttling. Doubtless even without such male advertisement, mating would eventually occur; but, as Darwin so clearly saw, the advantage may be to the male and not to the race—the male who did not display himself as such would not get mated and would leave no descendants.

(8) In the spiders, we find a very interesting difference between the hunters and the web-spinners. Among the former, who catch their prey by sight and stalking, males perform strange dances before the females, and often have the parts they thus display brightly coloured.

The latter are almost blind; and in them there are no dances, but the male comes up to the web of the female and vibrates one of the threads in a special manner, quite different from the vibrations made by trapped prey. In both cases it seems clear that the courtship's primary function is to indicate the existence of a "sexual situation." But here, to do so is a good deal more important than in the crab, for all the evidence goes to show that if this indication were not made, the female would simply treat the male like any other small living object, and eat him! In many species she actually does so after the act of mating (and this occurs too in the scorpions); and in some others she is definitely hostile at first, while the male, who is usually much smaller than she is, is always obviously very ready to run away during the early phases of courtship.

(9) In one hunting spider the male offers the female a nice fly, neatly wrapped in silk. If put in a box by himself with a fly, he will eat it; but if with a fly and a female, he will wrap and offer it; and if a box from which a female has recently been removed, and in which her odour still presumably lingers, he will still wrap it, and search, like Shelley with his bouquet, "That he might there present it!—Oh, to whom?"

(10) In the carnivorous flies of the family *Empidae*, strange developments of the love-gift have taken place. In some species the male offers an unadorned carcass to the female. In others, however, the prey is stuck in the front end of a glistening "balloon" made of bubbles of viscous liquid secreted by the male, larger than his own body, and carried in his legs as he flies to and fro; doubtless this makes the "sexual situation" more conspicuous from afar. Finally, in a few species there has been a refinement. The balloon is there, but prey is no longer carried in it; instead, the males stick a leaf or a flower petal in it—and indeed they will dart down and pick up any small conspicuous objects, such as fragments of paper, that you may choose to sprinkle on the surface of the water over which they hover. Here, in quite a different evolutionary line from our own, we find quite definitely the employment of a non-utilitarian "present" as gift from male to female.

(11) When we come to the vertebrates, matters become even more interesting, for it is among them, especially in the birds, that courtship

and display reach their highest elaboration. Only in a few fish is there much of a courtship, as would be expected from the fact that most species produce large numbers of eggs which are only fertilized after laying. The frogs and toads that make night pulse with sound in the warm regions of the earth use their voices, as do the grasshoppers their legs or wings, in the interests of reproduction; and if the grasshoppers were life's first instrumentalists, the frogs were the first vocalists.

(12) The male frog, however, merely broadcasts an advertisement of his presence; it is among the tailed amphibians that true display is found. Our common newts in the breeding season take to the water and develop a high fin all along the back and tail. This is much larger in the males, who in addition change their winter livery for one of brighter colours. They may also be seen performing their courtship—actively moving in front of the females, often scraping up against them, all the time vibrating the bent tail. The strange fact about this procedure, however, is that they do not begin their display until after they have emitted their fertilizing elements. These are deposited on the bottom of the pond or aquarium inside a special packet or spermatophore, which the female must pick up for fertilization to occur; and courtship begins when this deposition is completed.

(13) Here we see that display may have a racial function, adjuvant to successful fertilization, and not an affair between rival males. For even the most hardened Darwinian would hardly maintain that a female, if two males simultaneously deposited spermatophores and then began their display before her, would be able to remember which male had deposited which spermatophore even were she to be better pleased or more stimulated by the display of one rather than of the other; and of course unless the approved male were also to be the father of the young, his pleasing of the female could have no evolutionary effect. No: it seems clear that here the function of display has again to deal with the "sexual situation"; with the difference that it is not merely to advertise the male's presence and masculinity, but to generate a sexual situation in the mind of the female. As a matter of fact, Finkler has by experiment shown that in the absence of a male's display, the female will not pick up spermatophores, so that this conception of courtship's function being to facilitate fertilization via the

mind, by stimulating the mental mechanism into the right phase, seems justified.

(14) There is one species of bird for which Darwin's original theory has been definitely shown to hold good. That is the well-known shore bird, the ruff (*Machetes*). In the winter the sexes are only to be told apart by size, but in the breeding season the males grow a magnificent ruff—a tippet or collar—round the cheeks and neck, and two fine ear-tufts above. What is more, it is hard to find two males alike; not only do they develop different ground colours in their plumage, but the collar and ear-tufts may either or both be of some special colour or marking, one black, the other white; or chestnut, pepper and salt, buff, sandy, grey, sepia, and what not. Arrived at their breeding places, the males assemble at a definite spot, usually known as a "hill," though it may be but a dry area in the marsh. The females visit the hill from time to time, but the males never go near the nests out in the marshes, nor take any share in brooding or the cares of the young. On the hill each male usually keeps to a little private area of his own. When no females are present, the male birds will be dancing, whirring round like Dervishes, and sparring and jousting with each other. On the arrival of a female, the scene is changed. The males crouch down, immobile, sometimes flat on the ground with spread wings. The hen may simply stroll round and fly away again—on which the cock birds rise rather sheepishly from their prostrate posture, as if pretending that nothing had been going on. Or she may approach a male and nibble at his neck, on which mating will be consummated.

(15) Edmund Selous watched one particular ruff hill in Holland for weeks, arriving at his hide at or before dawn. Every male on the hill was distinguishable by his appearance; and so Selous was able to discover that some were more successful than others.

(16) Here is Darwin's theory in practice, working itself out in every detail—the adornments developed only by the male in the breeding season, and used only in sexual combat and sexual display; the male with no power to enforce his desires, the female completely arbiter of her choice; and, finally, the evidence that choice is exercised. The only puzzling point is the extreme variability of the males. This may be explained by some later discoveries. Various biologists, as we shall see

later, have found that display, combat, and threat have a direct physiological effect on birds of both sexes, actually helping to ripen the reproductive organs. And Fraser Darling and others have recently shown
that this effect is cumulative, some stimulus resulting from the sight of
other birds courting or fighting. This at once explains the frequent occurrence of communal display-grounds; they are arrangements for
heightening reproductive efficiency. But it also explains the ruff's variability. If, as seems reasonable, the unfamiliar is more exciting than the
familiar, variety will have a greater mass-stimulating effect than uniformity. So, granted a tendency to marked variation, variety will be
encouraged and preserved.

(17) This clear-cut case is of importance, because it enables us
to draw pretty definite conclusions in other similar cases. In the black-
cock, for instance, a handsome member of the grouse tribe, there are
similar assembly-places for mating—veritable temples of Venus. Here
the individual males cannot be distinguished, but each again appears
to have his own definite pitch or stand, and, both from direct watching
and by analogy with the ruff, it seems that here, too, there is true selection. Finally in some Birds of Paradise there are also mating-places, but
in the trees, where the males dance and display their gorgeous plumes.

(18) It is interesting to note that the evolution of such special
mating-places with assemblies of males and visits by females has taken
place at least three separate times in birds—in the waders, the game-
birds, and the birds of paradise. The influence of mode of life on type
of courtship is another problem that can be followed out in birds.
Where there is polygamy and where the female alone broods the eggs
and cares for the young, there we find the greatest disparity in colour
and courtship-behaviour between the sexes. The female is generally
drab, protectively coloured; the male, *per contra*, brilliant, and alone
participating in display. Since there is polygamy (or promiscuity), the
successful male will imprint his characters on a larger number of descendants—and so display-brilliance will be at a premium; while, since
he plays no biologically useful rôle after fertilization is once effected,
there is less need for protective colour, since it does not much matter
whether he be killed or no.

(19) Most birds are monogamous, however, at least for the season

(or sometimes only for a single brood—like the American wren, which as bird-banding experiments have shown, usually changes partners between the first and second broods of a single year). Most of the largest group of monogamous birds, the song-birds proper, have their whole sex-life hinge on what we may call the territorial system. They have their young hatched naked and helpless, needing abundant food for their growth, and liable to die of cold if left too long unbrooded. Hence it is necessary, first, for both parent birds to feed the young; second, for the presence round the nest of an area sufficiently large to supply the young's needs, and not trespassed upon by other food-seeking parents of the same species. This is ensured through an extension of the instinct, nearly universal among birds, to resent intrusion into the area round the actual or future nest-site.

(20) Even in colonial nesters, like egrets or guillemots, the defended area exists, though it may be only a couple of feet across. In what we may call the true territorial birds, or birds with feeding as well as nesting territory, the course of events is as follows (I follow in this particular Eliot Howard's admirable description of the course of events in the European warblers or *Sylviidae*). The males are first on the breeding-grounds. If the species be a spring migrant, the males generally migrate north a week or so ahead of the females. Arrived, they take possession of an area—a territory—sometimes without dispute, sometimes after a fight with a simultaneous arrival or a bird already in possession. Then they begin their singing. Contrary to usual belief, the song of most song-birds is at its best before the mate has even arrived. As Howard has I think convincingly shown, the prime function of song is an advertisement. It is an advertisement of eligibly-occupied territory, which serves the double purpose of attracting females and warning off other males. Similarly, many of the special display-characters of males are used in threat-display against other males as well as in courtship-display to females.

(21) When the females arrive on the scene, no immediate courtship on the part of the males is to be observed. If the female is alone, she simply takes her place in the territory, and the two are a pair for the season. Nature abhors a vacuum, and this particular vacuum, the ab-

sence of the female from a territory, is filled with the least possible fuss. If two rival females arrive together, it is they who fight for the possession of territory-plus-male, while he hovers about, an interested and even excited spectator, but without participating. Then follows the strange fact, which at first seems to upset the whole Darwinian apple-cart, namely that courtship and display now begin vigorously—only now, after the two birds are mated for the season. The male vibrates his wings, spreads his tail, puffs his feathers, bows and scrapes, runs before his mate, often with a leaf or twig or other piece of nest material in his beak, and his antics may be so extravagant as to testify to the most ardent excitement within. How can this be fitted in with Darwin's view that these antics and displays have been evolved in large measure through the female's selection? To this, what we have learned from the lowly newt provides the answer. Courtship and display need not always have as their chief result the choosing of a mate. They may be, and indeed normally appear to be, accessory to the act of pairing and fertilization itself. The mind of a bird is a complex thing, and so is its life; the bird cannot always be tuned to a sexual situation. The simplest way, it would appear, of ensuring that it is not always so tuned (with consequent excessive pairing), and yet of ensuring that both sexes shall be simultaneously ready to mate often enough, is that one sex—the male—shall be more constantly in the phase of sexual preparedness, and by his display shall both advertise the fact, and also help to stimulate the female to the proper emotional level.

(22) Finally, as we have mentioned, there is a more direct biological advantage in display. It appears that in seasons which have been inclement just before and during egg-laying, the number of eggs is often reduced and the percentage of infertility raised. It is also known that all the reproductive processes of birds are very much under the control of the higher, emotional centres of the brain. For instance, a female dove brought up in isolation from infancy will usually lay no eggs; but the presence of a male bird in a near-by cage, or even the caressing of her neck with a human finger in a way reminiscent of the caresses of the male's nibbling beak, will almost always cause an egg to be laid. It has now been demonstrated that display and threat promote the

ripening of the reproductive organs; this will be of advantage, and especially in bad seasons, since birds' emotions are very much at the mercy of the weather.

(23) Before leaving this group, mention should be made of the curious fact that in all-the-year residents who are also territory-birds, there is an "engagement" period in the spring. For some weeks after the pair are in possession of a territory, fertilization is not effected. The biological reason for this is plain—it is advantageous for a bird to be on its territory early, or it may not find one; but it must not breed before a date which will give the probability of there being plenty of food for the young. The physiological machinery by which it is effected resides in the female; it is only at a certain season (probably depending on a certain mean temperature) that the eggs in her ovary start to grow rapidly, and only then that her full sex-instincts arise.

(24) Finally, we come to the large group of birds in which both male and female not only help look after the young, but also share in incubation and in the building of the nest. Such are the herons, the pelicans, the grebes, the divers, and many others. In them, neither parent is biologically the more precious; so that if protective colour is needed, it is needed by both. Furthermore, their instincts have to be so similar in regard to nest, eggs, and young that the similarity, it appears, has spread to their courtship habits, too. For it is at any rate a fact that in a large number of this group of birds, and nowhere else, we find what we must call mutual courtship—both sexes developing bright colours and special structures for the breeding season, and both using them simultaneously in a mutual display (which, as with other monogamists among birds, begins only after pairing-up).

(25) Anyone who, like myself, has watched such birds by the hour day after day, must be struck by the fact of their enjoyment of the courtship ceremonies for their own sake, and the further fact that the ceremonies are often what we may call biologically self-exhausting, in that the birds' emotional tension is often liberated through them, instead of being stimulated and leading on to actual pairing. It would seem as if these strange and romantic displays—head-shaking, or diving for weed, or aquatic dances breast to breast, or relieving guard on the nest with ceremonies of parade, or presentation of a twig with wings

and crest a-quiver,—as if they constituted a bond between the two birds of the pair, binding them together so long as the breeding season lasted by emotional links. And after all, why not? Does not something similar obtain in human society? And does it not there play a valuable rôle, in cementing with love and joy the racially important edifice of the family? And if it has this value in man, why not in these birds, for whom too the co-operation of both parents for the good of the family is essential?

(26) Here then we see display pressed, not merely into the service of one male against the rest, not merely facilitating fertilization, but into that of the super-individual unit, the family. And it is interesting that the family life of birds attains its highest development in these forms which have, we may say, equal sex rights and duties.

(27) In yet other cases we see display becoming social, and courtship tending (as again sometimes in man) to be again diverted from its original character of individual wooing, this time toward the publicity of the dance. Among birds I myself have investigated, this is best seen in the oyster-catcher, the bold black-and-white shore bird, with red bill, sometimes known as sea-pie. Gatherings of eight or ten birds of this species may be seen in spring, all careering around together in their stiff courtship attitude with neck outthrust and long bill pointing vertically downwards, and a piercing noise of trilled piping issuing from their throats. Observation revealed that this is not only the commonest form of display, but the only one used while on the ground; that it may be employed by the male alone, or mutually by male and female together; and that, in addition to its courtship function, it expresses jealous hostility of other trespassing birds, whether trespassing on territorial or sexual rights. When, in a flock in early spring, courtship begins, other birds may join in the excitement; hostility re-enforces love, and soon the whole number are careering round in frenzied excitement which is, it seems, neither sexual nor hostile, but social. Here the social dance appears to have little or no special function, but is rather a biological accident.

(28) Psychologically, one of the most interesting things about bird courtship is the frequency with which in display the birds will carry in their beaks a piece of the material of which their nest is built. This

holds good even for the Adélie penguins, charmingly described by Dr. Levick. Here the nest is nothing but a rim of stones round a depression; and accordingly the male presents stones to his mate as part of his courtship. Interestingly enough, this action sometimes becomes diverted to serve other instincts and emotions, such as wonder—the birds will present stones to dogs and to men; and Dr. Levick confesses to having felt quite embarrassed the first time he was the recipient! Still another tale hangs by these stones. The sitting birds are all the time stealing stones from each other's nests. Levick painted a number of stones different colours, and placed them at one margin of the nesting area. After this he could mark the rate of their progress (all by theft!) across the colony; and found that the red stones travelled much quicker than the rest. This is of great theoretical interest, for red is a colour which is to all intents and purposes absent in the penguin's environment—and yet they prefer it above all others. If a male penguin could grow a red patch he would probably be very quick to gain a mate.

(29) Such an example also shows in what sort of way the extraordinary bowers of the bower-bird can have developed. These are a blend between art gallery and museum, usually a tunnel of twigs with a collection of shells, bones, berries, and flowers at one end. In one species a space of ground is cleared, and large leaves laid upon it, their silvery undersurface upwards. As they wither, they are replaced; if they are blown over, the silver side is turned up once more.

(30) Among the mammals, there is on the whole little courtship or display by the males, but correspondingly more fighting. This probably depends on the fact that the reproductive instincts of the female mammal are more rigidly under a definite physiological control, less under the fluid control of higher, emotional centres; the male deer or elephant-seal has but to guard his harem, and they will automatically accept him in due time. There is, however, a great deal still to be discovered of the courtships of monogamous mammals—a difficult subject, because so many are nocturnal or burrowers, but one that would well repay study. Among some intelligent quadrupeds, however, such as the elephant, a pleasant mutual courtship, of trunk-caresses, has been described; and when we move up towards *Homo sapiens* and reach the monkeys and apes, we find a number of display and threat

characters among the males. Some are to us repulsive, like the naked
scarlet and azure cheeks of the Mandril, or the blue of Stevenson's

> . . . . blue-behinded ape that skips
> about the trees of Paradise.

But others, like the orang or some of the marmosets with their mus-
tachios, or the Satan monkey with his fine beard, are curiously reminiscent of ourselves, and we are reminded of Mr. Hilaire Belloc's
baboon—

> The Big Baboon who lives upon
> The plains of Caribou,
> He goes about with nothing on
> —A shocking thing to do.
>
> But if he dressed respectably
> And let his whiskers grow,
> How like that Big Baboon would be
> To Mister—So-and-So!

(31) Courtship in animals is the outcome of four major steps in
evolution. First, the development of sexuality; secondly, the separation
of the sexes; thirdly, internal fertilization, or at least the approximation
of males and females; and finally, the development of efficient sense-
organs and brains. Without any one of these, there would never have
existed that host of strange and lovely features of life, summed up
under the head of courtship, which beautify the appearance and varie-
gate the existence of so many of the higher animals, including our own
species.

STUDY QUESTIONS

1. In presenting his examples of animal courtship, what principle of
order does Mr. Huxley use?

2. Mr. Huxley seems to be examining animal courtship from the point
of view of the truth of Charles Darwin's theory of sexual selection. What
is this theory? What logical procedure is Mr. Huxley following in carrying
out this aim?

3. Do the conclusions in the last paragraph grow out of the evidence
given? Are they logically justified?

4. Why does Mr. Huxley use such an abundance of illustrative material in this essay? Can it be justified in terms of his purpose?

5. What effect is achieved by the following words and phrases: *like Dervishes* (14), *lowly* (21), *sieve* (3), *adumbration of courtship* (5), *tiptoe attitude* (6), *unadorned carcass* (10), *livery* (12), and *colonial* (20)?

6. Does Mr. Huxley give the reader a sense of the complexity of the factors involved in animal courtship? If you think so, show what methods he uses to convey this sense.

7. On the basis of this essay, what would you say is Mr. Huxley's concept of man?

8. What attitude of the author is conveyed in the opening sentences of this essay? Does Mr. Huxley's subsequent development of his theme sustain that attitude?

WRITING ASSIGNMENTS

1. Write an imaginative essay giving a bird's-eye view of human courtship.

2. Write a light essay on male advertisement among *Homo sapiens*.

3. Develop into a full essay this quotation from Mr. Huxley's first paragraph: "Man is a vain organism, and likes to stand surrounded by mirrors."

4. Write a familiar essay on the courtship of man, as viewed in American advertising.

5. Write a research paper on one aspect of the life of a species of animal (social organization among bees, feeding habits of anteaters, building habits of beavers, etc.).

Courtship Through the Ages *

JAMES THURBER (1894–   ), *born in Columbus, Ohio, and graduate of* The Ohio State University, *is a cartoonist, humorist, and playwright. After working with the U.S. Department of State in World War I, he worked for the* Columbus Dispatch (1920–1924) *and briefly for the* Chicago Tribune, Paris edition. *He is best known, however, as a contributor of cartoons and essays to the* New Yorker. *He is author of* Is Sex Necessary? (1929, *with E. B. White*), My Life and Hard Times (1933), Let Your Mind Alone (1937), The Male Animal (1940, *a play written with Elliott Nugent*), My World—and Welcome to It (1942), The 13 Clocks (1950), *and* The Thurber Album (1952).

(1) Surely nothing in the astonishing scheme of life can have non-plussed Nature so much as the fact that none of the females of any of the species she created really cared very much for the male, as such. For the past ten million years Nature has been busily inventing ways to make the male attractive to the female, but the whole business of courtship, from the marine annelids up to man, still lumbers heavily along, like a complicated musical comedy. I have been reading the sad and absorbing story in Volume 6 (Cole to Dama) of the Encyclopaedia Britannica. In this volume you can learn all about cricket, cotton, costume designing, crocodiles, crown jewels, and Coleridge, but none of these subjects is so interesting as the Courtship of Animals, which recounts the sorrowful lengths to which all males must go to arouse the interest of a lady.

(2) We all know, I think, that Nature gave man whiskers and a mustache with the quaint idea in mind that these would prove attrac-

tive to the female. We all know that, far from attracting her, whiskers and mustaches only made her nervous and gloomy, so that man had to go in for somersaults, tilting with lances, and performing feats of parlor magic to win her attention; he also had to bring her candy, flowers, and the furs of animals. It is common knowledge that in spite of all these "love displays" the male is constantly being turned down, insulted, or thrown out of the house. It is rather comforting, then, to discover that the peacock, for all his gorgeous plumage, does not have a particularly easy time in courtship; none of the males in the world do. The first peahen, it turned out, was only faintly stirred by her suitor's beautiful train. She would often go quietly to sleep while he was whisking it around. The Britannica tells us that the peacock actually had to learn a certain little trick to wake her up and revive her interest: he had to learn to vibrate his quills so as to make a rustling sound. In ancient times man himself, observing the ways of the peacock, probably tried vibrating his whiskers to make a rustling sound; if so, it didn't get him anywhere. He had to go in for something else; so, among other things, he went in for gifts. It is not unlikely that he got this idea from certain flies and birds who were making no headway at all with rustling sounds.

(3) One of the flies of the family Empidae, who had tried everything, finally hit on something pretty special. He contrived to make a glistening transparent balloon which was even larger than himself. Into this he would put sweetmeats and tidbits and he would carry the whole elaborate envelope through the air to the lady of his choice. This amused her for a time, but she finally got bored with it. She demanded silly little colorful presents, something that you couldn't eat but that would look nice around the house. So the male Empis had to go around gathering flower petals and pieces of bright paper to put into his balloon. On a courtship flight a male Empis cuts quite a figure now, but he can hardly be said to be happy. He never knows how soon the female will demand heavier presents, such as Roman coins and gold collar buttons. It seems probable that one day the courtship of the Empidae will fall down, as man's occasionally does, of its own weight.

(4) The bowerbird is another creature that spends so much time courting the female that he never gets any work done. If all the male bowerbirds became nervous wrecks within the next ten or fifteen years,

it would not surprise me. The female bowerbird insists that a playground be built for her with a specially constructed bower at the entrance. This bower is much more elaborate than an ordinary nest and is harder to build; it costs a lot more, too. The female will not come to the playground until the male has filled it up with a great many gifts: silvery leaves, red leaves, rose petals, shells, beads, berries, bones, dice, buttons, cigar bands, Christmas seals, and the Lord knows what else. When the female finally condescends to visit the playground, she is in a coy and silly mood and has to be chased in and out of the bower and up and down the playground before she will quit giggling and stand still long enough even to shake hands. The male bird is, of course, pretty well done in before the chase starts, because he has worn himself out hunting for eyeglass lenses and begonia blossoms. I imagine that many a bowerbird, after chasing a female for two or three hours, says the hell with it and goes home to bed. Next day, of course, he telephones someone else and the same trying ritual is gone through with again. A male bowerbird is as exhausted as a night-club habitué before he is out of his twenties.

(5) The male fiddler crab has a somewhat easier time, but it can hardly be said that he is sitting pretty. He has one enormously large and powerful claw, usually brilliantly colored, and you might suppose that all he had to do was reach out and grab some passing cutie. The very earliest fiddler crabs may have tried this, but, if so, they got slapped for their pains. A female fiddler crab will not tolerate any caveman stuff; she never has and she doesn't intend to start now. To attract a female, a fiddler crab has to stand on tiptoe and brandish his claw in the air. If any female in the neighborhood is interested—and you'd be surprised how many are not—she comes over and engages him in light badinage, for which he is not in the mood. As many as a hundred females may pass the time of day with him and go on about their business. By nightfall of an average courting day, a fiddler crab who has been standing on tiptoe for eight or ten hours waving a heavy claw in the air is in pretty sad shape. As in the case of the males of all species, however, he gets out of bed next morning, dashes some water on his face, and tries again.

(6) The next time you encounter a male web-spinning spider, stop

and reflect that he is too busy worrying about his love life to have any desire to bite you. Male web-spinning spiders have a tougher life than any other males in the animal kingdom. This is because the female web-spinning spiders have very poor eyesight. If a male lands on a female's web, she kills him before he has time to lay down his cane and gloves, mistaking him for a fly or a bumblebee who has stumbled into her trap. Before the species figured out what to do about this, millions of males were murdered by ladies they called on. It is the nature of spiders to perform a little dance in front of the female, but before a male spinner could get near enough for the female to see who he was and what he was up to, she would lash out at him with a flat-iron or a pair of garden shears. One night, nobody knows when, a very bright male spinner lay awake worrying about calling on a lady who had been killing suitors right and left. It came to him that this business of dancing as a love display wasn't getting anybody anywhere except the grave. He decided to go in for web-twitching, or strand-vibrating. The next day he tried it on one of the nearsighted girls. Instead of dropping in on her suddenly, he stayed outside the web and began monkeying with one of its strands. He twitched it up and down and in and out with such a lilting rhythm that the female was charmed. The serenade worked beautifully; the female let him live. The Britannica's spider-watchers, however, report that this system is not always successful. Once in a while, even now, a female will fire three bullets into a suitor or run him through with a kitchen knife. She keeps threatening him from the moment he strikes the first low notes on the outside strings, but usually by the time he has got up to the high notes played around the center of the web, he is going to town and she spares his life.

(7) Even the butterfly, as handsome a fellow as he is, can't always win a mate merely by fluttering around and showing off. Many butterflies have to have scent scales on their wings. Hepialus carries a powder puff in a perfumed pouch. He throws perfume at the ladies when they pass. The male tree cricket, Oecanthus, goes Hepialus one better by carrying a tiny bottle of wine with him and giving drinks to such doxies as he has designs on. One of the male snails throws darts to entertain the girls. So it goes, through the long list of animals, from the bristle

worm and his rudimentary dance steps to man and his gift of diamonds and sapphires. The golden-eye drake raises a jet of water with his feet as he flies over a lake; Hepialus has his powder puff, Oecanthus his wine bottle, man his etchings. It is a bright and melancholy story, the age-old desire of the male for the female, the age-old desire of the female to be amused and entertained. Of all the creatures on earth, the only males who could be figured as putting any irony into their courtship are the grebes and certain other diving birds. Every now and then a courting grebe slips quietly down to the bottom of a lake and then, with a mighty "Whoosh!," pops out suddenly a few feet from his girl friend, splashing water all over her. She seems to be persuaded that this is a purely loving display, but I like to think that the grebe always has a faint hope of drowning her or scaring her to death.

(8) I will close this investigation into the mournful burdens of the male with the Britannica's story about a certain Argus pheasant. It appears that the Argus displays himself in front of a female who stands perfectly still without moving a feather. (If you saw "June Moon" some years ago and remember the scene in which the Songwriter sang "Montana Moon" to his grim and motionless wife, you have some idea what the female Argus probably thinks of her mate's display.) The male Argus the Britannica tells about was confined in a cage with a female of another species, a female who kept moving around, emptying ashtrays and fussing with lampshades all the time the male was showing off his talents. Finally, in disgust, he stalked away and began displaying in front of his water trough. He reminds me of a certain male (Homo sapiens) of my acquaintance who one night after dinner asked his wife to put down her detective magazine so that he could read her a poem of which he was very fond. She sat quietly enough until he was well into the middle of the thing, intoning with great ardor and intensity. Then suddenly there came a sharp, disconcerting *slap!* It turned out that all during the male's display, the female had been intent on a circling mosquito and had finally trapped it between the palms of her hands. The male in this case did not stalk away and display in front of a water trough; he went over to Tim's and had a flock of drinks and recited the poem to the fellas. I am sure they all told bitter stories of their own about how their displays had been inter-

rupted by females. I am also sure that they all ended up singing "Honey, Honey, Bless Your Heart."

STUDY QUESTIONS

1. In this essay what does Mr. Thurber say about women and human courtship? Is he concerned primarily with animals or with human beings? Does he discuss human courtship directly? What do you conceive to be the uses and the values of the indirect approach in exposition? What problems are involved in the use of this approach?

2. Are the biological facts in this article correct? How can one verify them? What bearing do the facts have upon the purpose and tone of this essay? What difference would it make if the details about animal courtship were fictitious?

3. Can you discern any reasons for the order in which Mr. Thurber discusses individual species? Could the order be changed about without fundamentally altering his effect? Why or why not?

4. Select several examples of Mr. Thurber's use of animal-human analogies for humorous purposes. How do these comparisons help to sustain the tone of the essay?

5. What is the effect of the parenthetical remark *Homo sapiens* in paragraph 8?

6. Select examples of personification used in paragraphs 1 and 2. What is their effect?

7. To what extent does Mr. Thurber's humor derive from his diction? How much of his diction is colloquial? What specific effect do his subject and his point of view give to his colloquial, homely phraseology?

8. On the basis of this essay, how would you characterize Mr. Thurber's humor?

WRITING ASSIGNMENTS

1. Read the article "Nest" in the *Encyclopaedia Britannica*, 14th Edition, and write a humorous essay employing a basic analogy with human behavior.

2. Write a familiar essay on campus conventions of dating.

3. Write an analysis, serious or humorous, of female use of display.

4. Write an argument for or against university courses in marriage.

5. Write a research paper on courtship as practiced in a specific primitive tribe, in a tribe of American Indians, in an Asiatic culture, or in ancient Greece or Rome.

The Poignancy of Neurotic Conflicts *

KAREN HORNEY (1885–1952), psychiatrist, was born in Germany and graduated from the Universities of Freiburg and Berlin. She came to the United States in 1932 and was naturalized in 1938. She wrote a number of books dealing with her particular interpretation of Freudian psychoanalysis, among them the following: Neurotic Personality of Our Time (1936), New Ways in Psychoanalysis (1939), Self-Analysis (1942), Our Inner Conflicts (1945), *and* Neurosis and Human Growth (1950).

(1) Let me say to begin with: It is not neurotic to have conflicts. At one time or another our wishes, our interests, our convictions are bound to collide with those of others around us. And just as such clashes between ourselves and our environment are a commonplace, so, too, conflicts within ourselves are an integral part of human life.

(2) An animal's actions are largely determined by instinct. Its mating, its care for its young, its search for food, its defenses against danger are more or less prescribed and beyond individual decision. In contrast, it is the prerogative as well as the burden of human beings to be able to exert choice, to have to make decisions. We may have to decide between desires that lead in opposite directions. We may, for instance, want to be alone but also want to be with a friend; we may want to study medicine but also to study music. Or there may be a conflict between wishes and obligations: we may wish to be with a lover when someone in trouble needs our care. We may be divided between a desire to be in accord with others and a conviction that would entail expressing an opinion antagonistic to them. We may be in conflict,

---

finally, between two sets of values, as occurs when we believe in taking on a hazardous job in wartime but believe also in our duty to our family.

(3) The kind, scope, and intensity of such conflicts are largely d - termined by the civilization in which we live. If the civilization is stable and tradition bound, the variety of choices presenting themselves are limited and the range of possible individual conflicts narrow. Even then they are not lacking. One loyalty may interfere with another; personal desires may stand against obligations to the group. But if the civilization is in a stage of rapid transition, where highly contradictory values and divergent ways of living exist side by side, the choices the individual has to make are manifold and difficult. He can conform to the expectations of the community or be a dissenting individualist, be gregarious or live as a recluse, worship success or despise it, have faith in strict discipline for children or allow them to grow up without much interference; he can believe in a different moral standard for men and women or hold that the same should apply for both, regard sexual relations as an expression of human intimacy or divorce them from ties of affection; he can foster racial discrimination or take the stand that human values are independent of the color of skin or the shape of noses—and so on and so forth.

(4) There is no doubt that choices like these have to be made very often by people living in our civilization, and one would therefore expect conflicts along these lines to be quite common. But the striking fact is that most people are not aware of them, and consequently do not resolve them by any clear decision. More often than not they drift and let themselves be swayed by accident. They do not know where they stand; they make compromises without being aware of doing so; they are involved in contradictions without knowing it. I am referring here to normal persons, meaning neither average nor ideal but merely non-neurotic.

(5) There must, then, be preconditions for recognizing contradictory issues and for making decisions on that basis. These preconditions are fourfold. We must be aware of what our wishes are, or even more, of what our feelings are. Do we really like a person or do we only think we like him because we are supposed to? Are we really sad if a parent

dies or do we only go through the motions? Do we really wish to become a lawyer or a doctor or does it merely strike us as a respectable and profitable career? Do we really want our children to be happy and independent or do we only give lip service to the idea? Most of us would find it difficult to answer such simple questions; that is, we do not know what we really feel or want.

(6) Since conflicts often have to do with convictions, beliefs, or moral values, their recognition would presuppose that we have developed our own set of values. Beliefs that are merely taken over and are not a part of us hardly have sufficient strength to lead to conflicts or to serve as a guiding principle in making decisions. When subjected to new influences, such beliefs will easily be abandoned for others. If we simply have adopted values cherished in our environment, conflicts which in our best interest should arise do not arise. If, for instance, a son has never questioned the wisdom of a narrow-minded father, there will be little conflict when the father wants him to enter a profession other than the one he himself prefers. A married man who falls in love with another woman is actually engaged in a conflict; but when he has failed to establish his own convictions about the meaning of marriage he will simply drift along the path of least resistance instead of facing the conflict and making a decision one way or the other.

(7) Even if we recognize a conflict as such, we must be willing and able to renounce one of the two contradictory issues. But the capacity for clear and conscious renunciation is rare, because our feelings and beliefs are muddled, and perhaps because in the last analysis most people are not secure and happy enough to renounce anything.

(8) Finally, to make a decision presupposes the willingness and capacity to assume responsibility for it. This would include the risk of making a wrong decision and the willingness to bear the consequences without blaming others for them. It would involve feeling, "This is my choice, my doing," and presupposes more inner strength and independence than most people apparently have nowadays.

(9) Caught as so many of us are in the strangling grip of conflicts —however unacknowledged—our inclination is to look with envy and admiration on people whose lives seem to flow along smoothly without being disturbed by any of this turbulence. The admiration may be

warranted. These may be the strong ones who have established their own hierarchy of values, or who have acquired a measure of serenity because in the course of years conflicts and the need for decision have lost their uprooting power. But the outward appearance may be deceptive. More often, due to apathy, conformity, or opportunism, the people we envy are incapable of truly facing a conflict or of truly trying to resolve it on the basis of their own convictions, and consequently have merely drifted or been swayed by immediate advantage.

(10) To experience conflicts knowingly, though it may be distressing, can be an invaluable asset. The more we face our own conflicts and seek out our own solutions, the more inner freedom and strength we will gain. Only when we are willing to bear the brunt can we approximate the ideal of being the captain of our ship. A spurious tranquillity rooted in inner dullness is anything but enviable. It is bound to make us weak and an easy prey to any kind of influence.

(11) When conflicts center about the primary issues of life, it is all the more difficult to face them and resolve them. But provided we are sufficiently alive, there is no reason why in principle we should not be able to do so. Education could do much to help us to live with greater awareness of ourselves and to develop our own convictions. A realization of the significance of the factors involved in choice would give us ideals to strive for, and in that a direction for our lives.

(12) The difficulties always inherent in recognizing and resolving a conflict are immeasurably increased when a person is neurotic. Neurosis, it must be said, is always a matter of degree—and when I speak of "a neurotic" I invariably mean "a person to the extent that he is neurotic." For him awareness of feelings and desires is at a low ebb. Often the only feelings experienced consciously and clearly are reactions of fear and anger to blows dealt to vulnerable spots. And even these may be repressed. Such authentic ideals as do exist are so pervaded by compulsive standards that they are deprived of their power to give direction. Under the sway of these compulsive tendencies the faculty to renounce is rendered impotent, and the capacity to assume responsibility for oneself all but lost.

(13) Neurotic conflicts may be concerned with the same general problems as perplex the normal person. But they are so different in kind that the question has been raised whether it is permissible to use the same term for both. I believe it is, but we must be aware of the differences. What, then, are the characteristics of neurotic conflicts?

(14) A somewhat simplified example by way of illustration: An engineer working in collaboration with others at mechanical research was frequently afflicted by spells of fatigue and irritability. One of these spells was brought about by the following incident. In a discussion of certain technical matters his opinions were less well received than those of his colleagues. Shortly afterward a decision was made in his absence, and no opportunity was given him subsequently to present his suggestions. Under these circumstances, he could have regarded the procedure as unjust and put up a fight, or he could have accepted the majority decision with good grace. Either reaction would have been consistent. But he did neither. Though he felt deeply slighted, he did not fight. Consciously he was merely aware of being irritated. The murderous rage within him appeared only in his dreams. This repressed rage—a composite of his fury against the others and of his fury against himself for his own meekness—was mainly responsible for his fatigue.

(15) His failure to react consistently was determined by a number of factors. He had built up a grandiose image of himself that required deference from others to support it. This was unconscious at the time: he simply acted on the premise that there was nobody as intelligent and competent in his field as he was. Any slight could jeopardize this premise and provoke rage. Furthermore, he had unconscious sadistic impulses to berate and humiliate others—an attitude so objectionable to him that he covered it up by overfriendliness. To this was added an unconscious drive to exploit people, making it imperative for him to keep in their good graces. The dependence on others was aggravated by a compulsive need for approval and affection, combined as it usually is with attitudes of compliance, appeasement, and avoidance of fight. There was thus a conflict between destructive aggressions—reactive rage and sadistic impulses—on the one hand, and on the other the need for affection and approval, with a desire to appear fair and rational in his own eyes. The result was inner upheaval that went un-

noticed, while the fatigue that was its external manifestation paralyzed all action.

(16) Looking at the factors involved in the conflict, we are struck first by their absolute incompatibility. It would be difficult indeed to imagine more extreme opposites than lordly demands for deference and ingratiating submissiveness. Second, the whole conflict remains unconscious. The contradictory tendencies operating in it are not recognized but are deeply repressed. Only slight bubbles of the battle raging within reach the surface. The emotional factors are rationalized: it is an injustice; it is a slight; my ideas were better. Third, the tendencies in both directions are compulsive. Even if he had some intellectual perception of his excessive demands, or of the existence and the nature of his dependence, he could not change these factors voluntarily. To be able to change them would require considerable analytical work. He was driven on either hand by compelling forces over which he had no control: he could not possibly renounce any of the needs acquired by stringent inner necessity. But none of them represented what he himself really wanted or sought. He would want neither to exploit nor to be submissive; as a matter of fact he despised these tendencies. Such a state of affairs, however, has a far-reaching significance for the understanding of neurotic conflicts. It means that no decision is feasible.

(17) A further illustration presents a similar picture. A free-lance designer was stealing small sums of money from a good friend. The theft was not warranted by the external situation; he needed the money, but the friend would gladly have given it to him as he had on occasion in the past. That he should resort to stealing was particularly striking in that he was a decent fellow who set great store by friendship.

(18) The following conflict was at the bottom of it. The man had a pronounced neurotic need for affection, especially a longing to be taken care of in all practical matters. Alloyed as this was with an unconscious drive to exploit others, his technique was to attempt both to endear and intimidate. These tendencies by themselves would have made him willing and eager to receive help and support. But he had also developed an extreme unconscious arrogance which involved a correspondingly vulnerable pride. Others should feel honored to be

of service to him: it was humiliating for him to ask for help. His aversion to having to make a request was reinforced by a strong craving for independence and self-sufficiency that made it intolerable for him to admit he needed anything or to place himself under obligation. So he could take, but not receive.

(19) The content of this conflict differs from that of the first example but the essential characteristics are the same. And any other example of neurotic conflict would show a like incompatibility of conflicting drives and their unconscious and compulsive nature, leading always to the impossibility of deciding between the contradictory issues involved.

(20) Allowing for an indistinct line of demarcation, the difference, then, between normal and neurotic conflicts lies fundamentally in the fact that the disparity between the conflicting issues is much less great for the normal person than for the neurotic. The choices the former has to make are between two modes of action, either of which is feasible within the frame of a fairly integrated personality. Graphically speaking, the conflicting directions diverge only 90 degrees or less, as against the possible 180 degrees confronting the neurotic.

(21) In awareness, too, the difference is one of degree. As Kierkegaard has pointed out: "Real life is far too multifarious to be portrayed by merely exhibiting such abstract contrasts as that between a despair which is completely unconscious, and one which is completely conscious." [1] We can say this much, however: a normal conflict can be entirely conscious; a neurotic conflict in all its essential elements is always unconscious. Even though a normal person may be unaware of his conflict, he can recognize it with comparatively little help, while the essential tendencies producing a neurotic conflict are deeply repressed and can be unearthed only against great resistance.

(22) The normal conflict is concerned with an actual choice between two possibilities, both of which the person finds really desirable, or between convictions, both of which he really values. It is therefore possible for him to arrive at a feasible decision even though it may be hard on him and require a renunciation of some kind. The neurotic person engulfed in a conflict is not free to choose. He is driven by

[1] From *The Sickness unto Death* (translated, 1941).

equally compelling forces in opposite directions, neither of which he wants to follow. Hence a decision in the usual sense is impossible. He is stranded, with no way out. The conflict can only be resolved by working at the neurotic trends involved, and by so changing his relations with others and with himself that he can dispense with the trends altogether.

(23) These characteristics account for the poignancy of neurotic conflicts. Not only are they difficult to recognize, not only do they render a person helpless, but they have as well a disruptive force of which he has good reason to be afraid. Unless we know these characteristics and keep them in mind, we shall not understand the desperate attempts at solution which the neurotic enters upon, and which constitute the major part of a neurosis.

STUDY QUESTIONS

1. Miss Horney's basic point about neurotic conflicts, which she gives in her title, is not again specifically referred to until her last paragraph. What method of organization does that fact suggest she is using?

2. What are the two major divisions of this essay?

3. What does Miss Horney accomplish in her opening paragraph?

4. What use does Miss Horney make of illustrations? What is their value for this particular essay?

5. What are the fourfold preconditions referred to in paragraph 5?

6. In paragraph 13 Miss Horney says the conflicts in a normal person and those in a neurotic person are different in kind. In paragraph 20 she says they are different in degree. Is this a genuine or an apparent contradiction?

7. What is the force of the word *analytical* in paragraph 16?

8. Does Miss Horney use many or few adjectives? What kind of adjectives does she use? How do the number and quality of the adjectives affect the general tone and purpose of her essay? Would more or fewer adjectives have been more effective for her purpose?

9. To what extent does Miss Horney make us feel the poignancy of neurotic conflicts? How could she have made us more deeply conscious of the conflict? What would she have lost by so doing? What would she have gained? Remember that this essay is the opening chapter of a whole book on the subject of neurosis, written by a practicing psychiatrist.

WRITING ASSIGNMENTS

1. Write an essay on the essentially human problem of choice, as briefly discussed by Miss Horney in the second paragraph of her essay.

2. On the basis of your own experience, write an essay on the conflicts which arise between the individual and his environment.

3. Write an analysis of yourself in terms of your conflicts.

4. Write an honest analysis of your own beliefs in the light of Miss Horney's discussion in paragraphs 5, 6, and 7.

5. Write an analysis of one specific conflict of loyalties which you have faced and solved. (Reread Miss Horney's third paragraph.)

What Opinion Polls Can and Can't Do*

Some Findings of the Post-Mortem on 1948

NATHAN GLAZER (1923–   ), *graduate of the College of the City of New York and of the University of Pennsylvania, is an associate editor of the monthly magazine* Commentary. *He has collaborated in the writing of two important sociological studies:* The Lonely Crowd (1950, *with David Riesman and R. Denney*) *and* Faces in the Crowd (1952, *with David Riesman*).

(1) Since 1948, public opinion polls have not been much in the public eye. The Great Miscalculation of 1948 [1] drove them from their favored places in the daily newspapers, and the experts in opinion and attitude research, commercial and academic, retired to the haven of the professional journals and specialized publications, where they could meditate at leisure on what had happened and why.

(2) Despite its recent fall from grace, there is no doubt that public opinion polling in its contemporary form is a far sturdier and solider plant than the straw poll, which was completely finished off by another great error, the *Literary Digest's* prediction in 1936 of a Landon "sweep." The straw poll, based on the wholesale and indiscriminate distribution of ballots, had no way of finding out what exactly had gone wrong when its prophecies fell flat. In contrast, the public opinion poll, even though it covered a few thousand individuals as against millions, was systematic enough to make it possible to figure out just where

* From *Commentary*, August, 1951. Copyright 1951 by the American Jewish Committee. Reprinted by permission of the author.
[1] The prediction by national polls that President Truman would be defeated in his campaign for return to the presidency in 1948.

it had fallen into error. It could retrace the steps of its operations: had the question been asked incorrectly?—it could then compare the effect of asking two different types of question; were interviewers' biases at fault?—it could compare the results obtained by different interviewers; had the sample been selected incorrectly?—it could calculate what the effect of differently constructed samples would have been.

(3) All this, and more, was done shortly after the election in a 396-page study published by the Social Science Research Council: *The Pre-Election Polls of 1948*, by Frederick Mosteller, Herbert Hyman, Philip J. McCarthy, Eli S. Marks, and David B. Truman.

(4) The discussions in this volume are impressive in their mathematical clarity and precision. At every point of the polling process, errors were possible, and at every point some checks exist by which it is possible to find out whether such errors actually occurred. How to evaluate the role of the different errors in the total picture is a different and more complicated matter, and indeed it is not attempted. But one over-all conclusion is perfectly clear: nothing really exceptional happened in the 1948 election. Working with the customary samples and procedures, errors *of this degree* must be expected. As Frederick Mosteller sums it up: "In the present state of polling, where systematic errors of 3 or 4 percentage points are common, it is not to be wondered that polling operations incorrectly predict elections. The wonder is that polls do as well as they do."

(5) This is, from the point of view of the social history of polling, a rather remarkable conclusion. After all, the reader is bound to exclaim, no one told us this before 1948!

(6) The mathematics leading to Mr. Mosteller's conclusion are interesting. Because of the peculiarities of the electoral college system, to forecast elections correctly one must correctly predict the vote in each of a large number of states. Many of these states split almost exactly 50-50 between the two parties, so that a small percentage shift can throw any of them into one or the other party's lap. Now statistical theory tells us how large a sample we need to achieve a certain level of precision in describing some characteristic of a population from a sample of this population. Thus, to get the same precision for the state of Iowa that a sample of 3,000 would give us for the entire United

States, we would need a sample of no less than 2,994! And if we wanted to get the same precision for a town of approximately 32,000 people, we would still need a sample of 2,743! It is financially quite out of the question to use samples for every state as large as the one we ordinarily use for the nation. Consequently, the estimates for the various states are bound to be precarious.

(7) There is a further theoretical complication. Any sample drawn from a larger population will not be an exact miniature of the larger population. For, leaving out all considerations of bias that may enter into the interviewing or question-construction or interpretation, which will produce what is called "systematic error," we must expect a certain "random error," the variation that we will get from sample to sample, even if we get perfect random samples with no bias. Let us suppose a not uncommon random error of 3 per cent (which means that any sample will be off from the true figure on the average 3 per cent) and consider a state which splits 51–49—a not unlikely occurrence. Under these circumstances, the poller would have six chances out of ten of hitting the winner right—he would not do much worse if he flipped a coin. A 48–52 split would give him seven chances out of ten, and only with a 55–45 split would he have nine chances out of ten.

(8) This is on the basis of the statistical theory alone—which assumes a pure random sample, and no bias. When we add the distortions inevitably produced by the variation in the sample actually interviewed from a true random sample, as well as other biases, it is clear that polls can predict elections with no great certainty.

(9) One further item of analysis by Mr. Mosteller is of interest. In order to test how good any system of prediction is, we have to compare it with some other system of prediction. This, it seems, is done in meteorology, where one compares the excellence of prediction with the results one would have got if one had simply assumed that any day's weather was going to be just what the preceding day's weather had been. Now suppose, says Mr. Mosteller, we try the same with election forecasts. Suppose we predicted at each presidential election that each state would go the way it went last time. Embarrassingly enough, this rather mechanical system of predicting does about as well as polling

for all the elections in which polling has been used, which means all those since 1936. It is true that the Democrats won every one of these elections—in other words, that things have not changed too much from one presidential election to the next since 1936, and we would have to expect this "persistence forecasting" to do quite well under the circumstances. If we go backwards, we find that "persistence forecasting" would have done a horribly botched job in such elections as 1920 and 1932, where there were changes of administration; polling might have done better in these elections.

(10) But, after all, the predicting of elections is a rather special task, and an exceptionally difficult one, and it would be unfair to judge polling by it alone. To quote Mr. Mosteller again: "It is a rare study that has a serious interest in the change from 49 to 51 per cent." It is in these fields other than elections, where the change from 49 to 51 per cent is of little interest, that polling has undoubtedly made a quite considerable contribution. The polls have performed a task similar to that of a geographical survey: they outline the social landscape, telling us how people in different areas and countries, of different age groups and classes, differ on a vast variety of questions. Of course they do only a rough topographical job, and we should only depend on them for broad outlines: they tell us there is a mountain here and a lake there, without giving exact dimensions.

(11) It is the poll as social survey that provides the chief interest—indeed, the fascination—of a huge volume, *Public Opinion, 1935–1946*, published by the Princeton University Press, under the editorial direction of Hadley Cantril, and prepared by Mildred Strunk. It contains 1,191 large double-columned pages and costs $25.00. It reports, with breakdowns, results of nation-wide polls conducted by twenty-three polling organizations in 16 countries that concern themselves with regular polling on public issues. Even at that, it does not include all the poll questions asked by these organizations; and it does not attempt to deal with the questions asked by market research agencies or public polling organizations for private clients.

(12) There is in this book a great deal that is astonishing, a great deal that is amusing, a great deal that reminds one, though hardly

nostalgically, of those distant days when the depression, Martin Dies, [2] and Father Coughlin [3] (in 1938 nine per cent of the population listened to him regularly) were all live issues. Many of the results are cause for speculation. Why do 39 per cent of Americans report they are very happy, and only 8 per cent of Frenchmen? Is it really possible that 22 per cent of the American people had read *Gone With the Wind* in 1939, and that at one point, in 1937, five per cent of the American people were engaged in reading it? One is impressed by the cultural level of the Scandinavian peoples: in Sweden, 42 per cent of the people own oil paintings (including 31 per cent of the workers); 21 per cent of the population in Sweden and Denmark own more than a hundred books; 25 per cent of the Swedes read one or more foreign languages (not counting Danish or Norwegian), and 12 per cent two or more; in 16 per cent of Swedish homes someone plays the piano, in 8 per cent the violin, in 6 per cent the organ. One is charmed to discover that more Danes like modern furniture than traditional furniture. And awed to discover the number of Bible readers in the United States: 5 per cent of the population read the Bible every day (that would be some five or six million); a further 35 per cent have read some of it in the past month; 26 per cent have read it through. And one sees the lay of the land in these United States when one discovers that 91 per cent of those in the South believe in immortality as against only 63 per cent of the residents of the Pacific Coast.

(13) To this reader, at least, it was more interesting to read about these matters, generally of only peripheral interest to pollsters, than about attitudes towards reciprocal trade agreements; naturally it is polls of this latter sort that make up the bulk of the volume. But, inevitably, one must turn from this type of intellectual grazing to consider what this huge volume, and the many-branched enterprise it represents, adds up to. How does it modify our intellectual horizons? What does it make possible? Perhaps the most interesting approach

[2] A member of the U.S. House of Representatives who made headlines as chairman of the House Committee Investigating Un-American Activities, 1938–1941.

[3] A Catholic priest who attracted national attention by his political speeches over the radio in the 1930's. Driven off the major networks, he organized his own network of some 47 stations, and continued his anti-Semitic, anti-Roosevelt campaign.

to these problems is to ask, as Hadley Cantril does in his brief introduction, what would have been the significance of similar types of polls
conducted during the French or American Revolution, or during the
Civil War, or in Germany before Hitler. Mr. Cantril does no more than
raise this question; another leading figure in the field, Paul F. Lazarsfeld, goes into the question in some detail in an address to the American
pollsters' professional association, "The Obligation of the 1950 Pollster
to the 1984 Historian" (*Public Opinion Quarterly*, Winter, 1950–51).

(14) Professor Lazarsfeld's article is filled with several examples of
the possible role of the polls in the illumination of history. For example: Lord Macaulay makes a distinction, in his essay on Machiavelli,
between the dominant values of Renaissance Italy and those of con-
temporaneous Northern Europe. Italy, a land of commercial towns,
had developed a culture in which ingenuity was a dominant value; the
still backward North continued to prize courage. Carrying through his
distinction, Macaulay suggests that to a Florentine audience seeing
Othello, Iago would have been the hero.

(15) Here, suggests Professor Lazarsfeld, Macaulay proposed a
hypothesis that falls squarely into the field of opinion research, and one
which could have been directly tested by a poll. After rather facetiously
considering the preliminary technical operations, Professor Lazarsfeld
says: "The crucial question would have been: how many Florentines
and Londoners, respectively, approve of Iago, and how many of
Othello, and how many say 'don't know'? Nothing less, but hardly
much more, would have been needed to provide empirical evidence for
Macaulay's brilliant conjecture."

(16) This is a rather breath-taking possibility. One thinks of all
the historical hypotheses that have been debated these many years and
whether poll data could have confirmed or refuted them. Certainly the
extension of the polling process into the past—even speculatively—
raises some interesting questions: who, for example, among the Londoners and Florentines would we have polled? Would we have questioned the theater-goers alone? Would we have compared only the
merchants of the two towns? What about the workers and *lumpen?* [4]
And what about the clergy and nobility? Whose opinion *mattered*

[4] Ragamuffins.

on this question? Our present-day election pollers have at least this problem settled for them: they poll those who are eligible to vote.

(17) What Professor Lazarsfeld is after, of course, is to get pollsters to look at history, both past and current, so they can be helpful to the historian of the future when he comes to consider the mood, the attitudes, and the opinions of the men of the 1950's. Professor Lazarsfeld sees the polling profession in a position where it can afford to let up on its almost single-minded concentration on technical problems and consider how it could be of value to other social scientists. A great deal of what the pollsters have already done is unquestionably of great value in this respect. In the volume *Public Opinion, 1936–1945*, for example, one can find series of questions, asked of the British at intervals of a month or two, to find out what they thought of Neville Chamberlain: [5] we can thus trace the rise and fall of his popularity more closely than by a study of the British press. Similarly, the series of questions testing American attitudes toward entry into the war, asked every few months in 1939, 1940, and 1941, forms valuable data for a historian of this period.

(18) But it is in the field of the rise and fall of values—the history of a "Protestant ethic," or of a "success ideology," or of the conflict of "courage" and "ingenuity"—that Professor Lazarsfeld is most interested in seeing the polls make their contribution: after all, the polls study attitudes and it is to the history of attitudes that they have the most to offer. Perhaps this highly speculative branch of history, based generally on isolated bits of literary evidence, might be transformed by polls into something as substantial as diplomatic or economic history. For example, Professor Lazarsfeld suggests that the polls may be able to test David Riesman's hypothesis (in *The Lonely Crowd*) that there has been a shift in America from dominance by an "inner-directed" type of person—self-willed, certain of his goals, relatively impervious to the views of those around him—to an "other-directed" type, to whom goals are less significant than approval by others. Now as a matter of fact a great deal of existing poll data can be taken as supporting such

[5] The British Prime Minister in 1937–1940, who negotiated an agreement with Hitler in Munich after the German army occupied the Sudetenland in Czechoslovakia.

a thesis. Riesman has written that the greatest fear of the "other-directed" type is of his own temper: both because the explosion of temper may lose him approval, and because the need to rein himself in builds up a pressure to explode, which he must restrain. And one poll does report that 14 per cent of the American people say that "temper" is their worst fault—twice as many as choose the next most popular fault. Can we consider this as offering validation for Riesman's thesis? Certainly no opponent of Riesman's would be convinced: he will simply reject the interpretation that "temper" is a good index of "other-direction" or that those questioned meant by "temper" what Riesman means.

(19) This, essentially, is the problem: we know, after a poll, that about three thousand persons in all spheres of life have been approached and had a single rather simple question put to them. But can one take their "yes" or "no" as sufficient proof for the existence of a subtle and complex attitude that it may take a book to expound? Consider another example from Professor Lazarsfeld's article. He refers to a finding in *The American Soldier* [6] that those soldiers who do not pray seem to be more mature and get along better with their fellow soldiers than those who do. What might explain this? Professor Lazarsfeld suggests that in an industrial society there is a bifurcation in attitudes to religion: one group clings to it because society is so incomprehensible, uncontrollable, and frightening; another group, more mature and capable of unblinkingly facing the disenchanted world, rejects it. Now no poll could have even suggested such an extensive theory: nor could any poll or even many of them demonstrate it. The poll may give plausibility to the theories developed by a historian; it adds a new type of evidence; but as long as men are interested in comprehensive interpretations of history, we cannot expect polls of themselves to refute or prove any single theory.

(20) Professor Lazarsfeld is quite aware of this: he does not think the introduction of evidence from polls does away with the historian's need to interpret. Polls are new evidence, and in the social sciences

---

[6] A two-volume study in the larger work *Studies in Social Psychology in World War II*, published in 1949 by the Special Committee of the Social Research Council.

evidence has always played a rather ambiguous role. Theories arise, are fiercely held, and pass away—and after it is all over, it is often hard to see that the weight of evidence was so overwhelming as to have led to their acceptance in the first place, or their abandonment in the second. Persuasiveness of argument, apt examples from history and experience, inner logic, and perhaps our simple need to have a part of our experience given satisfactory meaning—these have played a far greater role in the history of theories in the social sciences than strict canons of evidence and proof. It seems that we human beings want to believe we know more about our human state than a strict adherence to scientific method would allow. The thought that we will now be able to buttress our ideas with the solid foundations of the opinion poll is an exciting one, and in many individual cases we will be able to do just this. But when it comes to those large constructions, the few glories of the social sciences, that pull together many things in one flash of illumination, polls will give only some additional data, no worse than we had before, and not much better, but in any case very far from justifying the assurance with which each of us holds his theories, or seeks to persuade others to relinquish theirs.

STUDY QUESTIONS

1. This is a review article of two relatively recent books and an article on public opinion polls. That is, Mr. Glazer is writing an analysis of public opinion polls as a social instrument and uses as his point of departure three items dealing with the matter. In the process, he reviews the books and the article and at the same time presents his own convictions on their common theme. What problems in organization does his purpose present? How does he solve those problems?

2. How does Mr. Glazer effect a transition between his discussion of *The Pre-Election Polls of 1948* and that of *Public Opinion, 1935–1946*? How does he effect a transition between his discussion of the latter and his discussion of "The Obligation of the 1950 Pollster to the 1984 Historian"? What differences are there between the two transitions? What similarities?

3. What specific information does Mr. Glazer give about each of the items he reviews? What judgments does he make on their value?

4. Can you justify the order in which Mr. Glazer discusses the books and the article?

5. In what ways does the concluding paragraph pull together Mr. Glazer's comments on the three items under review?

6. How would you justify the brevity of paragraphs 1, 5, and 8?

7. What is the exact meaning of the following transition words and phrases: *despite* (2), *but* (10), *after all* (10), *at least* (13), *here* (15), *of course* (17), *essentially* (19)?

8. Much of this essay is straightforward reporting employing direct statements with little connotative flavor. There are places, however, where literal statements are given added force and meaning by the use of connotation. Among such connotative phrases are *retired to the haven* (1), *meditate at leisure* (1), *fall from grace* (2), *clings* (19), *unblinkingly facing the disenchanted world* (19), *pass away* (20). What, for you, is the full meaning of each of these phrases? Are they justified in their contexts? Can you see any reason why Mr. Glazer does not use more of such suggestive language?

9. Summarize, in one paragraph, Mr. Glazer's view on the final worth and significance of public opinion polls.

10. What do you think Mr. Glazer means by the following sentence from his concluding paragraph: "It seems that we human beings want to believe we know more about our human state than a strict adherence to scientific method would allow"? Try writing down your explanation in a paragraph.

WRITING ASSIGNMENTS

1. Write an exposition of what you conceive to be the function and value of public opinion polls in a democracy.

2. Write a prospectus of a hypothetical poll to be conducted among students on your campus. In this prospectus justify your poll in terms of its significance and its function and indicate in detail how you would conduct it.

3. Write an argument either for or against student evaluation of teachers.

4. Write an essay on the problems involved in the phrasing of questions for a public opinion poll.

5. Write a research paper on the public opinion polls on the presidential race in 1948 or the straw poll of the 1936 election.

Great Newspapers, if Any*

GERALD JOHNSON (1890–   ) is a newspaperman of varied experience. He worked on the Lexington, North Carolina, Dispatch (1911–1913), the Greensboro, North Carolina, News (1913–1924), the Baltimore Evening Sun (1926–1939) and the Sun (1939–1943). Since 1943 he has devoted himself to free-lance writing. Since 1925 he has written over a score of books, including such varied items as historical studies (Randolph of Roanoke, 1929, Andrew Jackson, 1927, The Secession of the Southern States, 1933), books on his profession (What is News, 1926, The Sunpapers of Baltimore, in collaboration with others), and a book of political analysis (Roosevelt: Dictator or Democrat?, 1941). From 1924 to 1926 he was a professor of Journalism at the University of North Carolina.

I

(1) An old and successful, if not too reputable, North Carolina politician once explained to me the basis of the national optimism.

(2) "A free-born, sovereign American citizen is never down and out," he proclaimed. "If he is too lazy to farm, too ignorant to keep books, too ornery to clerk in a store, and too trifling to work at a saw mill, there are always three lines he can fall back on that require no special ability. He can teach school, govern the state, or edit a newspaper."

(3) That this is, in fact, part of the American credo you can readily determine for yourself at the next dinner party you attend, simply by gently directing the conversation toward education, politics, or journalism. Everybody knows what is wrong with them, and almost everybody

* From Harper's Magazine, June, 1948. Copyright 1948 by Harper & Brothers. Reprinted by permission of the author and Harper & Brothers.

knows what to do about it. The qualification, "almost," is necessary, because wherever you find a creed, there also you find heretics. As regards this particular article, for instance, I am two-thirds of a heretic myself. I am sure that I should make an excellent governor, but that is all. Being governor is the one of the three occupations that I have never tried.

(4) As an unbeliever in the general assumption that anybody can teach school—which I tried briefly—or edit a newspaper—which I tried for many years—I have watched with rather more than average interest recent deliverances on American newspaperdom, notably the report of the Hutchins Commission and the comments thereon of the Nieman Fellows at Harvard. These documents should be of great value because their authors are all people with special information. The members of the Hutchins Commission are scholars, carefully chosen not merely for profound learning in their own fields, but because each has a reputation for poise and sound judgment in handling general ideas. A Nieman Fellow is by definition a newspaper man in active practice and with several years of experience behind him. Without those qualifications he cannot join the group guided by Louis Lyons at Harvard toward the goal of an improvement in American journalism. In addition to that, before he can receive an appointment his editor must adjudge him "promising"—which, if it means anything, must mean that he is a good newspaper man who seems to have the will and the ability to become better.

(5) Thus both groups, the scholars by the austere disciplines to which they are committed, the Fellows by the criteria governing their selection, may be assumed to be searchers after excellence. It is malapropos, therefore, to ask them, "What is a good newspaper?" One may ask merely, "What is a newspaper?" for such men would not concede that a thoroughly bad newspaper is worthy of the name.

(6) I submit, therefore, that it is a fact of prime significance that the efforts of both groups to define a newspaper lead in half a dozen directions. This has given rise to a certain amount of snickering within the craft, based on the assumption that it proves how helpless are the *illuminati* when it comes to defining their terms. But this is not true. Neither the scholars nor the Fellows had any difficulty in defining a

newspaper with reasonable precision. What it proves is simply that the good newspaper is multiform; it may assume any of at least half a dozen shapes—half a hundred is a more plausible estimate—and still remain good. A specified journal may not be good for you, or for me; but, really, you know, there are several other newspaper readers besides us two; and the very newspaper that makes us seasick may be the delight of millions. Is it, then, devoid of merit? I am not prepared to say so.

(7) I have done time as a regular inmate on five newspapers, ranging in type from a country weekly to a metropolitan daily. As a contributor, I have had fairly close relations with several others. In wandering about I have come into contact, or collision, with a great many newspaper men. In writing about men and events of the past, I have had occasion to read rather extensively in the files of old newspapers. I have thus had opportunity to gather a great deal of special information about American journalism; but the net result is that although the scholars and the Fellows have expressed diverse and sometimes contradictory ideas of what constitutes a good newspaper, I am not prepared to assert flatly that any of them is wrong.

II

(8) For the newspaper itself is contradictory, which is one way of saying that it is a very human enterprise. The newspaper is a social force. That is indubitable. It is also a manufactory. That is just as certainly true. Like the school, it purveys information, but its information, unlike that of the school, must be fresh, which is to say, it handles a product that deteriorates with unparalleled speed. The very conditions of its existence, therefore, are impossible of perfect fulfillment; for information to be sound must be true, and to be fresh must be disseminated at high speed. But in the process of learning and informing others, high speed and perfect accuracy are incompatible. It follows, therefore, that, judged by the ideal standard, all newspapers are bad newspapers and can't be anything else.

(9) The tendency of investigators, however, is to overlook the necessary conditions of the newspaper's existence and to measure its dis-

tance from the ideal standard absolutely. Many of them would elimi-
nate, for example, the newspaper's status as a profit-making enterprise.
The necessity of showing an operating profit every year, they assert,
inhibits any real freedom and only a newspaper subsidized, either by
the government or by private funds, can enjoy liberty.

(10) There is a certain plausibility in this, but the people who argue
along that line overlook the fact that a subsidized newspaper, like a
subsidized man, is no longer to be identified with the common herd,
and is therefore no longer a structural unit in the common culture. An
American who doesn't have to work for his own living may be very
valuable, and very admirable, but he is not very typical. A newspaper
in similar circumstances may be both useful and ornamental, but it
is inevitably a little apart from the craft of journalism; for a craft is a
means of livelihood. Hence, a newspaper that cannot pay its bills is
not a typical newspaper; whether it is good, bad, or indifferent, it tells
us little about the possibility of journalism as it is and must be practiced by the great majority of newspapers in this country. A subsidized
press is a controlled press; whether it is controlled by holy angels or
fiends in human form it remains a controlled press, exactly as the Russian and Spanish newspapers are controlled, and its experience has
few lessons applicable to a free press.

(11) A man who cannot stand on his own feet, or a newspaper that
cannot pay its own bills, enjoys freedom only on sufferance. If its un-
earned funds are cut off, its merit will not save it. Hence in a capitalistic
economy the ability to make a profit, or at least to stay in the black, is
one of the indispensable elements of a great newspaper. For this reason
I cannot agree with those who lament the extinction of the New York
World as the destruction of a truly great newspaper. It had been great,
without doubt, and it remained brilliant and useful; but when its books
went into the red, it lost one of the essential requisites of real newspaper
greatness. The same consideration applies to *PM* and the Chicago
Sun. They have never been more than hopeful experiments. They are
not truly great newspapers.

(12) Unfortunately, this same factor, essential to greatness, is quite
capable of destroying greatness in a public journal. It is another illustration of the intense humanity of the newspaper, for it is emphatically

true of a man. One of the most dismal facts of life in the United States of America is that here very few men indeed have a million dollars, but many a million dollars has a man. If it is impossible for a newspaper to be free without a bank account acquired by its own efforts, it is only just possible for it to be free *from* that bank account after it has been acquired.

(13) Within the past generation the newspaper has become Big Business and, because of its size, it has acquired, except in a very few places, the characteristics of a natural monopoly. The annual expenditures of such a newspaper as, for instance, the Baltimore *Sun*, published not in the largest but the seventh city, run into eight figures. Disregarding national advertising and some other minor sources of revenue, the expenditures of a newspaper are a charge upon the business activity of its city of publication. Few cities of less than two or three million people have business enough to support more than one really first-class newspaper. Washington, whose business is politics that involves the revenues of the whole country, is the only conspicuous exception. Outside of New York, Chicago, and perhaps Philadelphia, American cities cannot afford two ten-million-dollar newspapers any more than they can afford two telephone companies, or two water-supply systems.

(14) But Big Business in the nature of the case involves big profits. Newspaper proprietors—not newspaper editors who are, as a rule, hired men—are tycoons of the first order. Inevitably they tend to associate for the most part with other tycoons and to acquire the mental and emotional attitudes of other millionaires; and it is an unusual millionaire who is not to some extent the bond-slave of his own money.

(15) There are few things in this vale of tears more jittery than a million dollars, and the man who is owned by a million dollars inevitably shivers like an aspen leaf. The notion that it is advertisers that newspaper proprietors fear is usually a misconception; normally, the advertisers fear the newspaper more than it does them, for a well-established newspaper, dominating its field, can heavily damage, perhaps wreck, a department store, theater, or hotel simply by excluding its advertising and its name from the news columns. What newspaper proprietors fear is what all men fear, namely, the condemnation of public opinion; but the public opinion that presses most intimately

upon the owner of a big newspaper is the opinion of big business men, not of the man in the street.

(16) One of them—call him Carver, since that is not his name— once expressed it clearly and succinctly.

(17) "When I go around this town," he said, "and two or three leading men see me coming, I want them to say, 'Oh, here comes Carver, a sound man; call him over to join us.' I don't want them to say, 'Here comes that son-of-a-bitch Carver; let's duck around the corner before he sees us!'"

(18) Considering the environment in which they live and the pressure to which it subjects them, the marvel is not that American newspaper proprietors are so conservative but rather that they are not all reactionaries. It is much easier to be a howling Communist in Greenwich Village than it is to be even a Cleveland Democrat in the stately midtown clubs, yet respectable numbers of American newspaper owners manage it.

(19) For one thing some of them, but not all, have gained some, but not an adequate, conception of the responsibility that is irremovably attached to a monopoly position. Every respectable newspaper in the country now acknowledges its duty to print the news, even when the news is unfavorable or possibly ruinous to the policy it advocates. Republican newspapers published full accounts of the conviction of Albert B. Fall,[1] even though that case was damaging to the Republican party; Democratic newspapers recorded the conviction of Andrew J. May,[2] although that news certainly did not help the party. Sometimes newspapers bury unfavorable items in the back pages, but they print them, and really big stuff usually goes on the front page, although the newspaper may regret bitterly the necessity of having to print such news.

(20) But the notion that opinions, also, are news is one that is by no means universally accepted. Many newspapers regard it as no part of their duty to present their readers with a summary of all shades of

[1] President Harding's Secretary of the Interior who was sentenced to prison for taking bribes in the Teapot Dome Scandal.

[2] Andrew J. May, former prominent Congressman from Kentucky, was convicted in 1947 of accepting bribes for exerting influence in the awarding of war contracts during World War II.

opinion, even when they hold a monopoly position in their towns. A conservative paper that reported faithfully the election of Wallace's candidate in the Bronx may have never printed a line of the argument by which that candidate won the election. Such a paper's readers therefore know that the man was elected but, as far as their paper is concerned, they have never been told why he was elected. They are not well informed and the paper is not accepting the duty that lies upon every monopoly, whether of goods or of services, to serve all classes of its constituency without favoritism.

(21) I would not imply that it is the duty of a newspaper to open its editorial columns to opinions it deems false and pernicious. The editorial page is admittedly the place for the paper's own opinion, and no other. But in a one-newspaper town it is clearly the duty of the paper holding the monopoly to make room somewhere for the presentation of opinions challenging its own. Many newspapers today contrive this by carrying signed columns expressing opinions differing from, and sometimes flatly contradicting, those on its editorial page. This policy is doubly creditable, first, because it serves the constituency fairly, and, second, because it is sometimes distasteful to the paper. Not infrequently the signed columns are so much better written than the editorial page that they show it up rather dreadfully, and in that case it takes courage to continue them.

III

(22) No one, I take it, would question the assertion that it is the duty of a newspaper to offer its readers a true account of the day's events, and a supremely great newspaper would do it infallibly. But newspaper men, unfortunately, are no better at discerning truth than you and I. Jan Masaryk [3] is dead. There is no doubt about that. Every newspaper in the world reported it, and no one has denied it. But can any newspaper anywhere assert confidently that it printed the truth about Masaryk's death? It cannot, because no adequate test of the truth was available.

[3] Foreign Minister of the Czechoslovak Government-in-Exile during World War II and of postwar Czechoslovakia, and son of the first president of Czechoslovakia. The circumstances of his death in 1948 were never disclosed.

(23) In that case the newspapers were deliberately denied access to the truth; but it is frequently concealed just as effectively when all the objective facts are known. What made Roosevelt run again in 1940? All the facts are known, and all the really pertinent ones were known at the time, but the facts are susceptible of many different interpretations. Somewhere among those interpretations lies the truth, but the best newspaper man in the country can identify it with no more justifiable assurance than you can.

(24) People, especially exasperated liberals, are forever denouncing newspaper craftsmen for not answering instantly and authoritatively Pilate's question, "What is truth?" After all, though, Socrates and Plato combined couldn't answer it, nor Aristotle, nor Thomas Aquinas, nor Erasmus, nor Descartes, nor Spinoza. It would seem that people might consider the possibility that the average harried and harassed man in the slot of the copydesk is really not the intellectual superior of these.

(25) It is not to be denied that there are newspaper men who are arrant rogues. I myself have known some who were slippery customers, some who were venal, some who were incorrigible liars, and more than a few who were plain jackasses. But I have encountered comparable types in business and in the Army, in law, in medicine, even—God save the mark!—in holy orders. In short, to paraphrase David Harum,[4] there is as much human nature in newspaper men as there is in others, if not more. And as they are, so are their papers. The question is, are these types prevalent in journalism? And the answer is, look at America. As the population from which it is drawn, so is the craft.

(26) As Paracelsus used to discuss the Alkahest, so newspaper men are given to talking about a conceptual absolute that they call "impersonal journalism." It has no real existence. Journalism is and always was as intensely personal as taste in neckties. Personalities may be concealed by institutional organization as the fire is concealed in an automobile engine, but it is there, or the thing doesn't move. If you find a great newspaper, rest assured that somewhere in the works is at least

[4] A New England country banker in Westcott's novel of the same name, published in 1898. The remark which Johnson paraphrases is "The's as much human nature in some folks as th' is in others, if not more."

one great man. He may be the owner, or the chief editorial writer, or the managing editor, or any of a dozen other executives, but he is there and he has authority. Extinguish him and the paper instantly ceases to be great, even though it may remain for some time successful as a business enterprise.

(27) But this intensely personal craft necessarily turns out an intensely personal product. The result is that it is as difficult to apply objective standards to newspapers as it is to people, and the greatest newspaper is as difficult to identify as the greatest man. It all depends upon what you require. The greatest doctor cannot help you win an intricate lawsuit, nor will the mightiest of attorneys help much toward getting you into heaven.

IV

(28) Like every other man who has been long in the business, I am frequently called on to name the greatest newspaper, or the ten greatest newspapers in the United States. There is no such thing, for newspapers are not institutions, they are personalities, as illogical, perverse, and contradictory as other personalities, and they should be described, not statistically, but in terms of their personal traits.

(29) Consider, for example, the two newspapers that I prefer for my own information and edification, the *Times* and the *Herald Tribune*, both of New York. The *Times* carries more detailed information, but the *Herald Tribune* is written in a more interesting style. To accord superiority to either would lead to endless argument.

(30) They are more exactly pictured by reference to personalities. The *Times*, to me, is Miss Betsey Trotwood, David Copperfield's aunt, a lady of the most estimable character, if a trifle dry, and of impressive dignity until some lout speaks disrespectfully of private enterprise. But private enterprise is to the *Times* what donkeys were to Miss Trotwood; at mention of the term she blows up in terrifying and disconcerting fashion. Nevertheless, she is kindly, and most rigidly upright.

(31) By the same token, the *Herald Tribune* is Mr. Tulkinghorn,[5] solicitor to the nobility and gentry, able, suave, imperturbable, and

[5] The cunning old lawyer in Dickens' novel *Bleak House* (1852–53).

discreet, oh, how immeasurably discreet! The scandals of all the great families were sealed forever within the breast of Mr. Tulkinghorn; even so, all the ghastly secrets of the Republican party are known to the *Herald Tribune* but it will never, never whisper a word of them.

(32) These are unquestionably superior persons, very superior indeed, and far be it from me to intimate that either is superior to the other. I love them both and I love especially the circumspect dignity with which they approach each other. Let us rather observe them respectfully as they move together with wary politeness, Miss Trotwood and Mr. Tulkinghorn, sedately and decorously taking the air, while humbler folk, as is right and proper, pull their forelocks and nimbly step aside.

(33) Less impressive, but still commanding immense respect in the newspaper world, are three papers outside of New York, the St. Louis *Post-Dispatch*, the Chicago *Daily News*, and the Baltimore *Sun*. All three have courage and honor, and if there are any great newspapers in America they are in the list. The *Post-Dispatch*, old Joe Pulitzer's first love, has fought the battle of the common man with gallantry and persistence for half a century; but Missouri politics is still Missouri politics. The paper reminds me of a character quite forgotten now, but celebrated in my youth, Irving Bacheller's Eben Holden,[6] who always did what he thought was right, but sometimes with startling results, never cussed 'less 'twas necessary, and held hope for the future, but passed through the world a little hurt, a little bewildered.

(34) The Chicago *Daily News*, like Diana Warwick [7]—and that is probably a lost allusion; has anybody read George Meredith within the past twenty years?—once hoped faintly that men, having passed Seraglio Point, might eventually double Cape Turk, which is by interpretation that Chicago, having become relatively civilized, might eventually develop a high culture. The *Daily News* developed a splendid foreign service when most American newspapers had none worth mentioning; it strove valiantly to inform the people of the crossways of the republic about such things as the municipal art museums, sym-

---

[6] The resourceful hired man in the novel, published in 1900, which bears his name.

[7] A leading character in Meredith's novel *Diana of the Crossways* (1885).

phonic music, and the news of the literary world. This Diana of the Crossways was and is charming, intelligent, a protagonist of civilization; if she is also rather futile, isn't that the common lot of torch-bearers?

(35) For a hundred and eleven years the Baltimore *Sun*, one of the original "penny press," has kept in mind fairly consistently its function as a disseminator of news, but it still balks at the idea of spreading opinion, other than the conservative opinion that it approves. It has today a superb news service, both foreign and domestic, and its editorial policy, especially as regards foreign affairs, is intelligent, vigorous, highly enlightened. But the city of Baltimore has some of the foulest slums in America, the State of Maryland has one of the most cynically ruthless soak-the-poor taxation systems in existence, and the tight efficiency of the Tydings political machine makes those of Hague and Flynn [8] look like the work of blundering amateurs. The personality of the *Sun* is not hard to identify; it is the type of the pious Mrs. Jellyby,[9] who wore her life out sewing red flannel nightgowns for the infant Hottentots, while her own children went rapidly to hell.

(36) However, the palm for sheer, dogged courage, indisputably one element of greatness, must be awarded to none of these, but to a paper in other respects quite unlike them. This is the Chicago *Tribune*, as magnificent in dubious projects as was green-eyed Becky Sharpe [10] —and as shrewd, as hard, as bold, as antisocial.

(37) Business success, being essential to any newspaper that is to survive at all, is necessarily another element of a great newspaper. It would be fatuous, therefore, to omit from a list of this sort the most successful business enterprise, and that by long odds, in American daily journalism, the New York *Daily News*. True, its success was attained by acceptance of some weird ideas and some strange bedfellows, but financial success it was and of stupendous dimensions. But this, too, is a striking perdurable factor in the newspaper world as in human

[8] The Tydings, Hague, and Flynn machines operate in Maryland, New Jersey, and the Bronx respectively.

[9] The character in Dickens' *Bleak House* who lets her family starve while she devotes her attention to professional philanthropy.

[10] The heroine of Thackeray's novel *Vanity Fair* (1847–48), a magnificently clever, vicious social climber.

life. It has always existed and apparently it always will exist; there is no point in ignoring the fact that we have among us Forever Amber.[11]

(38) Any discussion of the salient personalities in American journalism must add to these seven three additional names that do not represent individuals, but families of papers—Hearst, Scripps-Howard, Gannett. It is not worthwhile to pick out any one newspaper as representative of these, because none stands alone, but each is braced by the resources and abilities of the tribe, as every duPont, every Vanderbilt, every Astor is not merely an individual, but also a representative of a powerful clan.

(39) But with the seven individual papers and one representative of each of the three chains, it is possible to compile a list of ten American newspapers, each of which is great in one way or another. Which is the greatest, or, indeed, whether any is great absolutely—well, there is where the scholars and the Fellows fall out, and this writer is certainly not the Nestor to compose their dispute.

(40) As a matter of fact, when it comes to competent, thorough, and conscientious editing, which surely is of the essence of good newspaper work, not one of the mighty ten is to be mentioned in the same breath with certain obscure little journals, scattered here and there throughout the country. Two of the best, in this respect, are village sheets whose annual budget probably does not approach the cost of producing a single issue of the New York *Times*. They are the *Gazette*, published on Martha's Vineyard, Massachusetts, and the *Weekly*, published at Chapel Hill, North Carolina. Neither is a rural journal, however. Martha's Vineyard is a great summer resort and Chapel Hill is the seat of the University of North Carolina. Both places are swept by the currents of modern thought, and both newspapers, despite a superficial simplicity, are as sophisticated as the New York *Sun* ever was under Dana [12] or the *Herald* under Bennett.[13] You will never find a filler in either the *Weekly* or the *Gazette*; every line that goes into

[11] *Forever Amber* (1944), Kathleen Winsor's best-selling novel, recounts the sensational adventures of Amber, a woman willing to use her physical charms freely in the pursuit of her social goals, during the days of Restoration England (1660–1688).

[12] Charles Anderson Dana, editor from 1867 to 1897.

[13] James Gordon Bennett, editor from 1872 to 1918.

those papers is put there for a purpose other than filling space, which is more than can be said of any great metropolitan daily.

(41) The omissions in this list are glaring, I admit. My reasons for leaving out the Marshall Field enterprises, the New York *PM* and the Chicago *Sun,* I have explained. In a sense they apply also to the Boston *Christian Science Monitor,* which has sectarian support not acquired strictly on its merits as a newspaper, and therefore belongs among the ghostly fathers rather than among the working colleagues of the press. But there are the immaculate, impeccable, irreproachable Colonel Carter of Cartersville,[14] the Richmond *Times Dispatch,* and that damsel in distress among the Ku Kluxers, the Atlanta *Constitution;* there are the Tinman [15] in search of a soul, the Denver *Rocky Mountain News,* and Jurgen,[16] doing what seems to be expected, the Portland *Oregonian;* all these and a dozen others are not mere news factories, but personalities with character and intelligence. I do not believe, however, that any of them affects the thinking of as many people as many times a week as those I have mentioned.

(42) That there is a really great newspaper in all America I am not prepared to assert unequivocally, but the doubt is not troublesome. We have something that I regard as preferable to a Thunderer,[17] to wit, a press that is intellectually rich and varied, full of faults, no doubt, but full of merits, too, and merits so diverse that they could hardly be incorporated in a single journal.

(43) Yet my judgment is certainly questionable, for I find myself taking no small delight in one newspaper for a reason that is not journalistic but crassly sentimental. It is the New York *Post,* which I admire for its liberalism, but which also delights me by its sheer survival value. The *Post* is, for an American paper, extremely old. In the

---

[14] The frank, generous southern gentleman down on his luck who is the hero of F. Hopkinson Smith's novelette, *Colonel Carter of Cartersville* (1891).

[15] The Tin Woodman in Frank Baum's *The Wonderful Wizard of Oz* (1900) journeyed to the Wizard to request he be given a heart.

[16] The middle-aged pawnbroker in James Branch Cabell's *Jurgen* (1919). When the Devil spirited away his much-talking wife, Jurgen set out to find her, reluctantly bowing to the pressure of his conscience and local gossip. After a long trip, involving many erotic adventures, through the worlds of fiction, he regained his wife and returned with her to their former prosaic existence.

[17] The name given to the London *Times* in the nineteenth century because of its influential and authoritative (and even authoritarian) power.

beginning Alexander Hamilton wrote for it, and in the end Samuel Grafton writes for it; during the long time between it has had editors of every type, except the huckster type, that journalism has produced— brilliant, dull, conservative, radical, learned, ignorant, everything. I like it as I like Montaigne's perhaps fabulous woman of Toulouse, because in spite of having passed through so many hands, it remains blithe, brisk, unabashed, and full of beans.

STUDY QUESTIONS

1. Formulate in one sentence the central idea of this essay. What are Mr. Johnson's major divisions of his subject? How does each division prepare for the next?

2. What is the function of paragraph 7?

3. What is the relevance of Section IV to the rest of Mr. Johnson's discussion?

4. Why does Mr. Johnson compare specific newspapers with specific characters from fiction? What does he accomplish by such comparisons?

5. What effect is achieved by each of the following words or phrases: *done time as a regular inmate* (7), *along that line* (10), *the common herd* (10), *of the first order* (14), *bond-slave* (14), *howling* (18), *big stuff* (19), *absolutely* (39), *full of beans* (43)?

6. Examine very closely the arguments employed by Mr. Johnson in Section II. What, briefly, is his position? Can you detect any inconsistencies or logical weaknesses in his arguments? What basic premises underlie his arguments?

7. How does Mr. Johnson define a great newspaper? What meaning does he give to the term *great?*

8. Mr. Johnson objects generally to judging newspapers in terms of an ideal standard. Does he completely disregard such a standard? If not, at what points are his own judgments governed by that standard?

9. How valid are Mr. Johnson's judgments in Section IV? What is the basis of his ratings?

10. What do paragraphs 40 and 41 contribute to Mr. Johnson's evaluation?

WRITING ASSIGNMENTS

1. Write an extended definition of a great newspaper, in terms not of existing papers, but in terms of an ideal standard.

2. Write an analysis of what you think should be the social function of a newspaper.

3. Write a critical evaluation of a commercial newspaper you know well from long reading.

4. Write an analysis of the purpose and/or achievement of your campus newspaper.

5. Write a research paper on the origin of the newspaper.

Principles of Modern Form—Economy *

LEWIS MUMFORD (1895–   ) *is a writer with a wide range of interests which may be incorporated under the general designation of social philosophy. Many of his activities have been in the direction of social and regional planning. A Guggenheim Fellowship in 1932 precipitated a series of books on the evolution of Western civilization as viewed through its arts and its institutions:* Technics and Civilization (1934), The Culture of Cities (1938), The Condition of Man (1944), *and* The Conduct of Life (1951). *Mr. Mumford has served as a visiting lecturer and professor of Dartmouth College, Harvard University, Stanford University, The Pacific School of Religion, and the University of North Carolina.*

(1) Perhaps the main guiding principle of modern architecture is economy: economy of material, economy of means, economy of expression. And the reason why economy occupies the very center of our thought is that it is a sign of orderly understanding and perfect control—like the cut of a diver's body through the air, hitting the water without a splash.

(2) Let us begin with the most elementary statement of economy: modern means of construction. Under past systems of architecture the actual strength and mass of a structure was determined by empiric practice: if a tower fell down, its foundations were too feeble or its top too heavy: a bad guess. Not merely is there a considerable range of difference between the strength of various natural materials; but there existed no reliable means for working out the tensile and compression strengths of various types of members: indeed, in some of their temples

the Greeks, eager to reinforce their stones, carved channels for iron rods that actually weakened the structure.

(3) During the last half century the creation of new manufactured building materials, like steel and reinforced concrete, with determinable strengths, determinable coefficients of expansion, radically altered the problem of building: it decreased the need for large solid members that built up into great sculptural masses. To use the least possible amount of material compatible with safety has become a mark of fine calculation and intelligent architectural insight: to be oversized, or overweight, is a sign of technical uncouthness, even if not immediately apparent to the eye. Building codes, framed according to the canons of guesswork, with an absurd margin of oversafety, do not generally recognize this change: but building codes, throughout the world, are overdue for revision.

(4) The very interest in economy has given a special sanction to the lighter materials, which are easier to transport and usually easier to erect: the metal framework, the glass or composite surface to serve as sheath for the inner space, the flexible partition, have taken the place of clumsier and more static members. The esthetic attitude that goes with these new materials was very well put by J. J. P. Oud, the Dutch architect, one of the most able exponents of the new form:

In place of the natural charm of walls and roofs of rough materials, unstable in their plasticity and uncertainly patined; in place of windows cut into small panes, nebulously glazed and irregularly colored; a new architecture will offer us the definite values of artificial materials, surfaces polished and finished, the scintillation of steel and the brilliance of paint, the transparent openness of large windows of plate glass. . . . Architectural evolution will lead us toward a style that will appear liberated from matter, although it is joined to it more completely than ever.

(5) The entire functional development of architecture from the fifteenth century on, as Meyer remarked, is a response to the demand: "More light!" This development has thrown the structural emphasis from the supporting wall or column to the interior skeleton, from the enclosing *mass* to the bounding surface, from architectural form as the sculpture of solids to architectural form as the definition and articulation of voids. The age of crustacean building has given way to

the age of vertebrates, and the wall, no longer a protective shell, has become a skin. Other organic changes within buildings have necessarily followed this development: a specialization of parts, a finer articulation of the various members, a system for maintaining a standard interior temperature and for renovating the air, which may be compared, roughly, with the action of heart and lungs in the body—while similarly the organization of the functions of ingestion (light, air, water, coal, gas, electricity) and that of excretion (inorganic and organic waste) has modified the nature of practically every structure.

(6) The building is no longer a passive shell: it is a functioning organization in which the primitive aspect of shelter, as embodied in the original cave, and of symbol, as embodied in the monument, have become secondary attributes of more complicated processes. Some of these functions have indeed been provided for in other systems of architecture: they reached a high point in the eotechnic wood-and-water culture of the Japanese. But now their range has been extended through new forms of industrial fabrication, and their integration and expression, in fresh form, had become imperative.

(7) To resist the use of these new materials and forms of construction is to resist the possibilities of order today. Not merely must one reject the decadent style-mongering of the suburban bourgeoisie, not merely must one throw over the obsolete grandiosities of height or expanse beloved by the conceited dictators of finance or government: one must reject, as still fundamentally inadequate, those more sensible stereotypes of traditional architecture embodied in the otherwise sound and generously planned cottages built by governmental agents, for example, in numerous English housing estates. Modern life has more to offer than these sober compromises and collective timidities would indicate. We do not glue feathers on the wings of airplanes because men have always associated flight with the forms of birds; and there is no reason why, to pay respect to traditional notions of domesticity, we should resort to similar practices in the building of houses— as if what architecture had now to offer the housewife were not something infinitely more attractive to her than slate roofs and roughly smeared stucco walls. The eighteenth century American farmhouse was a gracious traditional form: its fine lines and just proportions,

which owed none of their charm to ornamental superfluity, derived
from the same technics and culture that built its water mills and its
wooden ships. Such harmony between the various parts of the environment is what architecture today requires, worked out in terms of contemporary order.

(8) Even when, for the sake of harmony with the natural surroundings, natural materials may be appropriately used, the modern principle
of economy will dictate that they be used in their modern technical
form, not in more traditional shapes inherited from an incongruent
past: not heavy half-timbers and ponderous oak paneling, for example,
but sawed beams and light plywood paneling.

(9) What is true of materials and construction is naturally also true
of plan. Here, too, economy must prevail. A modern plan is successful
only when it embraces every human need appropriate to the structure
without waste of space, duplication, clumsy and inefficient means of
circulation. This principle of economy is socially the opposite of the
ancient canon of conspicuous waste. For the latter principle, in the
interest of pecuniary and caste distinctions, emphasized the rôle of
superfluity: rooms were scaled, not to their specific human uses, but
solely for the purpose of impressing the spectator, no matter how difficult they might be to heat, or how oppressive they might feel to the
individual occupant. Rooms were often duplicated on the plan, too,
on either side of an axis, merely for the sake of achieving a formal
balance for the eye of the observer outside. So, too, decoration would
overlay the structural form: the product of the woodturner was marked
with bulges, beads, indentations, which collected dust: the oak paneling was carved in floral or heraldic designs, and the ceiling was
plastered with complicated geometric figures. Wherever a clear space
remained, it was filled with some product of handicraft or *virtu*, partly
because the craftsman himself delighted in such fantasies, even more
because the patron took pleasure in sheer excess. Beauty? Perhaps.
Show? Decidedly. A barn, a kitchen, a fortress might be built according
to the canons of economy; but not works that symbolized social station
or social function.

(10) If economy today derives partly from the finer scientific cal-
culations and the complicated inventions that enter into modern

building—*inventions whose cost must be offset in other departments* —it has a social and esthetic basis as well. The social principle under-lying the canon of economy rests on the fact that there is no modern utility or machine that we do not conceive as universal in its applica-tion. We do not have one type of electric light for the rich and another for the poor; we do not have one type of telephone, carved out of some ornate and precious material for the rich, and another type made of inferior materials, for peasants and clerks. All these instruments have an objective standard of performance, determinable by experiment: they are the products of a collective economy and are meant to fit into a collective whole. One's economic position may entitle one to a greater or smaller quantity, but the quality is fixed.

(11) With respect to the fundamental goods of modern life, a basic equality has been partly established, and more and more goods and services are coming into line: this principle has even made its way into realms like clothes where class differences were once duly established by law, and where conspicuous differential waste for long went un-challenged. Such equalization rests in good part on the economies of mass production or on the no less important economies, as in municipal utilities, of collective distribution based on a social monopoly. Mass production itself demands, esthetically, an emphasis upon the generic, the standardized: upon forms freed from irregularity, superfluity, and imaginative caprice. *In order to make collective production and distri-bution possible on a scale that will embrace a whole society, economy must be a regulating principle in all design: for it is only by saving on the means and instrumentalities of life that a community can com-mand the necessary abundance at the higher levels of art, science, edu-cation, and expression.* Economy, which in an earlier culture signified niggardliness, now provides the means for collective largesse. Holding to this principle means having enough to go round.

(12) There is, however, an additional esthetic basis for economy in modern architecture. It lies in the fact that we live in a far more complicated world than that of the primitive craftsman and peasant: even the most limited person today in our urban communities is played upon by forces and stimuli so numerous, so insistent, so diverting, that he can achieve internal peace only by stripping to the essentials the

visual environment. When there were no textbooks of natural history, no museums, no scientific abstracts, no illustrated papers and magazines, it might be amusing and instructive to have the animals in Noah's ark carved on a cathedral: then, truly, in Hugo's phrase, the cathedral was the stone book of mankind. But such decoration today is for the most part a distraction, at best a stale repetition of something that exists in more adequate form in treatises on biology and in museums of science. We demand that our modern environment become more legible, and above all, more serene. The clean surface, the candid revelation of function, the plain conspicuous lettering or symbolism of a sign or a building—these are the conditions that redefine our sense of beauty in urban structures.

(13) To appreciate art and sculpture, as emotional experiences, we must detach them from the function of building: their permanent, non-detachable place has disappeared with the stone forms and the solid walls and stable relations which gave them their functional setting in other cultures. Much of the current demand for murals today is esthetically and socially atavistic: the mural that goes with the modern building is the poster: a form that can be duplicated, broadcast, and frequently renewed. The London Underground has been a more intelligent patron of modern art than more pompous public bodies—such as the United States Post Office—that choose to work in terms of an obsolete social situation.

(14) The true symbol of the modern age in architecture is the *absence* of visible symbols: we no longer seek on the surface that which we can obtain effectively only through penetration and participation in the function of a structure. As our sense of the invisible forces at work in the actual environment increases—not merely our sense of physical processes below the threshold of common observation, but psychological and social processes too—as this sense increases we will tend to ask architecture itself to assume a lower degree of visibility: spectator's architecture, show architecture, will give way to a more thoroughgoing sense of form, not so conspicuous perhaps on the surface, but capable of giving intellectual and emotional stimulus at every step in its revelation.

(15) Carried out imaginatively, the principle of economy becomes

a positive pleasure in building: a sign of right relationship with life. Ships show this sense of economy, from modern sailing craft to the ocean liner: so do a great variety of machines; so, for the greater part, do dams and power-stations and factories. Perhaps one of the finest examples, not merely of utilitarian accomplishment but of positive esthetic impulse, is the modern American kitchen, even in houses that frequently contradict all its good features in every other room. Such economy is the moral flower of that long discipline of the spirit which Western man has undertaken during the last millennium under the forms of monasticism, capitalism, militarism, and mechanism: forms in which life was denied, rather than enhanced, for the ulterior purpose of holiness or power. Today, as we slough off the skin of old social habits, economy is at last ready to flow out of these life-constraining departments into a more balanced, a less sterile, human habitat.

STUDY QUESTIONS

1. What is the thesis sentence of this essay?
2. Write a general outline of this essay, indicating by paragraph number where each major and minor division begins and ends. How is each new division brought to the reader's attention?
3. Some essays are built around a key word or key words. In this essay, *economy* is such a word. Study its use as a key word and embody your observations in a written paragraph. Begin by looking up the history of the word and its various meanings in the unabridged *New* (or *Oxford*) *English Dictionary*.
4. The word *means* occurs in the first sentence of both paragraphs 1 and 2. In both instances, is the word used with exactly the same sense? If not, wherein lies the difference? If Mumford uses the same word twice in close proximity with somewhat different senses, is it legitimate to criticize him for so doing?
5. Although you probably will not find the word *style-mongering* (7) in any dictionary, try defining it by examining the meaning of its parts. What connotation does *mongering* almost invariably have in English? In the same fashion, try defining *eotechnic* (6).
6. In the last sentence of paragraph 9, what is meant by "works that symbolized social station or social function"?
7. How appropriate is the imagery used in paragraph 5? What is its value?

8. In this essay Mr. Mumford makes extensive use of the colon. Is every such use justified? At what points might other marks of punctuation be used?

9. Mr. Mumford often develops his argument by the use of antithesis and contrast and by rising emphasis. Select examples of these rhetorical devices.

10. Select a few examples of sentences which are balanced in construction.

11. What are the underlying assumptions of Mr. Mumford's argument, assumptions which he does not here express or which he expresses only obliquely?

12. What fallacy of argument is contained in the second sentence of paragraph 7?

13. What arguments can be raised against Mr. Mumford's position?

WRITING ASSIGNMENTS

1. Write an essay on the advantages and/or disadvantages of standardized living. (Reread paragraph 10.)

2. On the basis of your answers to question 13 above, write an answer to Mr. Mumford.

3. Write an account of your own impressions of some one embodiment of modern form (private home, public building, furniture, etc.).

4. Write a familiar essay on modern design.

5. Write a research paper on the difficulties imposed on new methods by building codes.

*Taste in Music**

VIRGIL THOMSON (1896–   ) *is a composer and music critic. After graduation from Harvard in 1922, he spent some years studying music in Paris. He has written articles on music for the* American Mercury *and the* New Republic. *Formerly music critic for* Vanity Fair, Modern Music, *and the Boston* Transcript, *he now writes in that capacity for the New York* Herald Tribune. *His best-known composition is the opera* Four Saints in Three Acts (1934), *with the libretto by Gertrude Stein. He has also written music for the movies. His books include* The State of Music (1939) *and* The Musical Scene (1945), *a collection of his critical pieces on music.*

(1) A taste *for* music, a taste for anything, is an ability to consume it with pleasure. Taste *in* music is preferential consumption, a greater liking for certain kinds of it than for others. A broad taste in music involves the ability to consume with pleasure many kinds of it.

(2) Vast numbers of persons, many of them highly intelligent, derive no pleasure at all from organized sound. An even larger number can take it or leave it alone. They find it agreeable for the most part, stimulating to the sentiments and occasionally interesting to the mind. But music is not for them a passional experience, a transport, an auditory universe. Everybody, however, has some kind of taste *in* music, even persons with little or no taste *for* it. No subject, save perhaps the theory of money, is disputed about so constantly in contemporary life as the divers styles of musical expression, both popular and erudite, their nature and likability.

(3) There are often striking contradictions between what musical

* Reprinted from *The Musical Scene,* by Virgil Thomson, by permission of Alfred A. Knopf, Inc. Copyright 1945 by Virgil Thomson. Copyright 1945 by Hearst Magazines, Inc.

people admire and what they like. Admiration, being a judgment, is submissive to reason. But liking is an inspiration, a datum exigent, unreasonable, and impossible by any act of the will to alter. It will frequently alter itself, however, without warning. And loyalty to things we once loved dearly brings tension into everybody's taste. Persons whose musical experience is limited may, indeed, be more loyal to old likings than persons who deal with music all the time. The latter tend to reject and to accept with vehemence; they are choosy. And their choosiness is quite independent of their judgment; it is personal and profoundly capricious. They can switch from Beethoven to boogie-woogie, from Bach to barbershop, with a facility that is possible only to those who take all music for their clothes closet. For practical living, man needs to be free in his thought and responsible in his actions. But in dealing with art, responsibility of thought, which makes for slowness of judgment, and freedom of action, which makes for flexibility of taste, constitute the mechanics of vigor.

(4) The development of taste is not a major objective in musical education. What the young need is understanding, that whole paraphernalia of analysis and synthesis whereby a piece is broken up into its component details, mastered, restored to integrity, and possessed. Musical understanding depends not so much on the number of works one has learned in this fashion, provided examples from several schools have been included, as on the completeness with which the procedure has been carried out. Any student can be convinced by study that Mozart is a more accomplished workman than Grieg or Rachmaninoff. If he still likes Grieg and Rachmaninoff better, that is his privilege. Maturity is certain to alter, whatever they may be, his youthful predilections.

(5) Persons unprepared by training to roam the world of music in freedom but who enjoy music and wish to increase that enjoyment are constantly searching for a key, a passport that will hasten their progress. There is none, really, except study. And how far it is profitable to spend time cultivating talent where there is no vocation every man must decide for himself. But if there is any door-opener to taste it is knowledge. One cannot know whether one likes, can use, a work unless one has some method beyond mere instinct for tasting it. The only

known ways to taste a piece of music are to read it in score or to follow it in performance. And it is quite impossible to follow unfamiliar kinds of music without an analytical method, a set of aids to memory that enables one to discern the pattern of what is taking place.

(6) But an ability to hear is not the whole of musical reception. A vote seems to be required, a yes or no as to whether one desires, for the present, further acquaintance. Now, the enjoyment of old musical acquaintance is such a pleasant thing for all and so quite sufficiently absorbing for the unskilled that nearly everybody leans toward a timid conservatism with regard to unfamiliar music. The too old, the too new, the in-any-way strange we resist simply because we do not know how to take them on. The lay public will try anything; but it will be disappointed, on first hearing, in anything it has no method for remembering. We like the idea of being musically progressive, because progress is one of our national ideals; but we do not always know how to conduct a progress.

(7) Well, the way of that is long. It is nothing less, if one wishes to take part in America's musical growing-up, than learning to hear music correctly and learning to know one's mind. Persons who cannot follow music at all do well to admit the fact and let music alone. Persons who really hear it, whom *it* will not let alone, usually improve themselves by one means and another in their ability to hear patterns in sound; and with more and more music thus rendered available to them, they can choose at any moment their personal allegiances with a modicum of liberty. The tolerant but untrained, however, will always be a bit uncertain in their tastes. They will never know, for instance, whether they are entitled to vote publicly or not. They will consequently assume the privilege more proudly, more dogmatically, and more irresponsibly than musicians themselves are likely to do. And they will rarely know the difference between their tastes and their opinions.

(8) It is the ignorantly formed and categorically expressed opinions of the amateur, in fact, that make the music world companionable. Professional musicians express, for the most part, responsible opinions; and these show a surprising tendency to approach, within twenty-five years, unanimity. There is not much difference of opinion any more, for instance, about either the nature or the value of Debussy's music,

or of Puccini's, or of what Stravinsky wrote before 1914. But musicians' personal likings are eclectic; they imply no agreement of any kind. It is laymen who like to like together. Musicians' opinions influence nothing; they simply recognize, with a certain delay but correctly, the history of music. Lay opinion influences everything—even, at times, creation. And at all times it is the pronouncements of persons who know something about music but not much, and a bit more about what they like but still not too much, that end by creating those modes or fashions in consumption that make up the history of taste.

(9) There is no doubt that lay opinion is in large part organized and directed by knowledgeable persons—by critics, college instructors, conductors, publishers' employees, and leaders of fashion. It is nevertheless not wholly under their control. The leaders of taste can no more create deliberately a mode in music than advertising campaigns can make popular a product that the public doesn't want. They can only manipulate a trend. And trends follow folk patterns. Nobody connected with a trend in music—whether composer, executant, manager, critic, consumer, or even resister—is a free agent with regard to it. That is why unsuccessful or unfashionable music, music that seems to ignore what the rest of the world is listening to, is sometimes the best music, the freest, the most original—though there is no rule about that either.

(10) And so, thus caught up on the wheel of fatality, how can anybody really know anything about music, beyond its immediate practice or perception, least of all what he likes? Learning is a precious thing and knowing one's mind is even more so. But let none of us who think we belong to music fancy too highly our opinions about it, since in twenty-five years most of these will have either gone down the drain or become every man's private conviction. And please let none imagine, either, that his personal tastes are unique, indissoluble, and free. Those who think themselves most individual in their likings are most easily trapped by the appeal of chic, since chic is no more than the ability to accept trends in fashion with grace, to vary them ever so slightly, to follow a movement under the sincere illusion that one is being oneself. And those who imagine themselves most independent as judges make up the most predictable public in the world, that known to managements as the university trade, since intellectuals will always

pay for the privilege of exercising their intellectual powers. Rarities of any kind, ancient or modern, are merely stones to whet their minds against. You can always sell to the world of learning acquaintance with that which it does not know.

(11) In the long run, such freedom as anybody has is the reward of labor, much study, and inveterate wariness. And the pleasures of taste, at best, are transitory, since nobody, professional or layman, can be sure that what he finds beautiful this year may not be just another piece of music to him next. The best any of us can do about any piece, short of memorizing its actual sounds and storing it away intact against lean musical moments, is to consult his appetite about its immediate consumption, his appetite and his digestive experience. And after consumption to argue about the thing interminably with all his friends. *De gustibus disputandum est.*

STUDY QUESTIONS

1. What does Mr. Thomson believe to be the safest approach to the appreciation of music? How does he attempt to convince his readers of the validity of his approach?

2. How does Mr. Thomson make his transition from each paragraph to the next?

3. The point and wit of several of Mr. Thomson's sentences depend upon his deliberate deformation of a well-known quotation. What is the original form, for example, of the last sentence in this essay? If you do not know it, where can you look to find it? What famous line lies behind the sentence beginning "They can switch . . ." in paragraph 3? To what extent does this perverting of the well-known contribute to the style and tone of this essay?

4. Make a list of the concrete images and allusions which Mr. Thomson employs in this essay. What is their value? Would it have been in keeping with his purpose for Mr. Thomson to have used more of such concrete references? Why, or why not?

5. How would you describe the tone of this essay? Document your answer with evidence from the text.

6. Does Mr. Thomson use much colloquial and informal diction? Before answering this question, look up the word *colloquial* in a good standard dictionary. What bearing does the diction have on the tone of this essay? Compare you answer here with the one you gave to question 3.

WRITING ASSIGNMENTS

1. Write an analysis of your musical taste.
2. Write an account of your education in music.
   3. Write an analysis of what you think should be the importance of music in public school education. If your experience qualifies, include your recommendations on how it should be taught.
   4. Write an attack on, or defense of, required courses in music appreciation.
   5. On the basis of personal experience, write an essay on the values of listening to music or the values of playing a musical instrument.

"Three Strangers" *

ADOLPH DEUTSCH (1897–   ) *was born in London and studied composition and piano there at the Royal Academy of Music. He came to the United States at the age of thirteen and is now a citizen. In addition to his work for the movies, he has arranged for popular orchestras and has composed and conducted radio and stage productions. He has composed scores for over fifty films, of which the best known were* The Maltese Falcon *and* Three Strangers. *His symphonic compositions include* The Scottish Suite *and* March of the United Nations.

(1) *Three Strangers* is a perfect example of my pet theory that there ought to be much more writer-composer collaboration in films, so I might as well start from the beginning and describe exactly what happened—and generally happens—in the scoring of a motion picture. The telephone rings; it is Miss Samson of the Warner Brothers music department. I am notified that the rough cut of *Three Strangers* will be run in Projection Room 6 at ten o'clock tomorrow morning. Arriving a few minutes early, I wait outside of Room 6 to enjoy the morning sun, remembering that for the next two and a half hours I shall be breathing air conditioned by yesterday's cigars and cigarettes. A small group of people arrive: I recognize Jean Negulesco, the director; Wolfgang Reinhardt, the supervising producer; and George Amy, the cutter. Greetings are exchanged, and I am introduced to Howard Koch, one of the two writers of the screen play. I am surprised to learn that his collaborator is Major John Huston, who, at the time, is away on official business for the U.S. Signal Corps. Mention of his name brings

* Reprinted from Vol. I, No. 2 of the *Hollywood Quarterly* (now *The Quarterly of Film, Radio, and Television*), published by the University of California Press, Berkeley and Los Angeles. Copyright 1946 by Adolph Deutsch. Reprinted by permission of the author and *The Quarterly of Film, Radio, and Television*.

to my mind the stimulating experience I had in composing the musical score for *The Maltese Falcon*, which he adapted for the screen and also directed.

(2) Promptly at ten, Leo Forbstein, the music department head, arrives and we file into the dimly lit projection room. It resembles a small theater and seats about fifty. Halfway forward is a long desk upon which are telephones, a volume regulator to control the sound, a buzzer signal, and an intercommunication phone that connects with the projectionist's booth. There is an air of expectancy as we await the two buzzes which is Eddie's "ready" signal. Eddie Higgins is our projectionist (operator, in studio language), and he is an expert at handling work prints so that they don't come apart at the splices or tear at the sprocket holes. As the small group settles itself in the divan-like chairs it occurs to me that this is the first time any of us will have seen the entire picture in continuity. It is the end toward which writer, director, producer, actors, and technicians have been working for several months.

(3) I reflect upon their intimate knowledge of each scene and compare it with the few meager hints I had gleaned from reading the script, wondering if some day I would be invited to sit in at a story conference or the preparation of a shooting script. The phone at Mr. Forbstein's elbow rings. He is called away. Awaiting his return, we discuss the immediate musical problems of the picture. I am told that *Three Strangers* is a story that picks up the lives of three persons unknown to each other and follows each separately to a tragic denouement. One is a woman inclined toward Oriental mysticism and superstition; the second, a lawyer who is the trustee for several large estates; and the third, a down-at-heel but literate young man who plays classical piano pieces, quotes fragments of poetry, and contemplates life through an alcoholic haze. From George Amy, the cutter, I learn that in the process of editing the film he transposed several sequences to clarify the story line which wove in and out of the lives of the three people, and that more recutting may be necessary.

(4) "The music," Jean Negulesco says, "will be a big help in identifying the main characters"—"What do you think," interjects Mr. Reinhardt, "of having three distinct themes?" "Excellent," I agree,

recalling how well the leitmotif device served the operatic composers —a quaint old Wagnerian custom. At this point Mr. Forbstein returns, signals the operator with two buzzes, and we're off.

(5) As the lights dim we focus our eyes on the screen, where the first atmospheric shot of Piccadilly Circus fades in. My mind automatically registers: music must reflect cosmopolitan London, around 1938; that's easy, I was born there. The camera wanders through the crowd and picks out Geraldine Fitzgerald (the most prepossessing of the three strangers). I concentrate on her characterization, seeking clues for an appropriate theme. Even though she has spoken no words, I am influenced by her appearance, her bearing, and her facial expressions. All these must be reflected in the music. The second stranger looms out of the crowd; he is Sydney Greenstreet, "the Fat Man." The camera lingers on him as his eyes follow Miss Fitzgerald appraisingly. I ask myself, "What kind of music does one write for a susceptible barrister?" The question remains unanswered as the film progresses unfalteringly to the first meeting of the three strangers. The third stranger is an old projection-room friend of mine, he of the soft-boiled eyes, Peter Lorre.

(6) It is not long before the narrative, in the hands of such capable performers, absorbs my interest to the total exclusion of musical considerations. This is a healthy sign and I don't resist it. Music has no place in this scene, I register subconsciously. Hold on! Here's that Chinese image, Kwan Yin, the "Goddess of Mercy"—here a symbol of mysticism and superstition. Big Ben starts tolling. The wind whips the curtains. A candle goes out. "Make a light!—The matches!" Miss Fitzgerald cries. Aha! I think . . . looks like a music cue. George Amy volunteers some information. "The chimes ought to last longer." Nobody answers. It is a point for later discussion.

(7) The first episode, the meeting of the three strangers, comes to an end and we watch the unwinding and interweaving of the three separate story threads. This is a uniquely daring essay in screen craftsmanship. It is no easy task to tell part of a story, part of a second story, part of a third story; pick up the first story again, the second and the third where they left off, and finally merge the three in a gripping climax. To be sure, there were some sections where the meanings be-

came obscured, but they were not too opaque to be cleared up by recutting and by the proper handling of music and sound effects. One has to imagine the finished print with these elements added.

(8) The final reel is before us and the three strangers, propelled by an evil fate, are brought together. I see Miss Fitzgerald seated near a radio, listening transfixed and oblivious to the ranting of Sydney Greenstreet and the piano playing of Peter Lorre. This being the work print, the sound of the piano is indicated for only a measure or two; the complete piece will be added in the re-recording process. The same applies to the radio announcer who is presumed to be describing the Grand National Steeplechase. Inexorably the emotional stress of the scene increases; I have a momentary flash of the musical problems to be solved, but the threat of impending violence again commands my attention to the exclusion of technical problems. The film fades out on a bizarre note; the lights flash on, and we look at each other. To the question marks which I see in the eyes of the Messrs. Reinhardt and Negulesco I give an honest nod of approval. The looks give way to conversation. We voice our opinions in generally favorable terms, meanwhile standing and stretching. Once these preliminaries are out of the way, we settle down to a review of the picture in relation to musical treatment. The odds are very one-sided. Nine reels of picture (roughly ninety minutes of screen play) are not quickly assimilated. The writer, the director, and the producer have lived with the picture from its beginnings, whereas I am basing my opinions on the superficial impressions of a single screening. My only advantages are a fresh perspective and my past experience in scoring dramatic films.

(9) Thus begins a belated and makeshift collaboration. The music I am about to write is expected to become an integral part of the screen play, heighten the emotional appeal, be so deftly a part of the drama that it has effect upon an audience without their being conscious of it. "Unobtrusive" is the gold standard for a dramative score. In the weeks of preparation of the script and with the knowledge that music was going to play an important part in their film the writers did not discuss this basic component with the composer. The problem for me is now one of adapting music to the tempi of acting, the spaces between spoken lines, fade-ins and fade-outs, gestures, reactions, and a dozen

other conditions arbitrarily crystallized on the film. My job has become one of conforming rather than of collaborating.

(10) We begin with Mr. Reinhardt's suggestion of identifying each stranger with a distinctive theme. I add to the idea by naming specific instruments to characterize them further. Negulesco would like a violin for Miss Fitzgerald. I do not quarrel with the idea; a violin can express the kind of femininity portrayed by Miss Fitzgerald. In her more violent moods I can harden the string quality with a muted trumpet. We are debating the proper place at which to introduce these individual themes (a decision that should have been made before the picture started shooting). "If you would precede the main title with individual close-ups of the three principals and give each one footage enough, I could introduce their themes effectively before the story begins." There is some hesitancy over my suggestion, because it will involve a radical change in the format of the title. The idea appeals to all present, however, and we decide to use it if the "front office" authorizes the change.

(11) The discussion moves on to the sequence with the chimes in it; it is an involved one. Preceding the chimes there is a period of dramatic silence, the lights are switched out, Miss Fitzgerald lights some candles and the group intently watches the image of Kwan Yin. The script, I recall, directs that the first chime be heard as the picture cuts to a "BIG HEAD CLOSE-UP OF KWAN YIN," and the last chime, just before Mr. Greenstreet strikes a match. The picture wasn't shot to the accurate length of twelve chimes, and we are obliged to consider ways of stretching the chimes so that they begin and end in the right places. This, we decide, will be a job of manipulating the spacing of the music, and of the chimes, and some discreet cutting of the film. Messrs. Reinhardt and Negulesco are content to leave this in our hands.

(12) Our next point is the very important one of finding a suitable device to punctuate the beginnings and endings of the three stories that interweave throughout the play. The audience must see and, if possible, hear where one story is interrupted and another is begun. The visual problem can be solved by using any one of a variety of optical distortions; it is the oil dissolve that is chosen. To the audience it

will appear as a series of ripples across the screen that blur the images as they melt from one to the other. In matching this oil dissolve I must devise an unusual sound as if the music were being blurred by the same ripple. My inner ear suggests a small combination of instruments, some electric, that will produce an oily sound contrasting sharply with the legitimate instrumentation preceding it. Two vibraphones, two harps, marimba, and cymbal, recorded with a fluctuating volume control, will do the trick. The audience will see and hear the ripples, I assure my collaborators.

(13) The final scene now receives some attention. Here again the screen action dictates the handling of the accompanying sounds. We know that a radio announcer is describing the Grand National and that at a certain point in the sequence the screen characters react to his shout of "They're off." We see Lorre start and stop playing the piano, and we will record a suitable length of piano music to match his actions. The scene presents a rare problem in dynamic levels of sound. Our theater audience must hear the spoken lines of the cast, so these will have to be rerecorded at the top range of audibility. At a slightly lower level the piano must be heard; still lower, the radio announcer, and behind his voice the murmurs and exclamations of the crowd at the race. "The idea," Reinhardt says, "is to play Greenstreet's lines against a confusion of sound that seems intent on frustrating his desire to be heard. He is competing with the radio and the piano for the attention of the other two persons in the room." It is the kind of drama that is ideally suited to the film medium, where one has complete control over the elements of sound. "I'll work with George and Alex (a sound engineer) on this. It won't be easy, but I think we'll give you the effect." Having seen examples of sound wizardry in other pictures of ours, Reinhardt, Negulesco, and Koch are content to leave the scene to us.

(14) The ending of the picture presents no further problems and so our little group in Projection Room 6 begins to melt away. After a screening of this sort there is always some reluctance to break up a meeting before double-checking with each other to be sure that we all understand what was agreed upon during the running. Howard Koch, the writer, moves off. He is glad to have met me. "So am I," I

answer (fervently), considering myself fortunate to have had even one casual meeting with him. Mr. Reinhardt and Mr. Negulesco say their goodbyes fully confident that the music department will do a good job. Mr. Forbstein assures them that they will be happy with the music and suggests that, in view of a tentative preview date, we had better get right on the first three reels.

(15) "Getting right on the first three reels" means that we will run each one through several times, analyzing them carefully for music cues. Upon deciding which sequences are to be underscored, we look for the exact spot, within the fraction of a second, to begin and end the music. Each musical entrance must coincide with some significant event on the screen. Sometimes it comes in on a change of facial expression, the sharp reaction of a character, a threatening gesture, a walk, a change of scene, a sudden cut from long shot to close-up or vice versa, a meaningful remark, an off-screen noise, a letter, or a weapon, violent physical action, or some other dramatic reason.

(16) During this crucial stage of what really amounts to dramatic construction, my inventiveness is circumscribed and dominated by the preëstablished pace of direction and camera movement crystallized on the film now before me. Collaboration with the writer and director is no longer possible. The cutter will coöperate as far as he possibly can, but he, too, works within these limitations. For example, if a musical phrase cannot be uttered without undue distortion of tempo, either fast or slow, it might be possible for the cutter to cheat a foot of film to accommodate the music. The word "cheat" is used literally here because the cutter, in making changes after the reels have been approved by the producer, runs the risk of being called to task for making unauthorized changes. It is a significant commentary on standardized film production that so much composer-cutter collaboration is carried on furtively, like the Underground.

(17) When the reels have been analyzed, the actual task of composing music begins. To supplement the mental images formed in my mind I will have typewritten cue sheets. Every spoken word, action, camera movement, and cut is written down and measured; the timings are given both in footage and in fractions of seconds. The mysterious process by which composers create music has never been fathomed.

Add to this mystery the self-control, the discipline of subordinating one's inspiration to a cue sheet, and further complicate the procedure with a delivery deadline, and you gain some idea of the conditions under which I shall write approximately one hour's worth of music (the equivalent, in length, to one act of *Tristan*) in four weeks.

(18) The composer is not worth his salt who assumes that his obligations as a collaborator end after the music is written. A new and vital phase of mutual effort begins, on the sound-recording stage. My next collaborator is the recording engineer, David Forrest, whose handling of the sensitive microphones and volume controls on the music-recording stage is termed "mixing." The responsibility of getting the best possible music recording is placed squarely upon the mixer's shoulders by his department head. Left to his own judgment, Dave, who reads an orchestral score in addition to his volume indicators, will capture a picture of my music on the sound track that meets the required standards of the studio. He will not, however, plumb the inner dramatic meanings of the score unless I make them clear to him first. By exploiting the acoustic flexibilities of film recording I can invest my music with qualities that will complement the mystic atmosphere of *Three Strangers*. Parts of the score must be recorded with clarity, others with a diffused quality; some must sound intimate, others distant; here and there I take "stage liberty" and ask for excessive reverberation in one section of the orchestra, combined with natural presence in the others.

(19) The microphone is a camera that records sound, and, like the cameraman, the mixer will direct the placement of the microphones to obtain the quality of recording I have asked for. Many times during the playing of a piece of music the microphone becomes a mobile unit, swinging in to pick up at close range, then returning to a normal placement. If necessary, Dave will employ several microphones at varying distances from the source of sound. There is nothing static about a recording stage. Instruments are at times moved and regrouped for special results; in fact, the very walls of the room are mounted on hinged sections that can be adjusted to alter acoustic characteristics. Equipped with all these devices, the mixer is an important factor in

contemporary film technique and certainly a collaborator to be accepted by every writer as well as composer if screen plays are to possess a multidimensional aural quality rather than a flat single plane of sound.

(20) *Three Strangers* presented many opportunities for the manipulation of recording qualities. Right in the introduction, for instance, where the close-ups of the principals were used, we decided to match the photographic proximity with a corresponding close pickup of the solo instruments. The image on the screen was big and the tone of the instrument was big. Following the title came the London atmosphere, Piccadilly Circus at night, traffic and crowd noise. The music I had written attempted to sound British and at the same time to give the feeling of a lot of things going on simultaneously. Dave and I agreed that we should attempt to get as much clarity of recording as possible, to bring out the counterrhythms and contrapuntal lines in the orchestra. Later on in the picture we had a scene on the bank of the Thames, a night shot, damp and foggy. The orchestration reflected this mood, which we further enhanced by using a very reverberant pickup. The result was a diffused shimmer of sound like the distant murmur of a metropolis, a perfect accompaniment for the occasion. For the image of Kwan Yin I wanted a detached quality as if the Oriental strain, played by seven instruments, were coming from a great distance. This was accomplished by performing the music softly and picking it up at twice the normal distance.

(21) In one of the final sequences there was a frightening shot of Sydney Greenstreet walking into the camera, his huge hulk filling the screen. The full orchestra was used, but to heighten further the feeling of the demoniac characterization we "miked" the bass section of the orchestra to get a massive sound that became louder as the actor came closer. The result was a gripping combination of sight and sound.

(22) The deliberate distortion of musical balance and perspective is thus an important adjunct to film technique. The uses of this device should be fully exploited, not only by the composer working in collaboration with the mixer, but also by the screen writer in collaboration with the composer. A shooting script may very well incorporate nota-

tions on aural perspective to supplement the camera angle and all the descriptive material considered necessary to achieve a well-integrated and artistic result.

(23) Once all the music for *Three Strangers* is recorded on film, the negative goes to the laboratory to be developed. Usually this is an overnight job. The positive prints of the music tracks are sent to the Dupe Building to be cut into their respective reels.

(24) Let me take you to the Dupe Room where Jerry Alexander is dubbing the first reel of *Three Strangers*. Jerry and his assistant sit at a sound-control panel facing the screen. Each knob on the panel controls a different sound track, and the number of knobs required depends upon the complexity of the sound pattern in the reel. The speech of the principals, the shuffling of feet on the pavement, traffic sounds, crowd sounds, the tap-tap of a steel-ferruled cane, the chimes of Big Ben, a wind effect, and the musical score comprise the setup of the sound pattern for the first reel. Detailed cue sheets serve as a guide to indicate the exact footage at which the sounds and music will occur.

(25) Jerry signals his projectionist, the room is darkened, and we watch the illuminated footage meter at the right of the screen, which is synchronized with the projection machine. The meter serves as a warning guide for incoming and outgoing sounds, also as a quick check if any imperfection of quality or bad synchronization of sound with the picture is apparent. "This is only a rough rehearsal, so don't expect too much," Jerry always says when the composer is present, usually to forestall a request for more music—louder, louder. The rehearsal is rough; some effects are too loud, some too soft; music entrances are faded in too slowly and the whole reel seems a confused jumble. "Rewind," Jerry signals, "and we'll run it again." The second rehearsal is smoother and the pattern of sound begins to make more sense. While the reel is being rewound for a third rehearsal I talk over the musical dynamics with Jerry. "Hold it down a little so that the tapping of Greenstreet's cane comes over." "Fade in sooner when they sign their names." "Blend it with the wind effect and increase the volume as the candle goes out." "Hold the Kwan Yin theme down." The next rehearsal gets under way and my suggestions are tried; they all work out except the cane tapping; that is out of balance. Jerry is now becoming

familiar with the sound content of the reel, and each successive rehearsal shows a marked improvement. A few more adjustments and we
are ready for a final take. Overhead a red light indicates that this run is
a take; there will be no conversation in the room to distract the two
dubbers from their sensitive task. The picture fades in, the title music
starts, and we know that downstairs the light valve is recording on a
strip of film one-tenth of an inch wide a pattern of modulations that
will reproduce the speech, music, and noises in exactly the same relative
proportions as those in which Jerry is mixing them. The reel is over,
the lights brighten. "How do you like it?" "O.K. for me," I reply, and
the first thousand feet of *Three Strangers* is ready to print. "Lunch,"
announces Jerry. It has taken three hours to rehearse and record ten
minutes of sound.

(26) Returning from lunch, I notice the NO ADMITTANCE
sign on the door of the Dupe Building and ask Jerry whether that includes writers and directors. "It sure does; departmental rule," he re-
plies. "Hum," is my guarded comment, as I ponder the wisdom of
keeping these talents ignorant of this important phase of film making.

(27) The dubbing of the next seven reels moves along smoothly.
We have occasion to add an echo to the sounds in two places: one is
a scene under Battersea Bridge; the other, a corridor in a jail. We work
out an interesting transition from a train effect underscored with music
to a cracked phonograph record repeating a phrase monotonously.
We exaggerate an orchestral crescendo and punctuate it with the im-
pact of a weapon hitting the floor—pure cinematic liberty to shock an
audience.

(28) The final reel containing the critical scene of the Grand National coming over the radio, the tense dialogue in the room, and
Lorre's piano playing, commands our attention for the better part of
a day. We are occupied, for the most part, with finding the proper
dynamic levels, playing them higher or lower as the camera follows the
action from one side of the room to the other, and never once losing
the intelligibility of the on-screen dialogue. It is fascinating to watch
the hands of Jerry and his assistant as they play the multiple controls
during this scene. Satisfied with our last rehearsal, we decide to try our
luck. We have notified Leo Forbstein and George Amy that reel 9 is

ready for a take and they are in the room as the reel starts. Our audience is augmented by some sound cutters and technicians, since word has reached them that reel 9 of *Three Strangers* is up; they watch with critical attention. The take is made, but proves unsatisfactory. We ask for reactions and get them. Some discussion follows. It is decided to cheat the piano out sooner and play up the dramatic scoring in one spot. This time the take is good and our dubbing job is done.

(29) The completed sound track now goes to the laboratory to be developed, printed, and combined with the picture in a master negative. A positive print will be made as quickly as possible because our sneak preview deadline is two days away. The exact time and place of the sneak is a studio secret, known only to a few department heads. On the evening of the event, a favored few of us will receive two hours' advance notice, naming an outlying theater and an approximate starting time. "Eight-thirty tonight at the Cascade Theater." At eight-thirty we submit our work to the public. By ten o'clock we shall have its verdict, not in writing but through an intangible series of telepathic signals—"audience reaction."

(30) Outside the Cascade Theater the same group which four weeks ago met in Room 6 greet each other. Awaiting the arrival of Jack Warner and his associates, we make conversation, carefully avoiding the topic uppermost in our minds. My eye wanders over the line of cash customers—our jury. I am counting the infants in arms and the popcorn bags, wondering if their cacophony will obliterate the subtle nuances of our play.

(31) The arrival of the Jack Warner party is our signal to file into the theater. As the last newsreel clip thunders from the screen, we settle ourselves in the section reserved for us. Recorded several decibels higher than feature pictures, all newsreels leave the ears tingling. A normal recording following the news sounds puny, and if the proscenium curtains are closed the effect is that of an underwater performance.

(32) "Ladies and gentlemen, we present a Warner Brothers feature preview," the voice from behind the closed curtains announces, with an air of confidence not shared by us. A murmur of anticipation fills the house and as the close-up of Geraldine Fitzgerald fades in the

murmur surges into exclamations of approval. Another surge as the patrons recognize Sydney Greenstreet and his co-artist Peter Lorre. The musical themes of identification are lost in the shuffle, but I am not too concerned, knowing that the element of surprise will not be present in a regularly advertised performance. As the title fades out and the picture begins, we concentrate on the screen as though we had never seen *Three Strangers* before. This is not entirely because an audience is present; much of the unfamiliarity stems from the fact that the screen play has acquired a new aural dimension since it was run in Room 6.

(33) The background of music and sound against which the actors perform and speak their lines is at this time doubly conspicuous to the writer, the director, and the producer. Accustomed as they are to the simple picture-and-word form of the work print, these added sounds must seem obtrusive. More than once during the preview I glance in Howard Koch's direction as a piece of musical underscoring begins while his lines are being spoken. As we did not collaborate on the script, I am sure he is having many surprises. It is a disquieting thought.

(34) As the picture nears its end the cumulative result of the nine reels run in continuity before an audience manifests itself in a number of ways. We see our work in true perspective and all the details merged into a whole. Our senses of self-appraisal and criticism are sharpened; the glow of accomplishment is tempered by the sobering knowledge that some places might have been better. As for the score, I am acutely aware of some irritating musical mutilations and incoherences that could have been avoided if I had been able to work with Howard Koch, John Huston, and Jean Negulesco *before* the picture was shot. It is incongruous that two such vital ingredients as the music and sound effects should receive so little consideration in the plotting of the script. The musical score of this film was heard during two-thirds of the running time, more than 60 per cent of its total footage—by no means an inconsequential contribution. Is music the leavening in the loaf of bread, or merely the gaudy icing hastily poured over a cake to conceal some doubtful ingredients? Surely, it's the leavening.

(35) The curtain closes, the audience applauds, but long before this we are aware of its favorable verdict.

(36) Our group files out of the theater and assembles in the manager's office for the usual confab and review of notes made during the running. This time, the notes are few and the changes are slight. Jack Warner nods his approval to the circle of inquiring faces and, as if to confirm his feelings, offers Reinhardt a cigar. The tension eases, there are some pleasantries, and we gather our hats and coats. Reinhardt smiles from behind his Havana perfecto.

(37) In the lobby Howard Koch approaches me. Is he thinking that I have smothered some of his best lines? My momentary suspense is relieved by his smile. "The music helped a lot," he remarks quietly. Jean Negulesco joins us as we walk to the parking lot. "Beautiful score, Adolph"—his enthusiasm is sincere. "Thanks, Jean! Maybe on our next picture we won't have to work like *Three Strangers*."

STUDY QUESTIONS

1. This is an essay in which Mr. Deutsch explains a process by recounting the chronological steps involved. What were the successive steps in the scoring of *Three Strangers*? How is each new step announced?

2. What special thesis does Mr. Deutsch wish his essay to demonstrate? At what points does he stress that thesis? Does it provide the principal interest of the essay? If not, what does?

3. The first eight paragraphs constitute the first unit of this essay. How much of the actual process of scoring is explained in this unit? What introductory functions does the unit serve?

4. The account of the process of scoring the music for *Three Strangers* is concluded in paragraph 28, but the essay continues for nine more paragraphs. What does Mr. Deutsch accomplish in those last paragraphs (29–37)?

5. This essay is a good example of narrative exposition. What advantage does the use of the narrative form have over a more strictly expository form? What disadvantages? Why is the narrative form particularly appropriate for exposition of a process? Try summarizing the process which Mr. Deutsch narrates. Put your summary in such general terms that it would apply to any film.

6. You will notice that Mr. Deutsch uses the present tense consistently in his narrative. What effect does he gain thereby?

7. Can you see any justification for the very short, clipped sentences in paragraph 6?

8. A problem often involved in explaining a process is that of making technicalities clear to a reader unfamiliar with the process. Are there any points at which Mr. Deutsch does not sufficiently clarify his procedure? Does he define the technical terms he uses? Cite examples of such definition.

9. If you did not see *Three Strangers,* did you have any difficulty following Mr. Deutsch's explanation? How does Mr. Deutsch attempt to accommodate the readers who did not see the movie?

10. Do you think that the knowledge gained from this essay will in any way add to your appreciation of the movie as an art form? Write a one-paragraph explanation of your answer.

WRITING ASSIGNMENTS

1. Attend a movie, preferably one you have already seen, with the purpose of listening intently to its musical setting. Then write an analysis of the use of music in that movie.

2. Write an account of a simple process with which you are well-acquainted from personal experience.

3. Write a proposal for a change in a process you know something about (a change in fraternity or sorority procedures, a change in classroom procedures, a change in registration, a change in the system of military service, etc.).

4. Write an account, for the nonspecialist, of a scientific process you have learned about in a high school or college course.

5. Write a research paper on a process connected with the movies, radio, or television (the distribution of movies, technicolor, the actual process of making a movie, the process of television, the operation of a radio station, the preparation of a radio show, etc.).

Why Great Men Are Not Chosen Presidents *

JAMES BRYCE (1838–1922) *was a British jurist and historian who taught law at Oxford (1870–1893) and played a prominent part in British political life, serving several terms in Parliament and holding several offices in the British cabinet. In 1907 he was appointed British ambassador to Washington. His reputation as a historian was established in 1864 by his great* The Holy Roman Empire. *His greatest literary fame derives from* The American Commonwealth (1888), *now considered a classic study of American government. An important work which may be considered a sequel to that study is* Modern Democracies (1921). *Bryce wrote numerous other works on history, politics, law, travel, mountain-climbing, and personal impressions.*

(1) Europeans often ask, and Americans do not always explain, how it happens that this great office, the greatest in the world, unless we except the Papacy, to which any man can rise by his own merits, is not more frequently filled by great and striking men? In America, which is beyond all other countries the country of a "career open to talents," a country, moreover, in which political life is unusually keen and political ambition widely diffused, it might be expected that the highest place would always be won by a man of brilliant gifts. But since the heroes of the Revolution died out with Jefferson and Adams and Madison some sixty years ago, no person except General Grant has reached the chair whose name would have been remembered had he not been President, and no President except Abraham Lincoln has displayed rare or striking qualities in the chair. Who now knows or cares to know anything about the personality of James K. Polk or Franklin

* From *The American Commonwealth* by James Bryce, Vol. I, 1889 (2nd ed.).

Pierce? The only thing remarkable about them is that being so commonplace they should have climbed so high.

(2) Several reasons may be suggested for the fact, which Americans
are themselves the first to admit.

(3) One is that the proportion of first-rate ability drawn into politics
is smaller in America than in most European countries. This is a
phenomenon whose causes must be elucidated later: in the meantime
it is enough to say that in France and Italy, where half-revolutionary
conditions have made public life exciting and accessible; in Germany,
where an admirably-organized civil service cultivates and develops
statecraft with unusual success; in England, where many persons of
wealth and leisure seek to enter the political arena, while burning
questions touch the interests of all classes and make men eager observers of the combatants, the total quantity of talent devoted to
parliamentary or administrative work is far larger, relatively to the
population, than in America, where much of the best ability, both for
thought and for action, for planning and for executing, rushes into a
field which is comparatively narrow in Europe, the business of developing the material resources of the country.

(4) Another is that the methods and habits of Congress, and indeed
of political life generally, seem to give fewer opportunities for personal
distinction, fewer modes in which a man may commend himself to his
countrymen by eminent capacity in thought, in speech, or in administration, than is the case in the free countries of Europe. This is a point
to be explained in later chapters. I merely note here in passing what
will there be dwelt on.

(5) A third reason is that eminent men make more enemies, and
give those enemies more assailable points, than obscure men do. They
are therefore in so far less desirable candidates. It is true that the eminent man has also made more friends, that his name is more widely
known, and may be greeted with louder cheers. Other things being
equal, the famous man is preferable. But other things never are equal.
The famous man has probably attacked some leaders in his own party,
has supplanted others, has expressed his dislike to the crotchet of some
active section, has perhaps committed errors which are capable of being
magnified into offences. No man stands long before the public and

bears a part in great affairs without giving openings to censorious criticism. Fiercer far than the light which beats upon a throne is the light which beats upon a presidential candidate, searching out all the recesses of his past life. Hence, when the choice lies between a brilliant man and a safe man, the safe man is preferred. Party feeling, strong enough to carry in on its back a man without conspicuous positive merits, is not always strong enough to procure forgiveness for a man with positive faults.

(6) A European finds that this phenomenon needs in its turn to be explained, for in the free countries of Europe brilliancy, be it eloquence in speech, or some striking achievement in war or administration, or the power through whatever means of somehow impressing the popular imagination, is what makes a leader triumphant. Why should it be otherwise in America? Because in America party loyalty and party organization have been hitherto so perfect that any one put forward by the party will get the full party vote if his character is good and his "record," as they call it, unstained. The safe candidate may not draw in quite so many votes from the moderate men of the other side as the brilliant one would, but he will not lose nearly so many from his own ranks. Even those who admit his mediocrity will vote straight when the moment for voting comes. Besides, the ordinary American voter does not object to mediocrity. He has a lower conception of the qualities requisite to make a statesman than those who direct public opinion in Europe have. He likes his candidate to be sensible, vigorous, and, above all, what he calls "magnetic," and does not value, because he sees no need for, originality or profundity, a fine culture or a wide knowledge. Candidates are selected to be run for nomination by knots of persons who, however expert as party tacticians, are usually commonplace men; and the choice between those selected for nomination is made by a very large body, an assembly of over eight hundred delegates from the local party organizations over the country, who are certainly no better than ordinary citizens. How this process works will be seen more fully when I come to speak of those Nominating Conventions which are so notable a feature in American politics.

(7) It must also be remembered that the merits of a President are one thing and those of a candidate another thing. An eminent Ameri-

can is reported to have said to friends who wished to put him forward, "Gentlemen, let there be no mistake. I should make a good President, but a very bad candidate." Now to a party it is more important that its nominee should be a good candidate than that he should turn out a good President. A nearer danger is a greater danger. As Saladin says in *The Talisman*,[1] "A wild cat in a chamber is more dangerous than a lion in a distant desert." It will be a misfortune to the party, as well as to the country, if the candidate elected should prove a bad President. But it is a greater misfortune to the party that it should be beaten in the impending election, for the evil of losing national patronage will have come four years sooner. "B" (so reason the leaders), "who is one of our possible candidates, may be an abler man than A, who is the other. But we have a better chance of winning with A than with B, while X, the candidate of our opponents, is anyhow no better than A. We must therefore run A." This reasoning is all the more forcible because the previous career of the possible candidates has generally made it easier to say who will succeed as a candidate than who will succeed as a President; and because the wire-pullers with whom the choice rests are better judges of the former question than of the latter.

(8) After all, too, and this is a point much less obvious to Europeans than to Americans, a President need not be a man of brilliant intellectual gifts. Englishmen, imagining him as something like their prime minister, assume that he ought to be a dazzling orator, able to sway legislatures or multitudes, possessed also of the constructive powers that can devise a great policy or frame a comprehensive piece of legislation. They forget that the President does not sit in Congress, that he ought not to address meetings, except on ornamental and (usually) non-political occasions, that he cannot submit bills nor otherwise influence the action of the legislature. His main duties are to be prompt and firm in securing the due execution of the laws and maintaining the public peace, careful and upright in the choice of the executive officials of the country. Eloquence, whose value is apt to be overrated in all free countries, imagination, profundity of thought or extent of knowledge, are all in so far a gain to him that they make him "a bigger man," and help him to gain a greater influence over the nation, an

[1] Sir Walter Scott's historical novel on the Crusades (1825).

influence which, if he be a true patriot, he may use for its good. But they are not necessary for the due discharge in ordinary times of the duties of his post. A man may lack them and yet make an excellent President. Four-fifths of his work is the same in kind as that which devolves on the chairman of a commercial company or the manager of a railway, the work of choosing good subordinates, seeing that they attend to their business, and taking a sound practical view of such administrative questions as require his decision. Firmness, common sense, and most of all, honesty, an honesty above all suspicion of personal interest, are the qualities which the country chiefly needs in its chief magistrate.

(9) So far we have been considering personal merits. But in the selection of a candidate many considerations have to be regarded besides personal merits, whether they be the merits of a candidate, or of a possible President. The chief of these considerations is the amount of support which can be secured from different States or from different regions, or, as the Americans say, "sections," of the Union. State feeling and sectional feeling are powerful factors in a presidential election. The Northwest, including the States from Ohio to Dakota, is now the most populous region of the Union, and therefore counts for most in an election. It naturally conceives that its interests will be best protected by one who knows them from birth and residence. Hence *prima facie* a North-western man makes the best candidate. A large State casts a heavier vote in the election; and every State is of course more likely to be carried by one of its own children than by a stranger, because his fellow-citizens, while they feel honoured by the choice, gain also a substantial advantage, having a better prospect of such favours as the administration can bestow. Hence, *caeteris paribus*, a man from a large State is preferable as a candidate. New York casts thirty-six votes in the presidential election, Pennsylvania thirty, Ohio twenty-three, Illinois twenty-two, while Vermont and Rhode Island have but four, Delaware, Nevada, and Oregon only three votes each.[2] It is therefore, parties being usually very evenly balanced, better worth

2 The electoral vote in these states stands today as follows: New York 45, Pennsylvania 32, Ohio, 25, Illinois 27, Vermont 3, Rhode Island 4, Delaware 3, Nevada 3, Oregon 6.

while to have an inferior candidate from one of the larger States, who may carry the whole weight of his State with him, than a somewhat superior candidate from one of the smaller States, who will carry only three or four votes. The problem is further complicated by the fact that some States are already safe for one or other party, while others are doubtful. The North-western and New England States are most of them certain to go Republican: the Southern States are (at present) all of them certain to go Democratic. It is more important to gratify a doubtful State than one you have got already; and hence, *caeteris paribus*, a candidate from a doubtful State, such as New York or Indiana, is to be preferred.

(10) Other minor disqualifying circumstances require less explanation. A Roman Catholic, or an avowed disbeliever in Christianity, would be an undesirable candidate. Since the close of the Civil War, any one who fought, especially if he fought with distinction, in the Northern army, has enjoyed great advantages, for the soldiers of that army, still numerous, rally to his name. The two elections of General Grant, who knew nothing of politics, and the fact that his influence survived the faults of his long administration, are evidence of the weight of this consideration. It influenced the selection both of Garfield and of his opponent Hancock. Similarly a person who fought in the Southern army would be a bad candidate, for he might alienate the North.

(11) On a railway journey in the Far West in 1883 I fell in with two newspaper men from the State of Indiana, who were taking their holiday. The conversation turned on the next presidential election. They spoke hopefully of the chances for nomination by their party of an Indiana man, a comparatively obscure person, whose name I had never heard. I expressed some surprise that he should be thought of. They observed that he had done well in State politics, that there was nothing against him, that Indiana would work for him. "But," I rejoined, "ought you not to have a man of more commanding character. There is Senator A. Everybody tells me that he is the shrewdest and most experienced man in your party, and that he has a perfectly clean record. Why not run him?" "Why, yes," they answered, "that is all true. But you see he comes from a small State, and we have got that

State already. Besides, he wasn't in the war. Our man was. Indiana's vote is worth having, and if our man is run, we can carry Indiana."

(12) "Surely the race is not to the swift, nor the battle to the strong, neither yet bread to the wise, nor yet riches to men of understanding, nor yet favour to men of skill, but time and chance happeneth to them all." [3]

(13) These secondary considerations do not always prevail. Intellectual ability and force of character must influence the choice of a candidate, and their influence is sometimes decisive. They count for more when times are so critical that the need for a strong man is felt. Reformers declare that their weight will go on increasing as the disgust of good citizens with the methods of professional politicians increases. But for many generations past it is not the greatest men in the Roman Church that have been chosen Popes, nor the most brilliant men in the Anglican Church that have been appointed Archbishops of Canterbury.

(14) Although several Presidents have survived their departure from office by many years, only one, John Quincy Adams, has played a part in politics after quitting the White House. It may be that the ex-President has not been a great leader before his accession to office; it may be that he does not care to exert himself after he has held and dropped the great prize, and found (one may safely add) how little of a prize it is. Something, however, must also be ascribed to other features of the political system of the country. It is often hard to find a vacancy in the representation of a given State through which to re-enter Congress; it is disagreeable to recur to the arts by which seats are secured. Past greatness is rather an encumbrance than a help to resuming a political career. Exalted power, on which the unsleeping eye of hostile critics was fixed, has probably disclosed all a President's weaknesses, and has either forced him to make enemies by disobliging adherents, or exposed him to censure for subservience to party interests. He is regarded as having had his day; he belongs already to the past, and unless, like Grant, he is endeared to the people by the memory of some splendid service, he soon sinks into the crowd or avoids neglect by retirement. Possibly he may deserve to be forgotten; but more frequently he is

[3] From the Old Testament, Ecclesiastes 9:11.

a man of sufficient ability and character to make the experience he has gained valuable to the country, could it be retained in a place where he might turn it to account. They managed things better at Rome in the days of the republic, gathering into their Senate all the fame and experience, all the wisdom and skill, of those who had ruled and fought as consuls and praetors at home and abroad.

(15) "What shall we do with our ex-Presidents?" is a question often put in America, but never yet answered. The position of a past chief magistrate is not a happy one. He has been a species of sovereign at home. He is received—General Grant was—with almost royal honours abroad. His private income may be insufficient to enable him to live in ease, yet he cannot without loss of dignity, the country's dignity as well as his own, go back to practice at the bar or become partner in a mercantile firm. If he tries to enter the Senate, it may happen that there is no seat vacant for his own State, or that the majority in the State legislature is against him. It has been suggested that he might be given a seat in that chamber as an extra member; but to this plan there is the objection that it would give to the State from which he comes a third senator, and thus put other States at a disadvantage. In any case, however, it would seem only right to bestow such a pension as would relieve him from the necessity of re-entering business or a profession.

(16) We may now answer the question from which we started. Great men are not chosen Presidents, firstly, because great men are rare in politics; secondly, because the method of choice does not bring them to the top; thirdly, because they are not, in quiet times, absolutely needed. Subsequent chapters will, I hope, further elucidate the matter. Meantime, I may observe that the Presidents, regarded historically, fall into three periods, the second inferior to the first, the third rather better than the second.

(17) Down till the election of Andrew Jackson in 1828, all the Presidents had been statesmen in the European sense of the word, men of education, of administrative experience, of a certain largeness of view and dignity of character. All except the first two had served in the great office of secretary of state; all were well known to the nation from the part they had played. In the second period, from Jackson till the out-

break of the Civil War in 1861, the Presidents were either mere politicians, such as Van Buren, Polk, or Buchanan, or else successful soldiers, such as Harrison or Taylor, whom their party found useful as figureheads. They were intellectual pigmies beside the real leaders of that generation—Clay, Calhoun, and Webster. A new series begins with Lincoln in 1861. He and General Grant his successor, who cover sixteen years between them, belong to the history of the world. The other less distinguished Presidents of this period contrast favourably with the Polks and Pierces of the days before the war, but they are not, like the early Presidents, the first men of the country. If we compare the nineteen Presidents who have been elected to office since 1789 with the nineteen English prime ministers of the same hundred years, there are but six of the latter, and at least eight of the former whom history calls personally insignificant, while only Washington, Jefferson, Lincoln, and Grant can claim to belong to a front rank represented in the English list by seven or possibly eight names. It would seem that the natural selection of the English parliamentary system, even as modified by the aristocratic habits of that country, has more tendency to bring the highest gifts to the highest place than the more artificial selection of America.

STUDY QUESTIONS

1. Although Bryce's central thesis is given in his title, he does not plunge immediately into a partition of his subject, but instead devotes a full paragraph to a more elaborate introduction. Why? Does that paragraph contribute anything not stated or implied by the title?

2. What function is served by paragraph 2?

3. Into what divisions does Bryce divide his thesis? What principle governs the order in which they are discussed? Why is one of these topics discussed in much more detail than the others?

4. What is the relevance of paragraphs 14 and 15 to the central thesis of this essay?

5. Paragraphs 16 and 17 may both be regarded as concluding paragraphs. How do they differ? Could paragraph 17 be omitted? What is accomplished by its inclusion?

6. All the development of paragraph 3 is carried in the long second sentence. Analyze that sentence carefully to see how subordination is em-

ployed. Is the sentence compound or complex, or both? Is it loose, periodic, or balanced? Try recasting the sentence into several shorter sentences.

7. Paragraph 8 contains several series of adjective phrases, noun phrases, prepositional phrases, and noun clauses. Within each series, what principle governs the order of listing?

8. What bearing does the fact that Bryce was an Englishman have on his treatment of his subject? What advantages does it give him? What disadvantages? Can he be charged with bias? What is the general tone of his discussion?

9. If Bryce were writing on this same subject today, could he sustain the same thesis? If so, what modifications in his presentation might he wish to make?

10. This essay is essentially not a plea for reform, but an objective appraisal of an existing situation by a political scientist. What is its importance for you as an individual citizen who contributes, or will contribute, to the electing of presidents?

WRITING ASSIGNMENTS

1. Write a fully developed answer to the question, "What shall we do with our ex-Presidents?"

2. Write an analysis of the primary election as a part of the democratic process.

3. Write an argument for or against the idea of a program of educating men and women for political careers.

4. Write an analysis of some aspect of the operation of campus politics.

5. Write a research paper on the selection of a presidential candidate or candidates in a past presidential campaign.

The Fœderalist, No. 10 *

JAMES MADISON (1751–1836), *fourth President of the United States,
served in the Continental Congress (1779–1783) and the Virginia House
of Delegates. He played a leading role in the Constitutional Convention
of 1787, taking a prominent part in its debates and keeping careful notes
on them. He had a very important influence in shaping the draft of the
Constitution and then campaigned vigorously and successfully for its
adoption. He joined Alexander Hamilton and John Jay in writing* The
Fœderalist, *a series of eighty-five papers designed to win support for the
Constitution and gain its ratification. Madison served in the House of
Representatives from 1789 to 1797 and as Secretary of State in Jefferson's
cabinet from 1801 to 1809. In 1808 he was elected President and served
two terms.*

To the People of the State of New York: [1]

(1) Among the numerous advantages promised by a well-
constructed Union, none deserves to be more accurately developed
than its tendency to break and control the violence of faction. The
friend of popular Governments never finds himself so much alarmed
for their character and fate, as when he contemplates their propensity
to this dangerous vice. He will not fail, therefore, to set a due value on
any plan which, without violating the principles to which he is attached, provides a proper cure for it. The instability, injustice, and confusion introduced into the public councils, have, in truth, been the
mortal diseases under which popular governments have everywhere
perished; as they continue to be the favorite and fruitful topics from

---

* From the New York *Packet*, Friday, Nov. 23, 1787. This text is based on an
edition published in 1864, edited by Henry B. Dawson and based on the original
text of 1787.
[1] This essay was one of several letters written to urge the State of New York to
ratify the Constitution.

which the adversaries to liberty derive their most specious declamations. The valuable improvements made by the American Constitutions on the popular models, both ancient and modern, cannot certainly be too much admired; but it would be an unwarrantable partiality, to contend that they have as effectually obviated the danger on this side, as was wished and expected. Complaints are everywhere heard from our most considerate and virtuous citizens, equally the friends of public and private faith, and of public and personal liberty, that our governments are too unstable; that the public good is disregarded in the conflicts of rival parties; and that measures are too often decided, not according to the rules of justice, and the rights of the minor party, but by the superior force of an interested and overbearing majority. However anxiously we may wish that these complaints had no foundation, the evidence of known facts will not permit us to deny that they are in some degree true. It will be found, indeed, on a candid review of our situation, that some of the distresses under which we labor have been erroneously charged on the operation of our governments; but it will be found, at the same time, that other causes will not alone account for many of our heaviest misfortunes; and, particularly, for that prevailing and increasing distrust of public engagements, and alarm for private rights, which are echoed from one end of the continent to the other. These must be chiefly, if not wholly, effects of the unsteadiness and injustice, with which a factious spirit has tainted our public administrations.

(2) By a faction, I understand a number of citizens, whether amounting to a majority or minority of the whole, who are united and actuated by some common impulse of passion, or of interest, adverse to the rights of other citizens, or to the permanent and aggregate interests of the community.

(3) There are two methods of curing the mischiefs of faction: the one, by removing its causes; the other, by controlling its effects.

(4) There are again two methods of removing the causes of faction: the one, by destroying the liberty which is essential to its existence; the other, by giving to every citizen the same opinions, the same passions, and the same interests.

(5) It could never be more truly said than of the first remedy, that it

was worse than the disease. Liberty is to faction, what air is to fire, an aliment without which it instantly expires. But it could not be less folly to abolish liberty, which is essential to political life, because it nourishes faction, than it would be to wish the annihilation of air, which is essential to animal life, because it imparts to fire its destructive agency.

(6) The second expedient is as impracticable, as the first would be unwise. As long as the reason of man continues fallible, and he is at liberty to exercise it, different opinions will be formed. As long as the connection subsists between his reason and his self-love, his opinions and his passions will have a reciprocal influence on each other; and the former will be objects to which the latter will attach themselves. The diversity in the faculties of men, from which the rights of property originate, is not less an insuperable obstacle to an uniformity of interests. The protection of these faculties is the first object of Government. From the protection of different and unequal faculties of acquiring property, the possession of different degrees and kinds of property immediately results; and from the influence of these on the sentiments and views of the respective proprietors, ensues a division of the society into different interests and parties.

(7) The latent causes of faction are thus sown in the nature of man; and we see them everywhere brought into different degrees of activity, according to the different circumstances of civil society. A zeal for different opinions concerning religion, concerning Government, and many other points, as well of speculation as of practice; an attachment to different leaders ambitiously contending for preëminence and power; or to persons of other descriptions whose fortunes have been interesting to the human passions, have, in turn, divided mankind into parties, inflamed them with mutual animosity, and rendered them much more disposed to vex and oppress each other, than to coöperate for their common good. So strong is this propensity of mankind to fall into mutual animosities that, where no substantial occasion presents itself, the most frivolous and fanciful distinctions have been sufficient to kindle their unfriendly passions, and excite their most violent conflicts. But the most common and durable source of factions has been the various and unequal distribution of property. Those who hold, and

those who are without property, have ever formed distinct interests in society. Those who are creditors, and those who are debtors, fall under a like discrimination. A landed interest, a manufacturing interest, a mercantile interest, a moneyed interest, with many lesser interests, grow up of necessity in civilized nations, and divide them into different classes, actuated by different sentiments and views. The regulation of these various and interfering interests forms the principal task of modern Legislation, and involves the spirit of party and faction in the necessary and ordinary operations of the Government.

(8) No man is allowed to be a judge in his own cause; because his interest would certainly bias his judgment and, not improbably, corrupt his integrity. With equal, nay with greater reason, a body of men are unfit to be both judges and parties at the same time; yet what are many of the most important acts of legislation, but so many judicial determinations, not indeed concerning the rights of single persons, but concerning the rights of large bodies of citizens? and what are the different classes of Legislators, but advocates and parties to the causes which they determine? Is a law proposed concerning private debts? It is a question to which the creditors are parties on one side, and the debtors on the other. Justice ought to hold the balance between them. Yet the parties are, and must be, themselves the judges; and the most numerous party, or, in other words, the most powerful faction, must be expected to prevail. Shall domestic manufactures be encouraged, and in what degree, by restrictions on foreign manufactures? are questions which would be differently decided by the landed and the manufacturing classes; and probably by neither, with a sole regard to justice and the public good. The apportionment of taxes on the various descriptions of property is an act which seems to require the most exact impartiality; yet there is, perhaps, no legislative act in which greater opportunity and temptation are given to a predominant party, to trample on the rules of justice. Every shilling, with which they overburden the inferior number, is a shilling saved to their own pockets.

(9) It is in vain to say, that enlightened statesmen will be able to adjust these clashing interests, and render them all subservient to the public good. Enlightened statesmen will not always be at the helm: Nor, in many cases, can such an adjustment be made at all, without

taking into view indirect and remote considerations, which will rarely prevail over the immediate interest which one party may find in disregarding the rights of another, or the good of the whole.

(10) The inference to which we are brought is, that the *causes* of faction cannot be removed; and that relief is only to be sought in the means of controlling its *effects*.

(11) If a faction consists of less than a majority, relief is supplied by the republican principle, which enables the majority to defeat its sinister views by regular vote. It may clog the administration, it may convulse the society; but it will be unable to execute and mask its violence under the forms of the Constitution. When a majority is included in a faction, the form of popular Government, on the other hand, enables it to sacrifice to its ruling passion or interest both the public good and the rights of other citizens. To secure the public good, and private rights, against the danger of such a faction, and at the same time to preserve the spirit and the form of popular Government, is then the great object to which our inquiries are directed: Let me add, that it is the great desideratum, by which alone this form of Government can be rescued from the opprobrium under which it has so long labored, and be recommended to the esteem and adoption of mankind.

(12) By what means is this object attainable? Evidently by one of two only. Either the existence of the same passion or interest in a majority, at the same time, must be prevented; or the majority, having such coexistent passion or interest, must be rendered, by their number and local situation, unable to concert and carry into effect schemes of oppression. If the impulse and the opportunity be suffered to coincide, we well know that neither moral nor religious motives can be relied on as an adequate control. They are not found to be such on the injustice and violence of individuals, and lose their efficacy in proportion to the number combined together; that is, in proportion as their efficacy becomes needful.

(13) From this view of the subject, it may be concluded, that a pure Democracy, by which I mean a Society consisting of a small number of citizens, who assemble and administer the Government in person, can admit of no cure for the mischiefs of faction. A common pas-

sion or interest will, in almost every case, be felt by a majority of the whole; a communication and concert result from the form of Government itself; and there is nothing to check the inducements to sacrifice the weaker party, or an obnoxious individual. Hence it is, that such Democracies have ever been spectacles of turbulence and contention; have ever been found incompatible with personal security, or the rights of property; and have in general been as short in their lives, as they have been violent in their deaths. Theoretic politicians, who have patronized this species of Government, have erroneously supposed, that by reducing mankind to a perfect equality in their political rights, they would, at the same time, be perfectly equalized and assimilated in their possessions, their opinions, and their passions.

(14) A Republic, by which I mean a Government in which the scheme of representation takes place, opens a different prospect, and promises the cure for which we are seeking. Let us examine the points in which it varies from pure Democracy, and we shall comprehend both the nature of the cure, and the efficacy which it must derive from the Union.

(15) The two great points of difference, between a Democracy and a Republic, are, first, the delegation of the Government, in the latter, to a small number of citizens elected by the rest: Secondly, the greater number of citizens, and greater sphere of country, over which the latter may be extended.

(16) The effect of the first difference is, on the one hand, to refine and enlarge the public views, by passing them through the medium of a chosen body of citizens, whose wisdom may best discern the true interest of their country, and whose patriotism and love of justice will be least likely to sacrifice it to temporary or partial considerations. Under such a regulation, it may well happen, that the public voice, pronounced by the representatives of the People, will be more consonant to the public good, than if pronounced by the People themselves, convened for the purpose. On the other hand, the effect may be inverted. Men of factious tempers, of local prejudices, or of sinister designs, may by intrigue, by corruption, or by other means, first obtain the suffrages, and then betray the interests of the people. The question

resulting is, whether small or extensive Republics are most favorable to the election of proper guardians of the public weal; and it is clearly decided in favor of the latter by two obvious considerations.

(17) In the first place, it is to be remarked that however small the Republic may be, the Representatives must be raised to a certain number, in order to guard against the cabals of a few; and that however large it may be, they must be limited to a certain number, in order to guard against the confusion of a multitude. Hence, the number of Representatives in the two cases not being in proportion to that of the Constituents, and being proportionally greatest in the small Republic, it follows, that if the proportion of fit characters be not less in the large than in the small Republic, the former will present a greater option, and consequently a greater probability of a fit choice.

(18) In the next place, as each Representative will be chosen by a greater number of citizens in the large than in the small Republic, it will be more difficult for unworthy candidates to practice with success the vicious arts, by which elections are too often carried; and the suffrages of the People, being more free, will be more likely to centre in men who possess the most attractive merit, and the most diffusive and established characters.

(19) It must be confessed, that in this, as in most other cases, there is a mean, on both sides of which inconveniences will be found to lie. By enlarging too much the number of electors, you render the representative too little acquainted with all their local circumstances and lesser interests; as by reducing it too much, you render him unduly attached to these, and too little fit to comprehend and pursue great and National objects. The Fœderal Constitution forms a happy combination in this respect; the great and aggregate interests being referred to the National, the local and particular to the State Legislatures.

(20) The other point of difference is, the greater number of citizens and extent of territory which may be brought within the compass of Republican, than of Democratic Government; and it is this circumstance principally which renders factious combinations less to be dreaded in the former, than in the latter. The smaller the society, the fewer probably will be the distinct parties and interests composing it; the fewer the distinct parties and interests, the more frequently will

a majority be found of the same party; and the smaller the number of individuals composing a majority, and the smaller the compass within which they are placed, the more easily will they concert and execute their plans of oppression. Extend the sphere, and you take in a greater variety of parties and interests; you make it less probable that a majority of the whole will have a common motive to invade the rights of other citizens; or if such a common motive exists, it will be more difficult for all who feel it to discover their own strength, and to act in unison with each other. Besides other impediments, it may be remarked, that where there is a consciousness of unjust or dishonorable purposes, communication is always checked by distrust, in proportion to the number whose concurrence is necessary.

(21) Hence, it clearly appears, that the same advantage which a Republic has over a Democracy, in controlling the effects of faction, is enjoyed by a large over a small Republic,—is enjoyed by the Union over the States composing it. Does the advantage consist in the substitution of Representatives, whose enlightened views and virtuous sentiments render them superior to local prejudices, and to schemes of injustice? It will not be denied, that the Representation of the Union will be most likely to possess these requisite endowments. Does it consist in the greater security afforded by a greater variety of parties, against the event of any one party being able to outnumber and oppress the rest? In an equal degree does the increased variety of parties, comprised within the Union, increase this security. Does it, in fine, consist in the greater obstacles opposed to the concert and accomplishment of the secret wishes of an unjust and interested majority? Here, again, the extent of the Union gives it the most palpable advantage.

(22) The influence of factious leaders may kindle a flame within their particular States, but will be unable to spread a general conflagration through the other States: A religious sect may degenerate into a political faction in a part of the Confederacy; but the variety of sects dispersed over the entire face of it, must secure the National Councils against any danger from that source; A rage for paper money, for an abolition of debts, for an equal division of property, or for any other improper or wicked project, will be less apt to pervade the whole body of the Union, than a particular member of it; in the same proportion

as such a malady is more likely to taint a particular county or district, than an entire State.

(23) In the extent and proper structure of the Union, therefore, we behold a Republican remedy for the diseases most incident to Republican Government. And according to the degree of pleasure and pride we feel in being Republicans, ought to be our zeal in cherishing the spirit, and supporting the character, of Fœderalists.

PUBLIUS [2]

STUDY QUESTIONS

1. This essay is a closely reasoned argument in defense of a specific idea. What is it that Madison is defending? What kind of reasoning does he employ? How is the character of his approach reflected in his methods of paragraph development?

2. Write an outline of Madison's argument. What principle of organization does Madison use in presenting his argument? Could his separate points be presented in any other order? Try stating his argument as a syllogism.

3. What is the function of each of the following short paragraphs: 2, 3, 4, and 10?

4. In general, can you determine how Madison's style differs from modern style?

5. The word *faction* is a key word in the understanding of this essay. Why? What does Madison mean by the word? What is a modern equivalent for it?

6. To describe the principle enunciated in the first sentence of paragraph 11, what word would we use today instead of Madison's term *republican?* Compare with this use of the term here his use of *republic* in the first sentence of paragraph 14. In paragraph 15 how does he differentiate a republic from a democracy? Do we generally so distinguish the two words today?

7. Is the analogy in paragraph 5 sound? What does it tell us about Madison's own opinion on the question of destroying liberty?

8. The punctuation and capitalization of Madison's essay are given here essentially as they appeared in the original text of 1787. They obviously are based on principles different from those which govern modern practice. On the basis of your knowledge of modern punctuation, what

[2] This nom de plume was signed to all the Federalist Papers, separate numbers of which were written by Alexander Hamilton, John Jay, and James Madison.

specific changes would you make to modernize the punctuation in this text? Can you determine the basis of the use of capitals for words within sentences?

9. Who were the Federalists alluded to in the last sentence of this essay?

10. How does Madison believe the dangers of faction in popular government can be solved in the United States? (Look up the meaning of the word *popular*.)

11. This essay was written as a piece of propaganda. Are its arguments convincing? Would the strength of its arguments make it effective as propaganda today? If Madison were arguing his case over the radio today, would it be advisable for him to change his arguments and method of approach? If so, what kind of changes should he make?

12. What is the tone of Madison's argument?

WRITING ASSIGNMENTS

1. Write an analysis of the validity of Madison's theories in the light of the later development of the United States Government and of its operation today.

2. Write an essay on what you conceive to be the role of moral conscience in a democratic form of government.

3. Write an essay defending the value of "factions" in the functioning of a democracy.

4. Write an analysis of the problems involved in the selection of qualified and able representatives in our system of government and the means of solving such problems.

5. Write a research paper on the history of a political party in the United States.

A Modest Proposal*

For Preventing the Children of Poor People in Ireland from
Being a Burden to Their Parents or Country, and
for Making Them Beneficial to the Public

JONATHAN SWIFT (1667–1745), *born in Ireland of English parents,
spent most of his life there as a clergyman in the Church of England. His
fame as the greatest English prose satirist in the eighteenth century is
based on such works as* A Tale of a Tub *(1704),* The Battle of the Books
(1704), Gulliver's Travels *(1726), and a number of tracts on economic
and social conditions in Ireland. Of these latter,* A Modest Proposal *is
easily the most famous.*

(1) It is a melancholy object to those who walk through this great
town [Dublin] or travel in the country, when they see the streets, the
roads, and cabin doors crowded with beggars of the female sex, followed by three, four, or six children, all in rags and importuning every
passenger for an alms. These mothers, instead of being able to work
for their honest livelihood, are forced to employ all their time in stroll-
ing to beg sustenance for their helpless infants, who, as they grow up,
either turn thieves for want of work, or leave their dear native country
to fight for the Pretender in Spain,[1] or sell themselves to the Barbadoes.

(2) I think it is agreed by all parties that this prodigious number
of children in the arms, or on the backs, or at the heels of their mothers,
and frequently of their fathers, is in the present deplorable state of the

* First published in 1729.
[1] The Pretender to the English throne was James Stuart, the son of James II,
who had been deposed in the "Glorious Revolution" of 1688. Swift was probably
alluding here to the intrigues between Cardinal Alberini, the Spanish Minister to
England, and the supporters of James.

kingdom a very great additional grievance; and, therefore, whoever could find out a fair, cheap, and easy method of making these children sound, useful members of the commonwealth, would deserve so well of the public as to have his statue set up for a preserver of the nation.

(3) But my intention is very far from being confined to provide only for the children of professed beggars; it is of a much greater extent, and shall take in the whole number of infants at a certain age who are born of parents in effect as little able to support them as those who demand our charity in the streets.

(4) As to my own part, having turned my thoughts for many years upon this important subject, and maturely weighed the several schemes of our projectors, I have always found them grossly mistaken in their computation. It is true, a child just dropped from its dam may be supported by her milk for a solar year with little other nourishment, at most not above the value of two shillings, which the mother may certainly get, or the value in scraps, by her lawful occupation of begging; and it is exactly at one year old that I propose to provide for them in such a manner as instead of being a charge upon their parents or the parish, or wanting food and raiment for the rest of their lives, they shall, on the contrary, contribute to the feeding and partly to the clothing of many thousands.

(5) There is likewise another great advantage in my scheme, that it will prevent those voluntary abortions, and that horrid practice of women murdering their bastard children, alas! too frequent among us! sacrificing the poor innocent babes, I doubt, more to avoid the expense than the shame, which would move tears and pity in the most savage and inhuman breast.

(6) The number of souls in this kingdom being usually reckoned one million and a half, of these, I calculate there may be about two hundred thousand couples whose wives are breeders; from which number I subtract thirty thousand couples, who are able to maintain their own children (although I apprehend there cannot be so many, under the present distresses of the kingdom); but this being granted, there will remain one hundred and seventy thousand breeders. I again subtract fifty thousand for those women who miscarry, or whose children die by accident or disease within the year. There only remain an

hundred and twenty thousand children of poor parents annually born. The question therefore is, how this number shall be reared and provided for? which, as I have already said, under the present situation of affairs, is utterly impossible by all the methods hitherto proposed. For we can neither employ them in handicraft or agriculture; we neither build houses (I mean in the country) nor cultivate land; they can very seldom pick up a livelihood by stealing till they arrive at six years old, except where they are of towardly parts, although I confess they learn the rudiments much earlier, during which time, they can, however, be properly looked upon only as probationers, as I have been informed by a principal gentleman in the county of Cavan, who protested to me that he never knew above one or two instances under the age of six, even in a part of the kingdom so renowned for the quickest proficiency in that art.

(7) I am assured by our merchants that a boy or girl before twelve years old is no saleable commodity, and even when they come to this age they will not yield above three pounds or three pounds and half-a-crown at most on the exchange; which cannot turn to account either to the parents or the kingdom, the charge of nutriment and rags having been at least four times that value.

(8) I shall now therefore humbly propose my own thoughts, which I hope will not be liable to the least objection.

(9) I have been assured by a very knowing American [2] of my acquaintance in London, that a young healthy child well nursed is at a year old a most delicious, nourishing, and wholesome food, whether stewed, roasted, baked, or boiled; and I make no doubt that it will equally serve in a fricassee or a ragout.

(10) I do therefore humbly offer it to public consideration that of the hundred and twenty thousand children already computed, twenty thousand may be reserved for breed, whereof only one-fourth part to be males, which is more than we allow to sheep, black cattle or swine; and my reason is that these children are seldom the fruits of marriage, a circumstance not much regarded by our savages; therefore one male will be sufficient to serve four females. That the remaining hundred thousand may, at a year old, be offered in sale to the persons of quality

[2] American Indian.

and fortune through the kingdom, always advising the mother to let them suck plentifully in the last month, so as to render them plump and fat for a good table. A child will make two dishes at an entertainment for friends, and when the family dines alone, the fore or hind quarter will make a reasonable dish, and seasoned with a little pepper or salt will be very good boiled on the fourth day, especially in winter.

(11) I have reckoned upon a medium that a child just born will weigh twelve pounds, and in a solar year, if tolerably nursed, will increase to twenty-eight pounds.

(12) I grant this food will be somewhat dear, and therefore very proper for landlords, who, as they have already devoured most of the parents, seem to have the best title to the children.

(13) Infants' flesh will be in season throughout the year, but more plentiful in March, and a little before and after; for we are told by a grave author, an eminent French physician, that fish being a prolific diet, there are more children born in Roman Catholic countries about nine months after Lent than at any other season; therefore, reckoning a year after Lent, the markets will be more glutted than usual, because the number of popish infants is at least three to one in this kingdom, and therefore it will have one other collateral advantage, by lessening the number of papists among us.

(14) I have already computed the charge of nursing a beggar's child (in which list I reckon all cottagers, laborers, and four-fifths of the farmers) to be about two shillings per annum, rags included; and I believe no gentleman would repine to give ten shillings for the carcass of a good fat child, which, as I have said, will make four dishes of excellent nutritive meat, when he has only some particular friend or his own family to dine with him. Thus the squire will learn to be a good landlord, and grow popular among his tenants; the mother will have eight shillings net profit, and be fit for work till she produces another child.

(15) Those who are more thrifty (as I must confess the times require) may flay the carcass, the skin of which artificially dressed will make admirable gloves for ladies, and summer boots for fine gentlemen.

(16) As to our city of Dublin, shambles may be appointed for this

purpose in the most convenient parts of it, and butchers, we may be assured, will not be wanting, although I rather recommend buying the children alive, and dressing them hot from the knife as we do roasting pigs.

(17) A very worthy person, a true lover of his country, and whose virtues I highly esteem, was lately pleased, in discoursing on this matter, to offer a refinement upon my scheme. He said that many gentlemen of this kingdom, having of late destroyed their deer, he conceived that the want of venison might be well supplied by the bodies of young lads and maidens, not exceeding fourteen years of age nor under twelve, so great a number of both sexes in every country being now ready to starve for want of work and service, and these to be disposed of by their parents, if alive, or otherwise by their nearest relations. But with due deference to so excellent a friend and so deserving a patriot, I cannot be altogether in his sentiments; for as to the males, my American acquaintance assured me from frequent experience that their flesh was generally tough and lean, like that of our school-boys, by continual exercise, and their taste disagreeable; and to fatten them would not answer the charge. Then as to the females, it would, I think, with humble submission, be a loss to the public, because they soon would become breeders themselves; and besides, it is not improbable that some scrupulous people might be apt to censure such a practice (although indeed very unjustly) as a little bordering upon cruelty, which, I confess, has always been with me the strongest objection against any project, however so well intended.

(18) But in order to justify my friend, he confessed that this expedient was put into his head by the famous Psalmanazar,[3] a native of the island Formosa, who came from thence to London above twenty years ago, and in conversation told my friend, that in his country when any young person happened to be put to death, the executioner sold the carcass to persons of quality as a prime dainty, and that in his time the body of a plump girl of fifteen, who was crucified for an attempt to poison the emperor, was sold to his imperial majesty's prime minister of state and other great mandarins of the court, in

[3] George Psalmanazar (1679?–1762) was a literary impostor who pretended to have come to England from Formosa. He recorded his supposed experiences in *Description of the Island of Formosa* (1705).

joints from the gibbet, at four hundred crowns. Neither indeed can I deny that if the same use were made of several plump young girls in this town, who, without one single groat to their fortunes, cannot stir abroad without a chair,[4] and appear at the playhouse and assemblies in foreign fineries which they never will pay for, the kingdom would not be the worse.

(19) Some persons of a desponding spirit are in great concern about that vast number of poor people, who are aged, diseased, or maimed, and I have been desired to employ my thoughts what course may be taken to ease the nation of so grievous an encumbrance. But I am not in the least pain upon that matter, because it is very well known that they are every day dying and rotting by cold, and famine, and filth, and vermin, as fast as can be reasonably expected. And as to the younger laborers, they are now in as hopeful a condition; they cannot get work, and consequently pine away for want of nourishment, to a degree that if at any time they are accidentally hired to common labor, they have not strength to perform it; and thus the country and themselves are happily delivered from the evils to come.

(20) I have too long digressed, and therefore shall return to my subject. I think the advantages by the proposal which I have made are obvious, and many, as well as of the highest importance.

(21) For first, as I have already observed, it would greatly lessen the number of papists, with whom we are yearly overrun, being the principal breeders of the nation as well as our most dangerous enemies; and who stay at home on purpose with a design to deliver the kingdom to the Pretender, hoping to take their advantage by the absence of so many good protestants,[5] who have chosen rather to leave their country than stay at home and pay tithes against their conscience to an episcopal curate.

(22) Secondly, The poorer tenants will have something valuable of their own, which by law may be made liable to distress, and help to pay their landlord's rent, their corn and cattle being already seized, and money a thing unknown.

[4] A portable one-passenger vehicle without wheels, carried on poles by two men, one in front and one behind.
[5] Irish Dissenters, Protestants who refused to subscribe to the Church of Ireland, the Irish counterpart of the Church of England.

(23) Thirdly, Whereas the maintenance of an hundred thousand children, from two years old and upward, cannot be computed at less than ten shillings a-piece per annum, the nation's stock will be thereby increased fifty thousand pounds per annum, besides the profit of a new dish introduced to the tables of all gentlemen of fortune in the kingdom who have any refinement in taste. And the money will circulate among ourselves, the goods being entirely of our own growth and manufacture.

(24) Fourthly, The constant breeders, beside the gain of eight shillings sterling per annum by the sale of their children, will be rid of the charge of maintaining them after the first year.

(25) Fifthly, This food would likewise bring great custom to taverns, where the vintners will certainly be so prudent as to procure the best receipts for dressing it to perfection, and consequently have their houses frequented by all the fine gentlemen, who justly value themselves upon their knowledge in good eating; and a skilful cook, who understands how to oblige his guests, will contrive to make it as expensive as they please.

(26) Sixthly, This would be a great inducement to marriage, which all wise nations have either encouraged by rewards or enforced by laws and penalties. It would increase the care and tenderness of mothers toward their children, when they were sure of a settlement for life to the poor babes, provided in some sort by the public, to their annual profit instead of expense. We should see an honest emulation among the married women, which of them could bring the fattest child to the market. Men would become as fond of their wives during the time of their pregnancy as they are now of their mares in foal, their cows in calf, or sows when they are ready to farrow; nor offer to beat or kick them (as is too frequent a practice) for fear of a miscarriage.

(27) Many other advantages might be enumerated. For instance, the addition of some thousand carcasses in our exportation of barreled beef, the propagation of swine's flesh, and improvement in the art of making good bacon, so much wanted among us by the great destruction of pigs, too frequent at our tables; which are in no way comparable in taste or magnificence to a well-grown, fat yearling child, which roasted whole will make a considerable figure at a lord mayor's feast,

or any other public entertainment. But this and many others I omit, being studious of brevity.

(28) Supposing that one thousand families in this city would be constant customers for infants' flesh, beside others who might have it at merry-meetings, particularly weddings and christenings, I compute that Dublin would take off annually about twenty thousand carcasses, and the rest of the kingdom (where probably they will be sold somewhat cheaper) the remaining eighty thousand.

(29) I can think of no one objection that will possibly be raised against this proposal, unless it should be urged that the number of people will be thereby much lessened in the kingdom. This I freely own, and it was indeed one principal design in offering it to the world. I desire the reader will observe that I calculate my remedy for this one individual kingdom of Ireland, and for no other that ever was, is, or, I think, ever can be upon earth. Therefore let no man talk to me of other expedients: of taxing our absentees at five shillings a pound; of using neither clothes nor household furniture, except what is of our own growth and manufacture; of utterly rejecting the materials and instruments that promote foreign luxury; of curing the expensiveness of pride, vanity, idleness, and gaming in our women; of introducing a vein of parsimony, prudence, and temperance; of learning to love our country, in the want of which we differ even from Laplanders and the inhabitants of Topinamboo; [6] of quitting our animosities and factions, nor act any longer like the Jews, who were murdering one another at the very moment their city was taken; [7] of being a little cautious not to sell our country and consciences for nothing; of teaching landlords to have at least one degree of mercy toward their tenants; lastly, of putting a spirit of honesty, industry, and skill into our shop-keepers, who, if a resolution could now be taken to buy only our native goods, would immediately unite to cheat and exact upon us in the price, the measure, and the goodness, nor could ever yet be brought to make one fair proposal of just dealing, though often and earnestly invited to it. [8]

[6] A district of Brazil, inhabited supposedly by savages. Laplanders were also considered barbarous and uncivilized.

[7] At the fall of Jerusalem to the army of the Roman Titus in 70 A.D.

[8] Swift himself had made numerous proposals for improving conditions in Ireland.

(30) Therefore, I repeat, let no man talk to me of these and the like expedients, till he has at least some glimpse of hope that there will be ever some hearty and sincere attempt to put them in practice.

(31) But as to myself, having been wearied out for many years with offering vain, idle, visionary thoughts, and at length utterly despairing of success, I fortunately fell upon this proposal, which, as it is wholly new, so it has something solid and real, of no expense and little trouble, full in our own power, and whereby we can incur no danger in disobliging England. For this kind of commodity will not bear exportation, the flesh being of too tender a consistence to admit a long continuance in salt, although perhaps I could name a country which would be glad to eat up our whole nation without it.

(32) After all, I am not so violently bent upon my own opinion as to reject any offer proposed by wise men, which shall be found equally innocent, cheap, easy, and effectual. But before something of that kind shall be advanced in contradiction to my scheme, and offering a better, I desire the author or authors will be pleased maturely to consider two points. First, as things now stand, how they will be able to find food and raiment for an hundred thousand useless mouths and backs. And secondly, there being a round million of creatures in human figure throughout this kingdom, whose whole subsistence put into a common stock would leave them in debt two millions of pounds sterling, adding those who are beggars by profession to the bulk of farmers, cottagers, and laborers, with their wives and children, who are beggars in effect; I desire those politicians, who dislike my overture, and may perhaps be so bold as to attempt an answer, that they will first ask the parents of these mortals, whether they would not at this day think it a great happiness to have been sold for food at a year old in the manner I prescribe, and thereby have avoided such a perpetual scene of misfortunes as they have since gone through by the oppression of landlords, the impossibility of paying rent without money or trade, the want of common sustenance, with neither house nor clothes to cover them from the inclemencies of the weather, and the most inevitable prospect of entailing the like or greater miseries upon their breed for ever.

(33) I profess, in the sincerity of my heart, that I have not the

least personal interest in endeavoring to promote this necessary work, having no other motive than the public good of my country, by advancing our trade, providing for infants, relieving the poor, and giving some pleasure to the rich. I have no children by which I can propose to get a single penny; the youngest being nine years old, and my wife past child-bearing.

STUDY QUESTIONS

1. This essay is perhaps the most famous example of sustained irony in English. What does the term *irony* mean? Why is this essay considered ironical? What is the tone of Swift's irony?

2. What effect does Swift gain in his concluding paragaph? What contribution does this paragraph make to his total proposal?

3. This essay is a political pamphlet on the subject of Ireland's economic woes in the eighteenth century. Where does Swift introduce his own serious solution? How is it stated? Does it destroy the ironic tone?

4. What gives particular force to the pity shown in paragraph 5?

5. Coleridge said that one of the purposes of an author of fiction is to effect a "suspension of disbelief" in his readers. By that, he implied that we all are prone to believe that a literary work is not true and that the author must labor if not to make us believe, at least to make us suspend our disbelief. Try applying this concept to Swift's problem in this essay. How does he almost make us not disbelieve him?

6. This pamphlet has often been misunderstood. Why, do you think?

7. Swift states his problem in the opening paragraphs of his essay. What is the problem? Is it a serious one? How does Swift present it?

8. What is the role of specific details and statistics in this essay? Are they employed merely for developing points, or do they serve also to establish the author's tone?

9. List the words and phrases in this essay which are old fashioned, rarely used today, archaic, or obsolescent. To what extent do they make it difficult to understand the essay?

10. The quality of Swift's writing is not ornate but rather bare. How is this bareness appropriate to Swift's purpose?

WRITING ASSIGNMENTS

1. Write a modest proposal of your own for remedying an evil that you feel needs correcting. Try to make your presentation ironical.

2. Write an analysis of what you think would be the success of Swift's method of presentation today.

3. Write a serious, straightforward argument for a specific change you feel ought to be made on your campus.

4. Write a research paper on the economic and social conditions in Ireland which occasioned Swift's essay.

Sermons in Cats*

ALDOUS HUXLEY (1894–   ), *English novelist and essayist, is the brother of Julian, represented also in this collection, and grandson of Thomas Henry Huxley, the famous scientist. After graduation from Oxford, Aldous did some journalistic work and began his career as a novelist, which has produced such prominent works as* Crome Yellow (1921), Antic Hay (1923), Point Counter Point (1928), Brave New World (1932), Eyeless in Gaza (1935), After Many a Summer Dies the Swan (1939), *and* Ape and Essence (1949). *He has also written several volumes of essays and short stories. At present he lives in California.*

(1) I met, not long ago, a young man who aspired to become a novelist. Knowing that I was in the profession, he asked me to tell him how he should set to work to realize his ambition. I did my best to explain. "The first thing," I said, "is to buy quite a lot of paper, a bottle of ink, and a pen. After that you merely have to write." But this was not enough for my young friend. He seemed to have a notion that there was some sort of esoteric cookery book, full of literary recipes, which you had only to follow attentively to become a Dickens, a Henry James, a Flaubert—"according to taste," as the authors of recipes say, when they come to the question of seasoning and sweetening. Wouldn't I let him have a glimpse of this cookery book? I said that I was sorry, but that (unhappily—for what an endless amount of time and trouble it would save!) I had never even seen such a work. He seemed sadly disappointed; so, to console the poor lad, I advised him to apply to the professors of dramaturgy and short-story writing at some reputable university; if any one possessed a trustworthy cookery book

* From *Music at Night* by Aldous Huxley. Copyright 1931 by Aldous Huxley. Reprinted by permission of Harper & Brothers.

of literature, it should surely be they. But even this was not enough to satisfy the young man. Disappointed in his hope that I would give him the fictional equivalent of "One Hundred Ways of Cooking Eggs" or the "Carnet de la Ménagère," [1] he began to cross-examine me about my methods of "collecting material." Did I keep a notebook or a daily journal? Did I jot down thoughts and phrases in a card-index? Did I systematically frequent the drawing-rooms of the rich and fashionable? Or did I, on the contrary, inhabit the Sussex downs? or spend my evenings looking for "copy" in East End [2] gin-palaces? Did I think it was wise to frequent the company of intellectuals? Was it a good thing for a writer of novels to try to be well educated, or should he confine his reading exclusively to other novels? And so on. I did my best to reply to these questions—as non-committally, of course, as I could. And as the young man still looked rather disappointed, I volunteered a final piece of advice, gratuitously. "My young friend," I said, "if you want to be a psychological novelist and write about human beings, the best thing you can do is to keep a pair of cats." And with that I left him.

(2) I hope, for his own sake, that he took my advice. For it was good advice—the fruit of much experience and many meditations. But I am afraid that, being a rather foolish young man, he merely laughed at what he must have supposed was only a silly joke: laughed, as I myself foolishly laughed when, years ago, that charming and talented extraordinary man, Ronald Firbank,[3] once told me that he wanted to write a novel about life in Mayfair and so was just off to the West Indies to look for copy among the Negroes. I laughed at the time; but I see now that he was quite right. Primitive people, like children and animals, are simply civilized people with the lid off, so to speak—the heavy elaborate lid of manners, conventions, traditions of thought and feeling beneath which each one of us passes his or her existence. This lid can be very conveniently studied in Mayfair, shall we say, or Passy,[4] or Park Avenue. But what goes on underneath the lid in these polished and elegant districts? Direct observation (unless we happen to be endowed

---

[1] Housekeeper's Manual.
[2] A less respectable section of London.
[3] A British novelist of some prominence in the 1920's.
[4] A smart district in Paris.

with a very penetrating intuition) tells us but little; and, if we cannot infer what is going on under other lids from what we see, introspectively, by peeping under our own, then the best thing we can do is to take the next boat for the West Indies, or else, less expensively, pass a few mornings in the nursery, or alternatively, as I suggested to my literary young friend, buy a pair of cats.

(3) Yes, a pair of cats. Siamese by preference; for they are certainly the most "human" of all the race of cats. Also the strangest, and, if not the most beautiful, certainly the most striking and fantastic. For what disquieting pale blue eyes stare out from the black velvet mask of their faces! Snow-white at birth, their bodies gradually darken to a rich mulatto colour. Their forepaws are gloved almost to the shoulder like the long black kid arms of Yvette Guilbert; [5] over their hind legs are tightly drawn the black silk stockings with which Félicien Rops [6] so perversely and indecently clothed his pearly nudes. Their tails, when they have tails—and I would always recommend the budding novelist to buy the tailed variety; for the tail, in cats, is the principal organ of emotional expression and a Manx cat is the equivalent of a dumb man —their tails are tapering black serpents endowed, even when the body lies in Sphinx-like repose, with a spasmodic and uneasy life of their own. And what strange voices they have! Sometimes like the complaining of small children; sometimes like the noise of lambs; sometimes like the agonized and furious howling of lost souls. Compared with these fantastic creatures, other cats, however beautiful and engaging, are apt to seem a little insipid.

(4) Well, having bought his cats, nothing remains for the would-be novelist but to watch them living from day to day; to mark, learn, and inwardly digest the lessons about human nature which they teach; and finally—for, alas, this arduous and unpleasant necessity always arises— finally write his book about Mayfair, Passy, or Park Avenue, whichever the case may be.

(5) Let us consider some of these instructive sermons in cats, from which the student of human psychology can learn so much. We will begin—as every good novel should begin, instead of absurdly ending

[5] A famous French singer of topical songs.
[6] A Belgian-French painter, engraver, and lithographer (1833–1898).

—with marriage. The marriage of Siamese cats, at any rate as I have observed it, is an extraordinarily dramatic event. To begin with, the introduction of the bridegroom to his bride (I am assuming that, as usually happens in the world of cats, they have not met before their wedding day) is the signal for a battle of unparalleled ferocity. The young wife's first reaction to the advances of her would-be husband is to fly at his throat. One is thankful, as one watches the fur flying and listens to the piercing yells of rage and hatred, that a kindly providence has not allowed these devils to grow any larger. Waged between creatures as big as men, such battles would bring death and destruction to everything within a radius of hundreds of yards. As things are, one is able, at the risk of a few scratches, to grab the combatants by the scruffs of their necks and drag them, still writhing and spitting, apart. What would happen if the newly-wedded pair were allowed to go on fighting to the bitter end I do not know, and have never had the scientific curiosity or the strength of mind to try to find out. I suspect that, contrary to what happened in Hamlet's family, the wedding baked meats would soon be serving for a funeral. I have always prevented this tragical consummation by simply shutting up the bride in a room by herself and leaving the bridegroom for a few hours to languish outside the door. He does not languish dumbly; but for a long time there is no answer, save an occasional hiss or growl, to his melancholy cries of love. When, finally, the bride begins replying in tones as soft and yearning as his own, the door may be opened. The bridegroom darts in and is received, not with tooth and claw as on the former occasion, but with every demonstration of affection.

(6) At first sight there would seem, in this specimen of feline behaviour, no special "message" for humanity. But appearances are deceptive; the lids under which civilized people live are so thick and so profusely sculptured with mythological ornaments, that it is difficult to recognize the fact, so much insisted upon by D. H. Lawrence in his novels and stories, that there is almost always a mingling of hate with the passion of love and that young girls very often feel (in spite of their sentiments and even their desires) a real abhorrence of the fact of physical love. Unlidded, the cats make manifest this ordinarily obscure mystery of human nature. After witnessing a cats' wedding, no

young novelist can rest content with the falsehood and banalities which pass, in current fiction, for descriptions of love.

(7) Time passes and, their honeymoon over, the cats begin to tell us things about humanity which even the lid of civilization cannot conceal in the world of men. They tell us—what, alas, we already know—that husbands soon tire of their wives, particularly when they are expecting or nursing families; that the essence of maleness is the love of adventure and infidelity; that guilty consciences and good resolutions are the psychological symptoms of that disease which spasmodically affects every male between the ages of eighteen and sixty—the disease called "the morning after"; and that with the disappearance of the disease the psychological symptoms also disappear, so that when temptation comes again, conscience is dumb and good resolutions count for nothing. All these unhappily too familiar truths are illustrated by the cats with a most comical absence of disguise. No man has ever dared to manifest his boredom so insolently as does a Siamese tom-cat, when he yawns in the face of his amorously importunate wife. No man has ever dared to proclaim his illicit amours so frankly as this same tom caterwauling on the tiles. And how slinkingly—no man was ever so abject—he returns next day to the conjugal basket by the fire! You can measure the guiltiness of his conscience by the angle of his back-pressed ears, the droop of his tail. And when, having sniffed him and so discovered his infidelity, his wife, as she always does on these occasions, begins to scratch his face (already scarred, like a German student's, with the traces of a hundred duels), he makes no attempt to resist; for, self-convicted of sin, he knows that he deserves all he is getting.

(8) It is impossible for me in the space at my disposal to enumerate all the human truths which a pair of cats can reveal or confirm. I will cite only one more of the innumerable sermons in cats which my memory holds—an acted sermon which, by its ludicrous pantomime, vividly brought home to me the most saddening peculiarity of our human nature, its irreducible solitariness. The circumstances were these. My she-cat, by now a wife of long standing, and several times a mother, was passing through one of her occasional phases of amorousness. Her husband, now in the prime of life and parading that sleepy arrogance

which is the characteristic of the mature and conquering male (he was now the feline equivalent of some herculean young Alcibiades of the Guards), refused to have anything to do with her. It was in vain that she uttered her love-sick mewing, in vain that she walked up and down in front of him rubbing herself voluptuously against doors and chair-legs as she passed, it was in vain that she came and licked his face. He shut his eyes, he yawned, he averted his head, or, if she became too importunate, got up and slowly, with an insulting air of dignity and detachment, stalked away. When the opportunity presented itself, he escaped and spent the next twenty-four hours upon the tiles. Left to herself, the wife went wandering disconsolately about the house, as though in search of a vanished happiness, faintly and plaintively mewing to herself in a voice and with a manner that reminded one irresistibly of Mélisande in Debussy's opera.[7] "Je ne suis pas heureuse ici," [8] she seemed to be saying. And, poor little beast, she wasn't. But, like her big sisters and brothers of the human world, she had to bear her unhappiness in solitude, uncomprehended, unconsoled. For in spite of language, in spite of intelligence and intuition and sympathy, one can never really communicate anything to anybody. The essential substance of every thought and feeling remains incommunicable, locked up in the impenetrable strong-room of the individual soul and body. Our life is a sentence of perpetual solitary confinement. This mournful truth was overwhelmingly borne in on me as I watched the abandoned and love-sick cat as she walked unhappily round my room. "Je ne suis pas heureuse ici," she kept mewing, "je ne suis pas heureuse ici." And her expressive black tail would lash the air in a tragical gesture of despair. But each time it twitched, houp-la! from under the arm-chair, from behind the bookcase, wherever he happened to be hiding at the moment, out jumped her only son (the only one, that is, we had not given away), jumped like a ludicrous toy tiger, all claws out, on to the moving tail. Sometimes he would miss, sometimes he caught it, and getting the tip between his teeth would pretend to worry it, absurdly ferocious. His mother would have to jerk it violently to get it out of his mouth. Then, he would go back under his armchair again

[7] *Pelleas and Melisande,* 1902.
[8] "I am not happy here."

and, crouching down, his hindquarters trembling, would prepare once more to spring. The tail, the tragical, despairingly gesticulating tail, was for him the most irresistible of playthings. The patience of the mother was angelical. There was never a rebuke or a punitive reprisal; when the child became too intolerable, she just moved away; that was all. And meanwhile, all the time, she went on mewing, plaintively, despairingly. "Je ne suis pas heureuse ici, je ne suis pas heureuse ici." It was heartbreaking. The more so as the antics of the kitten were so extraordinarily ludicrous. It was as though a slap-stick comedian had broken in on the lamentations of Mélisande—not mischievously, not wittingly, for there was not the smallest intention to hurt in the little cat's performance, but simply from lack of comprehension. Each was alone serving his life-sentence of solitary confinement. There was no communication from cell to cell. Absolutely no communication. These sermons in cats can be exceedingly depressing.

STUDY QUESTIONS

1. Is Mr. Huxley's title appropriate to his essay? What are its full implications?

2. What method of organization does Mr. Huxley use in arranging his remarks on cats? What is the effect gained by his arrangement?

3. Much of this essay is devoted to narration, yet the essay cannot be considered a narrative. Why not? What purposes do the narrative portions serve? How is the basic parable enhanced by narrating the life of a cat in chronological terms?

4. How does Mr. Huxley move from the question of how to be successful to the subject of cats?

5. Except for paragraph 4, Mr. Huxley's paragraphs are relatively long. Could this essay be divided into more paragraphs? If not, why not? If so, where would you make further divisions? What does the length of paragraphs have to do with the effectiveness of this essay? Of essays in general?

6. What analogy does Mr. Huxley make between the Firbank story in paragraph 2 and the adventures of his Siamese cats? How does Mr. Huxley go a step beyond Firbank in his advice to a young novelist?

7. What structural purpose does the emphasis on tails in paragraph 3 have in the essay as a whole?

8. What, according to Mr. Huxley, do cats teach us about human beings? How does Mr. Huxley manage to give a sense of the sadness of human life?

WRITING ASSIGNMENTS

1. Write a supplementary essay to Mr. Huxley's in which you introduce further sermons in cats.

2. Write a familiar essay based on comparison between human beings and another form of animal (dog, horse, turtle, etc.).

3. Write a serious reflective essay around this quotation from Mr. Huxley's last paragraph: "Our life is a sentence of perpetual solitary confinement."

4. Reread Mr. Huxley's second paragraph, and then write an essay on "the heavy elaborate lid of manners" as you have experienced it.

5. Mr. Huxley speaks of the "falsehood and banalities which pass, in current fiction, for descriptions of love." Write an essay in which you analyze in detail such descriptions of love in fiction, in the movies, or on the radio and TV.

Dusk in Fierce Pajamas *

E. B. WHITE (1899–   ), *a graduate of Cornell University, was for many years associated with the* New Yorker *magazine, for which he wrote most of the "Talk of the Town" column. He also wrote the column "One Man's Meat" for* Harper's Magazine *for a few years. His published books include* Is Sex Necessary? (1929, *with James Thurber*), Quo Vadimus (1939), *and* One Man's Meat (1942), *a collection of his pieces for* Harper's. *With his wife, he edited* A Sub-Treasury of American Humor (1941).

(1) Ravaged by pink eye, I lay for a week scarce caring whether I lived or died. Only Wamba, my toothless old black nurse, bothered to bring me food and quinine. Then one day my strength began to return, and with it came Wamba to my bedside with a copy of *Harper's Bazaar* and a copy of *Vogue*. "Ah brought you couple magazines," she said proudly, her red gums clashing.

(2) In the days that followed (happy days of renewed vigor and re-awakened interest), I studied the magazines and lived, in their pages, the gracious lives of the characters in the ever-moving drama of society and fashion. In them I found surcease from the world's ugliness, from disarray, from all unattractive things. Through them I escaped into a world in which there was no awkwardness of gesture, no unsuitability of line, no people of no importance. It was an enriching experience. I realize now that my own life is by contrast an unlovely thing, with its disease, its banalities, its uncertainties, its toil, its single-breasted suits, and its wine from lesser years. I am aware of a life all around me of graciousness and beauty, in which every moment is a tiny pearl of

good taste, and in which every acquaintance has the common decency
to possess a good background.

(3) Lying here in these fierce pajamas, I dream of the *Harper's
Bazaar* world, the *Vogue* life; dream of being a part of it. In fancy I
am in Mrs. Cecil Baker's pine-panelled drawing-room. It is dusk. (It
is almost always dusk in the fashion magazines.) I have on a Gantner
& Mattern knit jersey bathing suit with a flat-striped bow and an all-
white buck shoe with a floppy tongue. No, that's wrong. I am in chiffon,
for it is the magic hour after bridge. Suddenly a Chippendale mahogany
hors-d'oeuvre table is brought in. In its original old blue-and-white
Spode compartments there sparkle olives, celery, hard-boiled eggs,
radishes—evidently put there by somebody in the employ of Mrs.
Baker. Or perhaps my fancy wanders away from the drawing-room: I
am in Mrs. Baker's dining-room, mingling unostentatiously with the
other guests, my elbows resting lightly on the dark polished oak of the
Jacobean table, my fingers twiddling with the early Georgian silver. Or
perhaps I am not at Mrs. Baker's oak table in chiffon at all—perhaps
instead I am at Mrs. Jay Gould's teak-wood table in a hand-knitted
Anny Blatt ensemble in diluted tri-colors and an off-the-face hat.

(4) It is dusk. I am dining with Rose Hobart at the Waldorf. We
have lifted our champagne glasses. "To sentiment!" I say. And the
haunting dusk is shattered by the clean glint of jewels by Cartier.

(5) It is dusk. I am seated on a Bruce Buttfield pouf, for it is dusk.

(6) Ah, magazine dreams! How dear to me now are the four evenings in the life of Mrs. Allan Ryan, Junior. I have studied them one
by one, and I feel that I know them. They are perfect little crystals of
being—static, precious. There is the evening when she stands, motionless, in a magnificent sable cape, her left arm hanging gracefully at
her side. She is ready to go out to dinner. What will this, her first of
four evenings, bring of romance, or even of food? Then there is the
evening when she just sits on the edge of a settee from the Modernage
Galleries, the hard bright gleam of gold lamé topping a slim-straight,
almost Empire skirt. I see her there (the smoke from a cigarette rising),
sitting, sitting, waiting. Or the third evening—the evening with books.
Mrs. Ryan is in chiffon; the books are in morocco. Or the fourth eve-

ning, standing with her dachshund, herself in profile, the dog in full face.

(7) So I live the lives of other people in my fancy: the life of the daughter of Lord Curzon of Kedleston, who has been visiting the Harold Talbotts on Long Island. All I know of her is that she appeared one night at dinner, her beauty set off by the lustre of artificial satin and the watery fire of aquamarine. It is all I know, yet it is enough; for it is her one perfect moment in time and space, and I know about it, and it is mine.

(8) It is dusk. I am with Owen Johnson over his chafing dish. It is dusk. I am with Prince Matchabelli over his vodka. Or I am with the Countess de Forceville over her bridge tables. She and I have just pushed the tables against the wall and taken a big bite of gaspacho.[1] Or I am with the Marquis de Polignac over his Pommery.[2]

(9) How barren my actual life seems, when fancy fails me, here with Wamba over my quinine. Why am I not to be found at dusk, slicing black bread very thin, as William Powell does, to toast it and sprinkle it with salt? Why does not twilight find me (as it finds Mrs. Chester Burden) covering a table with salmon-pink linens on which I place only white objects, even to a white salt shaker? Why don't I learn to simplify my entertaining, like the young pinch-penny in V*ogue*, who has all his friends in before the theatre and simply gives them champagne cocktails, caviar, and one hot dish, then takes them to the show? Why do I never give parties after the opera, as Mr. Paul Cravath does, at which I have the prettiest women in New York? Come to think of it, why don't the prettiest women in New York ever come down to my place, other than that pretty little Mrs. Fazaenzi, whom Wamba won't let in? Why haven't I a butler named Fish, who makes a cocktail of three parts gin to one part lime juice, honey, vermouth, and apricot brandy in equal portions—a cocktail so delicious that people like Mrs. Harrison Williams and Mrs. Goodhue Livingston seek him out to get the formula? And if I *did* have a butler named Fish, wouldn't I kid the pants off him?

[1] A dish made of bread, oil, vinegar, onions, salt, and red pepper, all mixed together in water.
[2] A champagne wine.

(10) All over the world it is dusk! It is dusk at Armando's on East Fifty-fifth Street. Armando has taken up his accordion; he is dreaming over the keys. A girl comes in, attracted by the accordion, which she mistakes for Cecil Beaton's camera. She is in stiff green satin, and over it she wears a silver fox cape which she can pull around her shoulders later in the evening if she gets feeling like pulling a cape around her shoulders. It is dusk on the Harold Castles' ranch in Hawaii. I have risen early to shoot a goat, which is the smart thing to do in Hawaii. And now I am walking silently through hedges of gardenias, past the flaming ginger flowers, for I have just shot a goat. I have on nothing but red sandals and a Martex bath towel. It is dusk in the Laurentians. I am in ski togs. I feel warm and safe, knowing that the most dangerous pitfall for skiers is *color*, knowing that although a touch of brilliance against the snow is effective, too much of it is the sure sign of the amateur. It is the magic hour before cocktails. I am in the modern penthouse of Monsieur Charles de Beistegui. The staircase is entirely of cement, spreading at the hemline and trimmed with padded satin tubing caught at the neck with a bar of milk chocolate. It is dusk in Chicago. I am standing beside Mrs. Howard Linn, formerly Consuelo Vanderbilt, formerly Sophie M. Gay, formerly Ellen Glendinning, formerly Saks-Fifth Avenue. It is dusk! a pheasant has Julian Street down and is pouring a magnificent old red Burgundy down his neck. Dreams, I'm afraid. It is really dusk in my own apartment. I am down on my knees in front of an airbound radiator, trying to fix it by sticking pins in the vent. Dusk in these fierce pajamas. Kneeling here, I can't help wondering where Nancy Yuille is, in her blue wool pants and reefer and her bright red mittens. For it is dusk. I said *dusk*, Wamba!. Bring the quinine!

STUDY QUESTIONS

1. What is Mr. White parodying in this essay? What devices does he use to make his parody effective?
2. What is the function of the character Wamba?
3. What role does repetition play in this essay?

4. Most of this essay is cast as a fictional daydream. How is this fact indicated?

5. By what principle does Mr. White arrange the many details in his daydream? Does his point of view remain static throughout, or does it shift?

6. How does Mr. White connect the last paragraph of this essay with the first?

7. What is the tone of paragraph 2? At what points in the essay is this tone repeated?

8. What is conveyed by the phrase *wine from lesser years* (2)? What does it say of the author in terms of the world he is parodying?

9. What advantages does this form of criticism have over a direct, literal attack? What disadvantages?

WRITING ASSIGNMENTS

1. In imitation of Mr. White, write a parody of a Western story magazine, a woman's magazine, the radio soap opera, etc.

2. Write an analysis of the human species as it may be deduced from radio, TV, or magazine advertising.

3. Write a serious, literal, evaluation of one of our leading magazines.

4. Write an account of contemporary civilization as it is reflected in your local newspaper.

5. Write a research paper on some specific aspect of the history of fashion magazines.

Some Unsentimental Confessions
of a Nature Writer*

JOSEPH WOOD KRUTCH (1893–   ) *is Brander Matthews Professor of Dramatic Literature at Columbia University. For several years he has served as dramatic critic and associate editor of* The Nation. *His many books include such well-known works as* Comedy and Conscience After the Restoration *(1924),* Edgar Allan Poe: A Study in Genius *(1926),* The Modern Temper *(1929),* Five Masters *(1930),* Samuel Johnson *(1944),* Henry David Thoreau *(1948),* The Twelve Seasons *(1949), and* The Desert Year *(1952). He was one of the founders of the Literary Guild of America.*

(1) A few years ago I first laid myself open to the charge of being a "nature writer." Perhaps in time I shall know better what it is that I am trying to do and why I do it. At the moment I still do not know precisely what a "nature writer" is.

(2) A great many people, I am afraid, do not even care to know. When they hear the phrase they think of "the birds and the bees"—a useful device in the sex education of children but hardly, they think, an occupation for a grown man. A biologist is all right and so is a sportsman. But a "nature writer" can hardly expect more than a shrug from the realistic and the robust.

(3) The more literary quote Wordsworth: "Nature never did betray the heart that loved her" or, "The meanest flower that blows for me oft holds a thought too deep for tears." But Darwin, they say, exploded

---

* From the New York *Herald Tribune Book Review*, June 15, 1952. Copyright 1952 by the New York *Herald Tribune*. Reprinted by permission of the author and the New York *Herald Tribune*.

such ideas nearly a century ago. Even Tennyson knew better: "Nature red in tooth and claw." We can't learn anything from all that. These are desperate times. The only hope for today lies in the study of politics, sociology, and economics. If a nature writer is some one who advocates a return to nature then he must be a sentimentalist and a very old-fashioned one at that.

(4) This is a serious charge. When I hear it I am tempted to reply only that if I discovered a certain pleasure in writing about nature and if a few like to read me, it at least does nobody any harm. My books will not contribute to juvenile delinquency, be banned in Boston, or investigated by any loyalty board. But though that satisfies some of my friends it does not entirely satisfy me. I have spent most of my life with literary criticism and history. Why should I have discovered that my week-ends and my summers in the country were becoming more and more important; that I spent more and more time looking at and thinking about plants and animals and birds; that I began to feel the necessity of writing about what I had seen and thought? Why, finally, when I saw fifteen free months ahead of me, should I have been sure that I wanted to go back to the Southwestern desert to see what an entirely different, only half known natural environment might have to say to me.

(5) It was more than a mere casual interest in natural history as a hobby. Certainly it was also more than the mere fact that the out-of-doors is healthful and relaxing. I was not merely being soothed and refreshed by an escape from the pressures of urban life. I was seeking for something, and got at least the conviction that there was something I was actually learning. I seemed to be getting a glimpse of some wisdom of which I had less than an inkling before.

(6) Perhaps I can put the answer abstractly and a little bit pompously something like this. Man is after all a part of nature. Life is a mystery and an adventure which he shares with all living things. The only clew to himself is in them. The universe is divided into two parts: that which is living and that which remains dead. We ought to be fully aware of which side we are on and of what it means to be on that side.

(7) Yet as civilization becomes more complicated we have less and less to do with the things which are on our side. We live in cities sur-

rounded by dead things. We deal far more with machines than we do with animals. The principal context of our lives has come to be dead matter, not living matter. And under these circumstances we tend more and more to lose sight of what we are and of what we are like. Even the graphic and plastic arts are forsaking nature so that the wheel and the lever are more familiar than the flower or the leaf. An attitude which became fully explicit at the Renaissance seems to be in the process of disappearing.

(8) Perhaps that is the real reason why we have tended more and more to think about man and society as though they were machines; why we have mechanistic theories about consciousness and about human behavior in general. Perhaps that fact is one of the things which make us unhappy and anxious because in our depths we know that we are not machines, that we are more like the animals with which we have so little to do than like the mechanical contrivances we have surrounded ourselves by. Perhaps it is even one of the reasons why totalitarianism spreads, since the theory of the totalitarian state is that men can and should be manipulated as though they were machines, not permitted to grow as organisms grow. The question used to be whether or not men had souls. The question now seems to be whether or not they are alive at all; but that is seldom asked any more. In a city we may doubt it. In the presence of nature we cannot.

(9) I do not mean that we should all go live on Walden Pond.[1] I am not any kind of crank or any kind of Utopian reformer. I do not believe that the solution to the world's ills is a return to some previous age of mankind. But I do doubt that any solution is possible unless we think of ourselves in the context of living nature.

(10) Perhaps that suggests an answer to the question what a "nature writer" is. He is not a sentimentalist who says that "nature never did betray the heart that loved her." Neither is he simply a scientist classifying animals or reporting on the behavior of birds just because certain facts can be ascertained. He is a writer whose subject is the natural context of human life, a man who tries to communicate his

[1] The pond in Massachusetts made famous by Henry David Thoreau, who built a hut near the pond, lived there for two years by the labor of his own hands, and recorded his observations in the book *Walden*, published in 1854.

observations and his thoughts in the presence of nature as part of his attempt to make himself more aware of that context. "Nature writing" is nothing really new. It has always existed in literature. But it has tended in the course of the last century to become specialized partly because so much writing that is not specifically "nature writing" does not present the natural context at all; because so many novels and so many treatises describe man as an economic unit, a political unit, or as a member of some social class but not as a living creature surrounded by other living things.

(11) There are few men who have never looked at a kitten and thought it was cute or looked at the stars and felt themselves small. Whoever has done either has been aware of the context of nature and that is good as far as it goes. But it does not go very far and there is little in modern life, not too much in modern literature or modern art, to make him go further. What the "nature writer" is really asking him to do is to explore what such thoughts and such feelings mean. Nearly every one admits that literature and art have something to say that science and sociology cannot. But nature in her turn has something to say beyond the reach of literature and art. To that something the nature writer asks us to open our minds and our hearts precisely as another kind of writer asks us to open them to art or music or literature.

(12) That is, at least, what I am asking myself to do when I write about a year in Connecticut or a year in the desert, about the courtship of lizards, or the desert toad who seems to spend four-fifths of his life holed up in the sand not dreading but waiting for a rainy day. He is interesting primarily because he is playing his part in an inconceivable adventure in which we are all somehow involved.

(13) One of the things which I remember best from my year in the West is a day spent alone on a mountain top looking down at a desert. Half seriously I said to myself that this was my great chance. Moses and Zarathustra did just that. Most of the prophets have retired either to a mountain or to a desert. If ever, I thought, you are to get The Answer it ought to be now.

(14) I did not get it. These days, I suppose, no one ever does. This is not an age when men appear to hear the voice of God. But I do not

think that I ever before understood myself so well and with the understanding came a conviction. We cannot understand other people or the world unless we do understand ourselves first. It is presumption and folly to advise, and direct, and legislate unless we at least know our own selves. But we do not understand ourselves unless we have been alone with ourselves and with that nature of which we are more a part than we usually seem to remember.

(15) Alone on a mountain top no one ever believed that Man is nothing but the product of economic forces or that production per man hour is a reliable index of human welfare. And surely no man on a mountain top ever believed that Good and Evil are nothing except the prejudices of a given society. Such dismal, such deadly, opinions are possible only to those who do not know human beings because they do not know themselves and do not know themselves because they have never been alone with themselves. This will never be a world in which a good life is possible for most people as long as dismal and deadly opinions predominate. And the nature writer, like the poet and like the priest, is their enemy.

(16) I do not mean to suggest that the nature writer always is or always should be on the mountain tops, either literally or figuratively. No one who actually looks at nature rather than at some fancy projected upon or read into her can ever fail to realize that she represents some ultimate things-as-they-are not some ideal of things-as-he-thinks-they-ought-to-be. There is in her what we call cruelty and also, even more conspicuously, what we call grotesqueness and what we call comedy. If she warns the so-called realist how limited his conception of reality is she is no less likely to bring the sentimentalist back, literally, to earth.

(17) How much of the cruelty, of the grotesqueness, or of the sublimity any given man will see depends no doubt to some considerable extent upon his own temperament and I suppose it is some indication of mine when I confess that what I see most often and relish the most is, first, the intricate marvel and, second, the comedy. To be reminded that one is very much like other members of the animal kingdom is often funny though it is never, like being compared to a machine, merely humiliating. I do not too much mind being somewhat

like a cat, a dog, or even an insect but I resent having it said that even an electronic calculator is like me.

(18) Not very long ago I was pointing out to a friend the courtship of two spiders in a web just outside my door. Most people know that the male is often much smaller than his mate and nearly everybody knows by now that the female of many species sometimes eats her husband. Both of these things were true of the common kind beside my door and the insignificant male was quite obviously torn between ardor and caution. He danced forward and then darted back. He approached now from one side and now from the other. He would and he wouldn't.

(19) My friend, no nature student and not much given to observing such creatures, was gratifyingly interested. Presently he could contain himself no longer.

(20) "You know," he said thoughtfully, "there is only one difference between that spider and a human male. The spider knows it's dangerous."

(21) That, I maintain, both is and ought to be as much grist for a nature writer's mill as a sunset or a bird song.

STUDY QUESTIONS

1. What do you think Mr. Krutch means by the term *unsentimental* in his title? What does the term *Confessions* suggest about the approach to be used?

2. Which paragraphs constitute the introduction of this essay? What idea or ideas is Mr. Krutch concerned with in his introduction?

3. Part of Mr. Krutch's development of his thesis consists of elaborating the contrast between his view of man and the view he opposes. What are these contrasting views? Could Mr. Krutch have presented his views without explicit discussion of the contrasting view? What is gained by developing the contrast?

4. In paragraph 4, Mr. Krutch mentions a line of defense he can use in justification of nature writing, but he indicates that it does not satisfy him. Why not?

5. In paragraph 17, Mr. Krutch remarks that he personally most relishes the intricacy and the comedy in nature. What do you think he means? Cite specific examples of natural events or phenomena which you think illustrate those aspects of nature.

6. What kind of development is employed in the following paragraphs: 5, 7, 8, 11? How is each of these paragraphs connected to the paragraph preceding it? Analyze one of those paragraphs closely to determine how much variety has been imparted to the sentence structure.

7. Is Mr. Krutch dogmatic in stating his views? Cite specific examples of his phraseology to support your answer.

8. How does the final anecdote sum up Mr. Krutch's point? Do you consider this an effective way of ending the essay? Why or why not?

WRITING ASSIGNMENTS

1. Write a defense of or an attack upon the topic of Mr. Krutch's seventh paragraph.

2. Write an essay on the comedy in nature.

3. Write an analysis of the role played in your life by machines.

4. Write an account of your reaction to a natural phenomenon (mountain-top, desert, river, etc.).

5. Write a research paper on one of the following nature writers: Joseph Wood Krutch, Henry David Thoreau, John Burroughs, John Muir, Donald Culross Peattie, Alan Devoe.

Preface to The Nigger of the Narcissus*

JOSEPH CONRAD (1857–1924), *famous English novelist, was born in Poland as Teodor Josef Konrad Korzeniowski. Instead of entering the university after finishing school at Cracow, he went to sea, where he served for twenty years, first as a sailor and finally as a master in the British merchant marine. In 1894 he retired from the sea to devote the remainder of his life to writing. Soon fame came to him with* The Nigger of the Narcissus, *which first appeared in serial form in the* New Review *in 1897. Appended to the last installment was the Preface which is printed here. Among his later novels are* Lord Jim (1900), Nostromo (1904), *and* Victory (1915). Youth (1902) *and* Typhoon (1903) *established his fame as a writer of short stories.*

(1) A work that aspires, however humbly, to the condition of art should carry its justification in every line. And art itself may be defined as a single-minded attempt to render the highest kind of justice to the visible universe, by bringing to light the truth, manifold and one, underlying its every aspect. It is an attempt to find in its forms, in its colours, in its light, in its shadows, in the aspects of matter and in the facts of life what of each is fundamental, what is enduring and essential—their one illuminating and convincing quality—the very truth of their existence. The artist, then, like the thinker or the scientist, seeks the truth and makes his appeal. Impressed by the aspect of the world the thinker plunges into ideas, the scientist into facts—whence, presently, emerging they make their appeal to those qualities of our being that fit us best for the hazardous enterprise of living. They speak authoritatively to our common-sense, to our intelligence, to our desire of

* From *The Nigger of the Narcissus,* 1897 (printed serially in the *New Review*), by Joseph Conrad. Reprinted by permission of J. M. Dent & Sons, Ltd.

peace or to our desire of unrest; not seldom to our prejudices, some-times to our fears, often to our egoism—but always to our credulity. And their words are heard with reverence, for their concern is with weighty matters: with the cultivation of our minds and the proper care of our bodies, with the attainment of our ambitions, with the perfection of the means and the glorification of our precious aims.

(2) It is otherwise with the artist.

(3) Confronted by the same enigmatical spectacle the artist descends within himself, and in that lonely region of stress and strife, if he be deserving and fortunate, he finds the terms of his appeal. His appeal is made to our less obvious capacities: to that part of our nature which, because of the warlike conditions of existence, is necessarily kept out of sight within the more resisting and hard qualities—like the vulnerable body within a steel armour. His appeal is less loud, more profound, less distinct, more stirring—and sooner forgotten. Yet its effect endures forever. The changing wisdom of successive generations discards ideas, questions facts, demolishes theories. But the artist appeals to that part of our being which is not dependent on wisdom: to that in us which is a gift and not an acquisition—and, therefore, more permanently enduring. He speaks to our capacity for delight and wonder, to the sense of mystery surrounding our lives; to our sense of pity, and beauty, and pain; to the latent feeling of fellowship with all creation—and to the subtle but invincible conviction of solidarity that knits together the loneliness of innumerable hearts, to the solidarity in dreams, in joy, in sorrow, in aspirations, in illusions, in hope, in fear, which binds men to each other, which binds together all humanity—the dead to the living and the living to the unborn.

(4) It is only some such train of thought, or rather of feeling, that can in a measure explain the aim of the attempt, made in the tale which follows, to present an unrestful episode in the obscure lives of a few individuals out of all the disregarded multitude of the bewildered, the simple and the voiceless. For, if any part of truth dwells in the belief confessed above, it becomes evident that there is not a place of splendour or a dark corner of the earth that does not deserve, if only a passing glance of wonder and pity. The motive then, may be held to justify the matter of the work; but this preface, which is simply an

avowal of endeavour, cannot end here—for the avowal is not yet complete.

(5) Fiction—if it at all aspires to be art—appeals to temperament. And in truth it must be, like painting, like music, like all art, the appeal of one temperament to all the other innumerable temperaments whose subtle and resistless power endows passing events with their true meaning, and creates the moral, the emotional atmosphere of the place and time. Such an appeal to be effective must be an impression conveyed through the senses; and, in fact, it cannot be made in any other way, because temperament, whether individual or collective, is not amenable to persuasion. All art, therefore, appeals primarily to the senses, and the artistic aim when expressing itself in written words must also make its appeal through the senses, if its high desire is to reach the secret spring of responsive emotions. It must strenuously aspire to the plasticity of sculpture, to the colour of painting, and to the magic suggestiveness of music—which is the art of arts. And it is only through complete, unswerving devotion to the perfect blending of form and substance; it is only through an unremitting never-discouraged care for the shape and ring of sentences that an approach can be made to plasticity, to colour, and that the light of magic suggestiveness may be brought to play for an evanescent instant over the commonplace surface of words: of the old, old words, worn thin, defaced by ages of careless usage.

(6) The sincere endeavour to accomplish that creative task, to go as far on that road as his strength will carry him, to go undeterred by faltering, weariness or reproach, is the only valid justification for the worker in prose. And if his conscience is clear, his answer to those who in the fulness of a wisdom which looks for immediate profit, demand specifically to be edified, consoled, amused; who demand to be promptly improved, or encouraged, or frightened, or shocked, or charmed, must run thus:—My task which I am trying to achieve is, by the power of the written word to make you hear, to make you feel—it is, before all, to make you *see*. That—and no more, and it is everything. If I succeed, you shall find there according to your deserts: encouragement, consolation, fear, charm—all you demand—and, perhaps, also that glimpse of truth for which you have forgotten to ask.

(7) To snatch in a moment of courage, from the remorseless rush of time, a passing phase of life, is only the beginning of the task. The task approached in tenderness and faith is to hold up unquestioningly, without choice and without fear, the rescued fragment before all eyes in the light of a sincere mood. It is to show its vibration, its colour, its form; and through its movement, its form, and its colour, reveal the substance of its truth—disclose its inspiring secret: the stress and passion within the core of each convincing moment. In a single-minded attempt of that kind, if one be deserving and fortunate, one may perchance attain to such clearness of sincerity that at last the presented vision of regret or pity, of terror or mirth, shall awaken in the hearts of the beholders that feeling of unavoidable solidarity; of the solidarity in mysterious origin, in toil, in joy, in hope, in uncertain fate, which binds men to each other and all mankind to the visible world.

(8) It is evident that he who, rightly or wrongly, holds by the convictions expressed above cannot be faithful to any one of the temporary formulas of his craft. The enduring part of them—the truth which each only imperfectly veils—should abide with him as the most precious of his possessions, but they all: Realism, Romanticism, Naturalism, even the unofficial sentimentalism (which like the poor, is exceedingly difficult to get rid of), all these gods must, after a short period of fellowship, abandon him—even on the very threshold of the temple—to the stammerings of his conscience and to the outspoken consciousness of the difficulties of his work. In that uneasy solitude the supreme cry of Art for Art itself, loses the exciting ring of its apparent immorality. It sounds far off. It has ceased to be a cry, and is heard only as a whisper, often incomprehensible, but at times and faintly encouraging.

(9) Sometimes, stretched at ease in the shade of a roadside tree, we watch the motions of a labourer in a distant field, and after a time, begin to wonder languidly as to what the fellow may be at. We watch the movements of his body, the waving of his arms, we see him bend down, stand up, hesitate, begin again. It may add to the charm of an idle hour to be told the purpose of his exertions. If we know he is trying to lift a stone, to dig a ditch, to uproot a stump, we look with

a more real interest at his efforts; we are disposed to condone the jar of his agitation upon the restfulness of the landscape; and even, if in a brotherly frame of mind, we may bring ourselves to forgive his failure. We understood his object, and, after all, the fellow has tried, and perhaps he had not the strength—and perhaps he had not the knowledge. We forgive, go on our way—and forget.

(10) And so it is with the workman of art. Art is long and life is short, and success is very far off. And thus, doubtful of strength to travel so far, we talk a little about the aim—the aim of art, which, like life itself, is inspiring, difficult—obscured by mists. It is not in the clear logic of a triumphant conclusion; it is not in the unveiling of one of those heartless secrets which are called the Laws of Nature. It is not less great, but only more difficult.

(11) To arrest, for the space of a breath, the hands busy about the work of the earth, and compel men entranced by the sight of distant goals to glance for a moment at the surrounding vision of form and colour, of sunshine and shadows; to make them pause for a look, for a sigh, for a smile—such is the aim, difficult and evanescent, and reserved only for a very few to achieve. But sometimes, by the deserving and the fortunate, even that task is accomplished. And when it is accomplished—behold!—all the truth of life is there: a moment of vision, a sigh, a smile—and the return to an eternal rest.

STUDY QUESTIONS

1. What is *The Nigger of the Narcissus?* To what extent is that information necessary for an understanding of this essay?

2. State the topic of each paragraph in one sentence. With those topic sentences as a guide, summarize Conrad's concept of literary art in a short paragraph.

3. What effect is gained by the brevity of paragraph 2?

4. How does Conrad use the imaginary scene in paragraph 9 in the remainder of the essay?

5. Take any paragraph from this essay (except 2) and list its adjectives and verbs. Which part of speech carries more force? Why?

6. Study carefully Conrad's use of parallelism in the sentence begin-

ning "They speak authoritatively . . ." in paragraph 1. How does he avoid monotony in his listing of prepositional phrases? What principle of order does he follow in his listing?

7. Study carefully the first sentence in paragraph 11. What kind of sentence is it: simple, complex, or compound? What use is made of parallelism of structure? How is the rhythm of the sentence related to its structure? Rewrite the sentence with *the aim* as its subject followed by the verb and the series of infinitives as the predicate. Can you feel the rhythmic difference between the original and the rewritten versions?

8. What is the difference in meaning between the words *gift* and *acquisition* in paragraph 3? What point does the contrast so simply make?

9. Because Conrad writes largely in terms of general concepts, the reader must study his statements with great care to get at their meaning. What, for instance, do you think Conrad means by the following terms: *justice* (1), *truth* (1), *our less obvious capacities* (3)? Select a few other examples of such general terms. Try writing a one-paragraph definition of one of them.

10. On the basis of this essay, what would you say Conrad means by *art*?

WRITING ASSIGNMENTS

1. Upon the basis of the distinction which Conrad makes in paragraphs 1–3 between the ways in which the scientist and the artist make their respective appeals, write an analysis of the social value of the artist.

2. Write an analysis of the problems which an artist of Conrad's description faces today in trying to practice his art.

3. Write an analysis of the relationship between the artist and the scientist, a paper in which you decide whether they are opposed in their interests and their accomplishments or whether instead they can profitably collaborate in their endeavors.

4. Write a fully developed essay on the subject of Conrad's third paragraph.

5. Write a research paper on Joseph Conrad.

Nobel Prize Award Speech*

WILLIAM FAULKNER (1897–   ), one of the foremost American novelists today, was born and educated in Mississippi. During the first World War he served in the British Royal Air Force. His fame in America and abroad has arisen from such novels as Soldiers' Pay (1926), The Sound and the Fury (1929), As I Lay Dying (1930), Sanctuary (1931), Light in August (1932), The Hamlet (1940), Intruder in the Dust (1948), and Requiem for a Nun (1951). In recognition of his achievement as an artist, he was awarded the Nobel Prize for Literature in 1949.

(1) I feel that this award was not made to me as a man but to my work—a life's work in the agony and sweat of the human spirit, not for glory and least of all for profit, but to create out of the materials of the human spirit something which did not exist before. So this award is only mine in trust. It will not be difficult to find a dedication for the money part of it commensurate with the purpose and significance of its origin. But I would like to do the same with the acclaim too, by using this moment as a pinnacle from which I might be listened to by the young men and women already dedicated to the same anguish and travail, among whom is already that one who will some day stand here where I am standing.

(2) Our tragedy today is a general and universal physical fear so long sustained by now that we can even bear it. There are no longer problems of the spirit. There is only the question: when will I be blown up? Because of this, the young man or woman writing today

* Given by Mr. Faulkner upon acceptance of the Nobel Prize for Literature in Stockholm, Sweden, on December 10, 1950. Reprinted by courtesy of Random House, Inc.

has forgotten the problems of the human heart in conflict with itself which alone can make good writing because only that is worth writing about, worth the agony and the sweat.

(3) He must learn them again. He must teach himself that the basest of all things is to be afraid; and, teaching himself that, forget it forever, leaving no room in his workshop for anything but the old verities and truths of the heart, the old universal truths lacking which any story is ephemeral and doomed—love and honor and pity and pride and compassion and sacrifice. Until he does so he labors under a curse. He writes not of love but of lust, of defeats in which nobody loses anything of value, of victories without hope and worst of all without pity or compassion. His griefs grieve on no universal bones, leaving no scars. He writes not of the heart but of the glands.

(4) Until he relearns these things he will write as though he stood among and watched the end of man. I decline to accept the end of man. It is easy enough to say that man is immortal simply because he will endure; that when the last ding-dong of doom has clanged and faded from the last worthless rock hanging tideless in the last red and dying evening, that even then there will still be one more sound: that of his puny inexhaustible voice, still talking. I refuse to accept this. I believe that man will not merely endure: he will prevail. He is immortal, not because he alone among creatures has an inexhaustible voice, but because he has a soul, a spirit capable of compassion and sacrifice and endurance. The poet's, the writer's, duty is to write about these things. It is his privilege to help man endure by lifting his heart, by reminding him of the courage and honor and hope and pride and compassion and pity and sacrifice which have been the glory of his past. The poet's voice need not merely be the record of man, it can be one of the props, the pillars to help him endure and prevail.

ings he made directly from visions (we have no reason to doubt his own testimony) bear the marks of automatic transcripts; they look like tracings and are less expressive in outline than those which he perfected by conscious labor.

(5) If then it is true, as these examples seem to suggest, that criticism can be a creative force in the very making of a work of art, it is not surprising to find that the finished work embodies a critical canon. This canon defines the aesthetic rules by which the particular work is to be judged, but in so doing, it implicitly reflects on the canons adopted by other artists. There is thus a persistent contention in progress, a "battle of the books," as Swift so happily put it, or in Hogarth's words a "battle of the pictures," a great *paragone* [4] which in the field of music as well divides composers into camps and factions. While the polemical labeling of these camps may be a comparatively recent custom (so far as I know, it has been a fairly regular practice only for the last three hundred and fifty years), the cause for these divisions is far from frivolous. If the artist is an intelligent craftsman, he will want to explore the principles of his craft; and it is only natural that those "rules" and "devices," once the guarded treasure of cautious guilds, should be debated with dialectical zest by a liberally emancipated profession.

(6) A work of art is thus loaded with critical matter, with technicalities to agitate the grammarians. And I hope I am not disrespectful in suggesting that every artist of stature harbors within himself not only a critic but one or two hidden grammarians as well. But when these come to the fore, the battle may deteriorate into an argument about syntax, a travesty of Balzac's "Comme un sentiment est logique!" [5] The work of art then becomes a specimen that is prepared for inspection by the curious, and proves readily acceptable to professional botanists who divide the specimens into classes, arrange each class as a perfect series, and discover that each member of the series produces new members by a mysterious form of parthenogenesis.

(7) But fortunately works of art are not made for artists alone, nor (which would be worse) for historians of art, but for a public on which

[4] Comparison.
[5] "How logical a feeling is!"

they have an immediate, occasionally a profound, and at times a radically disturbing effect. They intrude into our so-called normal life, upset our standards, confuse our perspectives, arouse emotions we never knew, ignore sensibilities we have learned to cherish. In short, art is a vital form of interference, a "nuisance" which, if carried far enough, may extend even to the sacred regions generally entrusted to men of affairs and which are hence supposed to be well-secured against any inroads by the imagination. If I understood my assignment correctly, it is this mischievous nature of art, its role as a critical *enfant terrible*, which was primarily intended by the title of this paper. I shall attempt to do it justice, but I am afraid that this will lead me into offending some of the idols of the schools.

(8) We have all been told by our aesthetic masters that the artist transfigures whatever he touches, that the all-too solid matter of this world melts away in the crucible of artistic creation. We have been promised, if only we submit to the conjuror's spell, that he will remove us from all terrestrial concerns and leave us transfixed in the contemplation of an ideal figment, which we can retain in its purity only so long as we allow it to subsist in perfect isolation. It is awkward to disturb such a happy dream; but idealism in matters of art has a family resemblance with its more common sister—it tells the truth, but only half of it. No one would wish to deny the strictly aesthetic qualities of a work of art, or to detract from its cathartic power. But while it is true that the artist transfigures our sensations, it is equally certain that they are also intensified by him. Consequently, the work of art has the power not merely to purge but also to incite emotions, to arouse a higher sense of awareness which may far outlast the artistic experience and become a force in shaping our conduct.

(9) When Baudelaire wrote his prefaces to *Les Fleurs du Mal*,[6] he protested in vain that this book was but an innocent exercise, designed to demonstrate how an exquisite artistry can transfigure an offensive theme. While he derided the vulgarity of those scribblers who make it a business to "mix up ink with virtue" ("à confondre l'encre avec la vertu"), his own desire to mix up ink with vice and infuse a poetic glory into evil, entailed commitments which he did

---

[6] *The Flowers of Evil.*

not care to evade: "Le sujet fait pour l'artiste une partie du genie, et pour moi, barbare malgré tout, une partie du plaisir." [7] The most sophisticated of poets, "barbare malgre tout," thus conceded his affinity to a savage. Like a primitive chieftain, he sensed that he could mold the conduct of a tribe by the sheer force of an incantation.

(10) For the "critical nature of a work of art," this barbaric strain is of the utmost importance; for it invests the artist with a unique power to sting. There is no appeal against a verdict clad in a song. Hence the insouciant vitality of polemic art as illustrated, for instance, in Heine. In a political fantasy, which he called *Ein Wintermärchen*,[8] he warned the king of Prussia that if he did not rescind his reactionary policies, he would write a poem in the manner of Dante's *Inferno*, where the king would find himself roasting in hell. And Heine took this occasion to inform the king that the hell of the poets is far more terrible than the fires prepared by theologians; for no god can redeem those who are incarcerated in Dante's awful tercets (*schreckliche Terzetten*).

(11) Theologians, it is true, have made equally extravagant claims for their own doctrine of eternal damnation, but even the most orthodox would have to admit that there has been an occasional exception. The emperor Trajan, a pagan and hence unbaptized, was at first quite fittingly placed in hell; but when St. Gregory read of his singular merits, and realized that these could not save him from perpetual languishment, he was so moved by pity that he began to cry, and his tears served as a posthumous baptism, by which the emperor was cleansed and released. But even St. Gregory might find it difficult to rescue anyone from the *Inferno*. The perfect cadence of the poet's phrase, the precision and vigor of his image, impress themselves upon the memory of men, from which they cannot be dislodged. From great art there is no redemption.

(12) If this is true, the poet's "singing flames" may prove a very

[7] From an essay on landscape painting in the "Salon of 1859." The sentence quoted is actually the last half of Baudelaire's sentence, which may be translated as follows: "You see, my dear friend, that I can never consider the choice of subject as a matter of indifference, and that in spite of the love necessary to impregnate the humblest piece, I believe that for the artist the subject is a part of his genius and for me, a barbarian in spite of everything, a part of my pleasure."

[8] A *Winter Fairytale*.

perilous way of dispensing justice; for there is no certainty that his power of expression is always matched by his power of insight. Beauty is not always Truth; and when it becomes the vehicle of falsehood or error, it endows them with an attractiveness which the imagination of centuries may be unable to resist. To this day, for example, it is proper to think of Lucrezia Borgia as a kind of incestuous monster. Yet, as a matter of plain historical fact, Lucrezia Borgia was modest, well-behaved, and inclined to be humble rather than assertive. She was a faithful wife and an affectionate mother. As duchess of Ferrara, she was respected and beloved, and sufficiently versed in the art of government to serve as a competent regent in the absence of her husband. Altogether her conduct was so irreproachable that Ercole d'Este's [9] rather critical ambassador could only report that she was somewhat colorless. How then did this fantastic legend originate? It was the invention of a poet—Sannazzaro. The Aragonese, engaged in a good political quarrel with the Borgias, were not satisfied with fighting them on the battlefield. They also enlisted in their service this most excellent of Italian versifiers, who wrote epigrams so vicious and at the same time so brilliant that even the skepticism of Guiccardini [10] could not resist the poetic contagion. The infection spread as far as the nineteenth century, when Victor Hugo wrote a drama, Donizetti composed an opera, and Rossetti painted a picture of Lucrezia Borgia, all of them glorifying her legendary vices.

(13) Against this conspiracy of the arts the truth proved powerless, even though temporal interests were no longer served by the fiction. The polemic point had completely vanished. Only the aesthetic image remained. In vain did a succession of meticulous scholars—Roscoe, Campori, Gregorovius—attempt to explode the fable. It was left for John Addington Symonds, the celebrated historian of the Italian Renaissance, to obscure their efforts by a dazzling somersault. Determined to show that he could fly like a poet along an elegant curve, and yet land on his feet like an historian, he placed the evidence squarely before the reader, explaining that "history has at last done justice to the memory of this woman"; but as he elaborated the theme, the poet

[9] The father of Lucrezia Borgia's husband, Anthony d'Este.
[10] Sixteenth-century Italian historian and statesman.

got the better of him, and he concluded his account with the Pythian [11] remark: "It is even probable that the darkest tales about her are true."

> Les dieux eux-mêmes meurent,
> Mais les vers souverains
> Demeurent
> Plus forts que les airains.[12]

(14) It might be argued that there is a simple remedy for these abuses. Why not plainly separate fiction from fact, and let each of them reign in its proper sphere? Let Victor Hugo declaim, and Donizetti sing, and Rossetti paint their figments. There can be no harm in their distortion of the truth, as long as we understand this to be *poetic license*. Meanwhile, truth can proceed on its sober path, unperturbed by the rage of poets.

(15) The remedy sounds plausible enough in the abstract, but the pity is that it will not work. When imagination and understanding are applied to the same object (as they often happily are), they cannot fail to reflect on each other. Sannazzaro's epigrams acquire a new facet of wit by our knowing that he was a liar, but the effect of Hugo's oratory is impaired if we begin to question his good sense. In other words, what we *know* about Lucrezia Borgia, has some influence on what we are willing to *believe* about her, and affects even our acceptance of *make-believe*. And conversely, the fancies with which artists have filled our minds cannot be banished by an act of will or safely quarantined when we begin to think in earnest. Nor is it desirable that it should be otherwise. The cure proposed, if it were effective, would produce a really fatal disease, a kind of schizophrenia, in which the intellect ignores what the imagination pictures, and the imagination disregards what the intellect knows; both functions helplessly coexisting in a distracted mind.

(16) But even at its best, as a brief of freedom, an absolute grant of poetic license would fatally narrow the scope of art. It would reduce art to the level of an irrelevant pastime, a pleasant caprice unrelated to any basic impulse, suited perhaps for embellishing our leisure, but

[11] I.e., with the authority of an oracle.
[12] "The gods themselves die, but sovereign verses remain, stronger than bronze." A stanza from Theophile Gautier's poem "L'Art" first published in 1857.

quickly forgotten when we settle down to serious business. The artist would be thus deprived of his greatest function, that of an explorer who can widen the understanding by probing into those darker repositories of experience which are not directly accessible to the intellect, and yet are indispensable to its working.

(17) While the power of art to shape our judgment is quite unmistakable when the aim of the artist is avowedly polemic, we have seen that the polemic intent can vanish and the infectious process continue unimpaired. The image exerts by itself a kind of barbaric fascination. And the same applies, I believe, to the power of pure music, that is, to an art which no longer depends on either words or images to arouse our passions, but on sounds and rhythms alone. It might seem, indeed, that pure aesthetics would be safe in this particular field. But despite the detachment of sounds from things, the artist retains even here his peculiar capability to affect our understanding and mold our conduct. Let us suppose we had never heard Sarastro [13] speak or sing, but knew Mozart's music only in its pure form, in chamber music or symphonies. Would it not be permissible to argue that the particular kind of sensibility and attention which is developed by listening to these works, has a natural affinity with the humane morality of Sarastro? Though not verbally equivalent to Sarastro's philosophy, the music of Mozart may perhaps be said to be favorable to a similar blending of rationality with compassion, and of relentless penetration with good humor and wit. And conversely: Do we require the verbal ejaculations of Tristan to sense that Wagner's music, by itself, has a raw potency of emotion which, if regularly inhaled, may prove singularly conducive to those pungently amorphous processes of thought which are characteristic of Wagner's heroes? The answer depends upon whether or not we admit that even in the evasive realm of musical expression there are certain limits of compatibility, so that a man who has trained himself thoroughly to feel like Tristan, may find it impossible to think like Sarastro, assuming that he concedes Sarastro to think at all.

(18) And so we are back at the old battle of the Muses and the Sirens, and may have to decide which of the two parties we are to serve: the Muses who are so difficult to court, or the Sirens who make us so

[13] An Egyptian priest in Mozart's opera *The Magic Flute*.

easily their prey. Certainly, to enter this battle is to become exposed to both; and possibly we must know the Siren before we can recognize the Muse. At least this seems to have been the opinion of Plato when he rebuked the Spartans for subjecting their youths to the hardships of pain, but not to the hazards of pleasure: "And those who drink from these two sources at the right time and in the right measure will be blessed . . . but those who do not, will be otherwise."

(19) But what are the right time and the right measure? This is a question which, Plato insists, the artist should not be permitted to decide for himself; for if art were allowed to follow its own impulse, free from the restraints of a judicious control, it would produce bedevilment in us and around us, releasing the anarchic forces on which it plays. In Plato's view, the artist can transform us into whatever he pleases; and if given free scope, will use his power to the full. By the proper choice of modes in music, he will make us alternatively heroic and cowardly, harsh and pliant. By the use of suitable words, he will persuade us that bad things are good, and good things are bad, like the worst of all possible sophists. By inventing weird characters for a mime, he will make us relish them as dramatic parts, and induce us to adopt their objectionable manners until we are transformed by the playful force of imitation; for there is an insidious sorcery in so-called innocent games. In the words of James Harris, the Platonist: "What began in fiction, terminates in reality."

(20) To modern ears, this indictment of the artist sounds a little frenzied in its fear. Having retained some of our Latin schooling and forgotten most of our Greek, we are always ready to acknowledge the *genius* in an artist without suspecting that this may be a *daemon*. Plato knew better. With Alcibiades [14] among his elders, he saw witchcraft emanating from an artist turned statesman, and he witnessed the ensuing disaster. But the phenomenon is not purely Greek. Bolingbroke [15] was English, yet he felt himself—possibly made himself—a reincarnation of Alcibiades. And is there anything extravagant in the

[14] An Athenian general of the fifth century B.C., notorious for his duplicity and opportunism.

[15] Henry St. John, Viscount Bolingbroke (1678–1751), according to Jonathan Swift, wished to be considered the Petronius or Alcibiades of his age in mixing licentious orgies with political duties.

suggestion that this plastic power, working a ruinous enchantment, is essentially that of the artist? Perhaps there is more truth than we care to admit in Plato's enigmatic warning: "When the modes of music change, the fundamental laws of the State always change with them." Obviously, an artist must be very great to produce such a profound effect; and this is precisely Plato's opinion. The greater the artist, the more he is to be feared. No witchcraft ever issued from a feeble imagination.

(21) Modern legal opinion has not taken to Plato's conclusions. When a work of art is indicted in court for having a demoralizing effect, a not uncommon judicial procedure is to enquire whether it has any artistic merit; and if it can be established that it has, its innocence is regarded as proved. The practice is, of course, only to be applauded, for it tends to keep artists out of jail; but the reasoning is exceedingly faulty. It forgets that art intensifies what it transfigures, and that a great artist can do more harm than a little one. Plato was far more circumspect: "And if any such man will come to us to show us his art, we shall kneel down before him and worship him as a rare and holy and wonderful being; but we shall not permit him to stay. And we shall anoint him with myrrh and set a garland of wool upon his head, and shall send him away to another city."

(22) This is the most bewildering point about Plato's "fear." Animated by an unfailing sensibility to art and by an extreme estimation of its power, he is driven to conclusions which seem treacherously close to the reforms envisaged by Anti-Vice Crusaders whose fear is nourished by ignorance. It would be tempting to treat the two cases as one; for this would quickly rid us of the entire problem, and we could peacefully return to pure aesthetics. But there are some difficulties about throwing Plato into one category with Anthony Comstock; for Plato proposes reforms not exactly in keeping with the character of an abstemious moralist. While he aims at arousing in us a "divine fear" (θεῖος φόβος) so that we may not be unduly swayed by a poetic incantation, he is scornful of what he calls a "limping virtue" (χωλὴ ἀνδρία), a state of mind so hardened against the influence of art that it is no longer exposed to its dangers. He suspects that this failing creeps

in with advancing age, when men have ceased to be carried away by their passions and begin to enjoy that righteous sense of security which is even blinder than passion itself. For this ailment Plato has a radical cure; he advises old men to get drunk, so that they may be newly exposed to the dangers they have forgotten, and rejoin the chorus of the young.

(23) Plato's fear of art is thus counterbalanced by his abhorrence of the "limping virtue." To instill the fear without acquiring the limp, this appeared to Plato as such a difficult task, and so vitally important for the body politic, that he believed it would be necessary to invest the magistrate with the power to regulate, control, and censor. But this counsel of despair is so remarkably unpersuasive that one is inclined to suspect that it never quite persuaded Plato himself. He implicitly admits that the magistrate cannot be safely entrusted with this function unless he happens to be omniscient; and given this miracle in Plato's premise, our conclusion of course is a commonplace: As long as magistrates are not omniscient, we had better not entrust them with such powers.

(24) But while we reject Plato's utopian remedy, I wonder whether we can afford to disregard his diagnosis. We shall certainly not trust the infallibility of our magistrates. But should we risk the confusions of blind chance? And if not, to whom are we to assign the role for which Plato required an omniscient legislator?

(25) This role, I think, should be assigned to that most fallible of men, the critic. It is he who, in pronouncing on a work of art, should instill into us a sacred fear or castigate our limping virtue. And if he errs, as he must, there are other critics to rise up against him, and there is the artist himself who can produce a new work to confound the critic and force him to recant. For we are in no need of a final verdict. A sense of awareness is what we require. But that sense of awareness will not develop if criticism is confined to the quality of artistic workmanship, and is not allowed to extend to those human commitments which the workmanship cannot fail to entail. According to the doctrine of the autonomy of art, there is only one question which a critic may legitimately discuss: Has the artist achieved the effect at which he

aimed? But I would argue that he should also ask the forbidden question: Should this kind of effect be aimed at, and what should be its place in our experience?

(26) The habitual evasion of these issues shows not only a want of spirit; it is also very imprudent, and has in fact led in the recent past to a number of curious inconveniences. A few years ago, the hallway of Rockefeller Center in New York was to be decorated with frescoes. Mexican frescoes were very much in fashion, and the commission was given to Rivera. Presumably, those responsible for this choice were not unaware that Rivera held opinions which, if acted upon, would slightly alter the function of Rockefeller Center. But as they were dealing with art, they were animated by superior sentiments and willing to accept a decorative edification regardless of its import. In other words, they placed their trust in a limping virtue. But when Rivera's frescoes were completed, they proved too embarrassing to be retained. Without wishing to seem facetious, I would suggest that in having these frescoes removed, the liberal-minded patrons paid the artist a greater tribute than by commissioning them. Somewhat belatedly they had begun to fear that his art might convey his convictions.

(27) A precisely converse dilemma arose at Dartmouth College where frescoes were ordered from Orozco. In this case, no fear of the artist's power prevailed, in spite of the relentless violence of his message and the ferocity of his designs. The frescoes decorate a room in the Baker Library, where students are expected to sit quietly and read, unperturbed (I presume) by the revolutionary phantoms attacking them from all sides. A more solid faith in the ineffectuality of art is difficult to imagine; and the result is that this room is pervaded by a glacial atmosphere which deprives it of any living function. Officially it is called a "reserved book room," but the students are permitted to remove books if they prefer to read them elsewhere, which they are sensibly inclined to do.

(28) These two extremes—iconoclasm and dereliction—are likely to occur when the fear of art either awakens too late or has vanished altogether. In the interest of a living art, it is essential to retain a sense of the risks involved in artistic expression; and this is to recognize the human force behind the aesthetic disguise. It might be objected that

an extension of art criticism beyond the accepted boundaries of art would be a threat to artistic freedom; for the artist would be held responsible for acts which are imaginative and therefore noncommittal. But the association of the imaginative with the noncommittal is a cardinal fallacy in aesthetics, and a cause of irrelevancies in art. The critic might help to cure these failings by attacking them at their source. Unquestionably, a debate about human commitments might prove more awkward, and possibly more violent, than one confined to pure sensibility; but as a disciple of Machiavelli put it: "Those who want God to reside in their house, must admit the devil into the antechamber."

STUDY QUESTIONS

1. What are the two senses in which the title is used?
2. This essay is a refutation of the arguments and point of view advanced by Mr. E. M. Forster earlier in the symposium at which this article was read. What is Mr. Forster's argument? How does Mr. Wind manage to be complimentary and still firm in opposing that argument? How does he establish his own point of view?
3. In one paragraph summarize Mr. Wind's argument for the critical effects of music in paragraphs 17–20. Why is music a particularly crucial subject for the establishment of his case?
4. What do the examples in paragraphs 26 and 27 contribute to the argument? In what way do they represent a contrast? How does Mr. Wind interpret this contrast?
5. What is the relevance of the concluding quotation to Mr. Wind's argument?
6. To what extent is Mr. Wind's development of his thesis one of progression? Do his paragraphs follow logically from their antecedent paragraphs? Select examples of paragraph openings to illustrate your answer.
7. How many different kinds of variety in sentence structure can you detect in paragraph 17?
8. Define the exact sense, or senses, in which Mr. Wind uses the following words: *cathartic* (8), *awful* (10), *temporal* (13), *quarantined* (15), *sophists* (19), *iconoclasm* (28).
9. Make a list of words and phrases which convey irony. Before doing so, look up the word *irony* in a good dictionary.

10. This essay was given orally before a learned audience. What influence has that fact had on the style, diction, and tone of this essay?

11. On the basis of this essay, how would you say Mr. Wind defines a work of art?

WRITING ASSIGNMENTS

1. Write an extended definition of the word *criticism*, as you think Mr. Wind uses it.

2. Write an essay on the social force of art, using as your thesis the second sentence of Mr. Wind's seventh paragraph.

3. Write an analysis of the importance of a study of art in college education.

4. Write an essay on the morality of a work of art.

5. Write a research paper on Lucrezia Borgia.

"Useless" Knowledge*

BERTRAND RUSSELL (1872–   ) is the famous English philosopher, essayist, logician, and mathematician. He has taught at various universities, including the Universities of Peking, Chicago, California, and Harvard University. A foremost thinker of our time, he is regarded with A. N. Whitehead as the founder of modern mathematical logic. Of the many books he has written, those of general interest for the student are Education and the Good Life (1926), Education and the Social Order (1932), In Praise of Idleness (1935), A History of Western Philosophy (1945), *and* Unpopular Essays (1950).

(1) Francis Bacon, a man who rose to eminence by betraying his friends, asserted, no doubt as one of the ripe lessons of experience, that "knowledge is power." [1] But this is not true of *all* knowledge. Sir Thomas Browne wished to know what song the sirens sang,[2] but if he had ascertained this it would not have enabled him to rise from being a magistrate to being High Sheriff of his county. The sort of knowledge that Bacon had in mind was that which we call scientific. In emphasizing the importance of science, he was belatedly carrying on the tradition of the Arabs and the early Middle Ages, according to which knowledge consisted mainly of astrology, alchemy, and pharmacology, all of which were branches of science. A learned man was one who, having mastered these studies, had acquired magical powers. In the early eleventh century, Pope Silvester II, for no reason except that he read books, was universally believed to be a magician in league with

* Reprinted from *In Praise of Idleness and Other Essays* by Bertrand Russell. By permission of W. W. Norton & Company, Inc. Copyright 1935 by Bertrand Russell.

[1] From *Sacred Meditations* (1597).
[2] From *Urn Burial* (1658).

the devil. Prospero, who in Shakespeare's time was a mere phantasy, represented what had been for centuries the generally received conception of a learned man, so far at least as his powers of sorcery were concerned. Bacon believed—rightly, as we now know—that science could provide a more powerful magician's wand than any that had been dreamed of by the necromancers of former ages.

(2) The Renaissance, which was at its height in England at the time of Bacon, involved a revolt against the utilitarian conception of knowledge. The Greeks had acquired a familiarity with Homer, as we do with music-hall songs, because they enjoyed him, and without feeling that they were engaged in the pursuit of learning. But the men of the sixteenth century could not begin to understand him without first absorbing a very considerable amount of linguistic erudition. They admired the Greeks, and did not wish to be shut out from their pleasures; they therefore copied them, both in reading the classics and in other less avowable ways. Learning, in the Renaissance, was part of the *joie de vivre*, just as much as drinking or love-making. And this was true not only of literature, but also of sterner studies. Every one knows the story of Hobbes's first contact with Euclid: opening the book, by chance, at the theorem of Pythagoras, he exclaimed, "By God, this is impossible," and proceeded to read the proofs backwards until, reaching the axioms, he became convinced. No one can doubt that this was for him a voluptuous moment, unsullied by the thought of the utility of geometry in measuring fields.

(3) It is true that the Renaissance found a practical use for the ancient languages in connection with theology. One of the earliest results of the new feeling for classical Latin was the discrediting of the forged decretals and the donation of Constantine.[3] The inaccuracies which were discovered in the Vulgate and the Septuagint made Greek and Hebrew a necessary part of the controversial equipment of Protestant divines. The republican maxims of Greece and Rome were invoked to justify the resistance of Puritans to the Stuarts and of Jesuits to monarchs who had thrown off allegiance to the Pope. But all this was an effect, rather than a cause, of the revival of classical learning,

[3] Medieval spurious documents employed in advancing the temporal power of the papacy.

which had been in full swing in Italy for nearly a century before Luther. The main motive of the Renaissance was mental delight, the restoration of a certain richness and freedom in art and speculation which had been lost while ignorance and superstition kept the mind's eye in blinkers.

(4) The Greeks, it was found, had devoted a part of their attention to matters not purely literary or artistic, such as philosophy, geometry, and astronomy. These studies, therefore, were respectable, but other sciences were more open to question. Medicine, it was true, was dignified by the names of Hippocrates and Galen; but in the intervening period it had become almost confined to Arabs and Jews, and inextricably intertwined with magic. Hence the dubious reputation of such men as Paracelsus. Chemistry was in even worse odor, and hardly became respectable until the eighteenth century.

(5) In this way it was brought about that knowledge of Greek and Latin, with a smattering of geometry and perhaps astronomy, came to be considered the intellectual equipment of a gentleman. The Greeks disdained the practical applications of geometry, and it was only in their decadence that they found a use for astronomy in the guise of astrology. The sixteenth and seventeenth centuries, in the main, studied mathematics with Hellenic disinterestedness, and tended to ignore the sciences which had been degraded by their connection with sorcery. A gradual change towards a wider and more practical conception of knowledge, which was going on throughout the eighteenth century, was suddenly accelerated at the end of that period by the French Revolution and the growth of machinery, of which the former gave a blow to gentlemanly culture while the latter offered new and astonishing scope for the exercise of ungentlemanly skill. Throughout the last hundred and fifty years, men have questioned more and more vigorously the value of "useless" knowledge, and have come increasingly to believe that the only knowledge worth having is that which is applicable to some part of the economic life of the community.

(6) In countries such as France and England, which have a traditional educational system, the utilitarian view of knowledge has only partially prevailed. There are still, for example, professors of Chinese in the universities who read the Chinese classics but are unacquainted

with the works of Sun Yat-sen, which created modern China. There
are still men who know ancient history in so far as it was related by
authors whose style was pure, that is to say, up to Alexander in Greece
and Nero in Rome, but refuse to know the much more important later
history because of the literary inferiority of the historians who related
it. Even in France and England, however, the old tradition is dying, and
in more up-to-date countries, such as Russia and the United States,
it is utterly extinct. In America, for example, educational commissions
point out that fifteen hundred words are all that most people employ
in business correspondence, and therefore suggest that all others should
be avoided in the school curriculum. Basic English, a British invention,
goes still further, and reduces the necessary vocabulary to eight hundred words. The conception of speech as something capable of aesthetic
value is dying out, and it is coming to be thought that the sole purpose of words is to convey practical information. In Russia the pursuit
of practical aims is even more whole-hearted than in America: all that
is taught in educational institutions is intended to serve some obvious
purpose in education or government. The only escape is afforded by
theology: the sacred Scriptures must be studied by some in the original
German, and a few professors must learn philosophy in order to defend
dialectical materialism [4] against the criticisms of bourgeois metaphysi-
cians. But as orthodoxy becomes more firmly established, even this
tiny loophole will be closed.

(7) Knowledge, everywhere, is coming to be regarded not as a good
in itself, or as a means of creating a broad and humane outlook on life
in general, but as merely an ingredient in technical skill. This is part
of the greater integration of society which has been brought about by
scientific technique and military necessity. There is more economic
and political interdependence than there was in former times, and
therefore there is more social pressure to compel a man to live in a
way that his neighbors think useful. Educational establishments, except those for the very rich, or (in England) such as have become in-
vulnerable through antiquity, are not allowed to spend their money as
they like, but must satisfy the State that they are serving a useful purpose by imparting skill and instilling loyalty. This is part and parcel

---

[4] A school of philosophy founded by Karl Marx and Friedrich Engels.

of the same movement which has led to compulsory military service, boy scouts, the organization of political parties, and the dissemination of political passion by the Press. We are all more aware of our fellow-citizens than we used to be, more anxious, if we are virtuous, to do them good, and in any case to make them do us good. We do not like to think of any one lazily enjoying life, however refined may be the quality of his enjoyment. We feel that everybody ought to be doing something to help on the great cause (whatever it may be), the more so as so many bad men are working against it and ought to be stopped. We have not leisure of mind, therefore, to acquire any knowledge except such as will help us in the fight for whatever it may happen to be that we think important.

(8) There is much to be said for the narrowly utilitarian view of education. There is not time to learn everything before beginning to make a living, and undoubtedly "useful" knowledge is *very* useful. It has made the modern world. Without it, we should not have machines or motor cars or railways or aeroplanes; it should be added that we should not have modern advertising or modern propaganda. Modern knowledge has brought about an immense improvement in average health, and at the same time has discovered how to exterminate large cities by poison gas. Whatever is distinctive of our world, as compared with former times, has its source in "useful" knowledge. No community as yet has enough of it, and undoubtedly education must continue to promote it.

(9) It must also be admitted that a great deal of the traditional cultural education was foolish. Boys spent many years acquiring Latin and Greek grammar, without being, at the end, either capable or de-sirous (except in a small percentage of cases) of reading a Greek or Latin author. Modern languages and history are preferable, from every point of view, to Latin and Greek. They are not only more useful, but they give much more culture in much less time. For an Italian of the fifteenth century, since practically everything worth reading, if not in his own language, was in Greek or Latin, these languages were the indispensable keys to culture. But since that time great literatures have grown up in various modern languages, and the development of civili-zation has been so rapid that knowledge of antiquity has become much

less useful in understanding our problems than knowledge of modern nations and their comparatively recent history. The traditional schoolmaster's point of view, which was admirable at the time of the Revival of Learning, became gradually unduly narrow, since it ignored what the world has done since the fifteenth century. And not only history and modern languages, but science also, when properly taught, contributes to culture. It is therefore possible to maintain that education should have other aims than direct utility, without defending the traditional curriculum. Utility and culture, when both are conceived broadly, are found to be less incompatible than they appear to the fanatical advocates of either.

(10) Apart, however, from the cases in which culture and direct utility can be combined, there is indirect utility, of various different kinds, in the possession of knowledge which does not contribute to technical efficiency. I think some of the worst features of the modern world could be improved by a greater encouragement of such knowledge and a less ruthless pursuit of mere professional competence.

(11) When conscious activity is wholly concentrated on some one definite purpose, the ultimate result, for most people, is lack of balance accompanied by some form of nervous disorder. The men who directed German policy during the War made mistakes, for example, as regards the submarine campaign which brought America on to the side of the Allies, which any person coming fresh to the subject could have seen to be unwise, but which they could not judge sanely owing to mental concentration and lack of holidays. The same sort of thing may be seen wherever bodies of men attempt tasks which put a prolonged strain upon spontaneous impulses. Japanese Imperialists, Russian Communists, and German Nazis all have a kind of tense fanaticism which comes of living too exclusively in the mental world of certain tasks to be accomplished. When the tasks are as important and as feasible as the fanatics suppose, the result may be magnificent; but in most cases narrowness of outlook has caused oblivion of some powerful counteracting force, or has made all such forces seem the work of the devil, to be met by punishment and terror. Men as well as children have need of play, that is to say, of periods of activity having no purpose beyond

present enjoyment. But if play is to serve its purpose, it must be possible to find pleasure and interest in matters not connected with work.

(12) The amusements of modern urban populations tend more and more to be passive and collective, and to consist of inactive observation of the skilled activities of others. Undoubtedly such amusements are much better than none, but they are not as good as would be those of a population which had, through education, a wider range of intelligent interests not connected with work. Better economic organization, allowing mankind to benefit by the productivity of machines, should lead to a very great increase of leisure, and much leisure is apt to be tedious except to those who have considerable intelligent activities and interests. If a leisured population is to be happy, it must be an educated population, and must be educated with a view to mental enjoyment as well as to the direct usefulness of technical knowledge.

(13) The cultural element in the acquisition of knowledge, when it is successfully assimilated, forms the character of a man's thoughts and desires, making them concern themselves, in part at least, with large impersonal objects, not only with matters of immediate importance to himself. It has been too readily assumed that, when a man has acquired certain capacities by means of knowledge, he will use them in ways that are socially beneficial. The narrowly utilitarian conception of education ignores the necessity of training a man's purposes as well as his skill. There is in untrained human nature a very considerable element of cruelty, which shows itself in many ways, great and small. Boys at school tend to be unkind to a new boy, or to one whose clothes are not quite conventional. Many women (and not a few men) inflict as much pain as they can by means of malicious gossip. The Spaniards enjoy bullfights; the British enjoy hunting and shooting. The same cruel impulses take more serious forms in the hunting of Jews in Germany and kulaks in Russia. All imperialism affords scope for them, and in war they become sanctified as the highest form of public duty.

(14) Now while it must be admitted that highly educated people are sometimes cruel, I think there can be no doubt that they are less often so than people whose minds have lain fallow. The bully in a

school is seldom a boy whose proficiency in learning is up to the average. When a lynching takes place, the ringleaders are almost invariably very ignorant men. This is not because mental cultivation produces positive humanitarian feelings, though it may do so; it is rather because it gives other interests than the ill-treatment of neighbors, and other sources of self-respect than the assertion of domination. The two things most universally desired are power and admiration. Ignorant men can, as a rule, only achieve either by brutal means, involving the acquisition of physical mastery. Culture gives a man less harmful forms of power and more deserving ways of making himself admired. Galileo did more than any monarch has done to change the world, and his power immeasurably exceeded that of his persecutors. He had therefore no need to aim at becoming a persecutor in his turn.

(15) Perhaps the most important advantage of "useless" knowledge is that it promotes a contemplative habit of mind. There is in the world much too much readiness, not only for action without adequate previous reflection, but also for some sort of action on occasions on which wisdom would counsel inaction. People show their bias on this matter in various curious ways. Mephistopheles tells the young student [5] that theory is gray but the tree of life is green, and every one quotes this as if it were Goethe's opinion, instead of what he supposes the devil would be likely to say to an undergraduate. Hamlet is held up as an awful warning against thought without action, but no one holds up Othello as a warning against action without thought. Professors such as Bergson, from a kind of snobbery towards the practical man, decry philosophy, and say that life at its best should resemble a cavalry charge. For my part, I think action is best when it emerges from a profound apprehension of the universe and human destiny, not from some wildly passionate impulse of romantic but disproportioned self-assertion. A habit of finding pleasure in thought rather than in action is a safeguard against unwisdom and excessive love of power, a means of preserving serenity in misfortune and peace of mind among worries. A life confined to what is personal is likely, sooner or later, to become unbearably painful; it is only by windows into a larger and less fretful cosmos that the more tragic parts of life become endurable.

[5] Faust, who sold his soul to the devil in exchange for all earthly knowledge.

(16) A contemplative habit of mind has advantages ranging from the most trivial to the most profound. To begin with minor vexations, such as fleas, missing trains, or cantankerous business associates. Such troubles seem hardly worthy to be met by reflections on the excellence of heroism or the transitoriness of all human ills, and yet the irritation to which they give rise destroys many people's good temper and enjoyment of life. On such occasions, there is much consolation to be found in out-of-the-way bits of knowledge which have some real or fancied connection with the trouble of the moment; or even if they have none, they serve to obliterate the present from one's thoughts. When assailed by people who are white with fury, it is pleasant to remember the chapter in Descartes' *Treatise on the Passions* entitled "Why those who grow pale with rage are more to be feared than those who grow red." When one feels impatient over the difficulty of securing international coöperation, one's impatience is diminished if one happens to think of the sainted King Louis IX, before embarking on his crusade, allying himself with the Old Man of the Mountain, who appears in the Arabian Nights as the dark source of half the wickedness in the world. When the rapacity of capitalists grows oppressive, one may be suddenly consoled by the recollection that Brutus, that exemplar of republican virtue, lent money to a city at 40 per cent, and hired a private army to besiege it when it failed to pay the interest.

(17) Curious learning not only makes unpleasant things less unpleasant, but also makes pleasant things more pleasant. I have enjoyed peaches and apricots more since I have known that they were first cultivated in China in the early days of the Han dynasty; that Chinese hostages held by the great King Kaniska [6] introduced them into India, whence they spread to Persia, reaching the Roman Empire in the first century of our era; that the word "apricot" is derived from the same Latin source as the word "precocious," because the apricot ripens early; and that the A at the beginning was added by mistake, owing to a false etymology. All this makes the fruit taste much sweeter.

(18) About a hundred years ago, a number of well-meaning philanthropists started societies "for the diffusion of useful knowledge," with the result that people have ceased to appreciate the delicious savor of

[6] King of Kabul, Kashmir, and Northwest India in the second century A.D.

"useless" knowledge. Opening Burton's *Anatomy of Melancholy* at haphazard on a day when I was threatened by that mood, I learnt that there is a "melancholy matter," but that, while some think it may be engendered of all four humors, "Galen holds that it may be engendered of three alone, excluding phlegm or pituita, whose true assertion Valerius and Menardus stiffly maintain, and so doth Fuscius, Montaltus, Montanus. How (say they) can white become black?" In spite of this unanswerable argument, Hercules de Saxonia and Cardan, Guianerius and Laurentius, are (so Burton tells us) of the opposite opinion. Soothed by these historical reflections, my melancholy, whether due to three humors or to four, was dissipated. As a cure for too much zeal, I can imagine few measures more effective than a course of such ancient controversies.

(19) But while the trivial pleasures of culture have their place as a relief from the trivial worries of practical life, the more important merits of contemplation are in relation to the greater evils of life, death and pain and cruelty, and the blind march of nations into unnecessary disaster. For those to whom dogmatic religion can no longer bring comfort, there is need of some substitute, if life is not to become dusty and harsh and filled with trivial self-assertion. The world at present is full of angry self-centered groups, each incapable of viewing human life as a whole, each willing to destroy civilization rather than yield an inch. To this narrowness no amount of technical instruction will provide an antidote. The antidote, in so far as it is matter of individual psychology, is to be found in history, biology, astronomy, and all those studies which, without destroying self-respect, enable the individual to see himself in his proper perspective. What is needed is not this or that specific piece of information, but such knowledge as inspires a conception of the ends of human life as a whole: art and history, acquaintance with the lives of heroic individuals, and some understanding of the strangely accidental and ephemeral position of man in the cosmos—all this touched with an emotion of pride in what is distinctly human, the power to see and to know, to feel magnanimously and to think with understanding. It is from large perceptions combined with impersonal emotion that wisdom most readily springs.

(20) Life, at all times full of pain, is more painful in our time than

in the two centuries that preceded it. The attempt to escape from pain drives men to triviality, to self-deception, to the invention of vast collective myths. But these momentary alleviations do but increase the sources of suffering in the long run. Both private and public misfortune can only be mastered by a process in which will and intelligence interact: the part of will is to refuse to shirk the evil or accept an unreal solution, while the part of intelligence is to understand it, to find a cure if it is curable, and, if not, to make it bearable by seeing it in its relations, accepting it as unavoidable, and remembering what lies outside it in other regions, other ages, and the abysses of interstellar space.

STUDY QUESTIONS

1. Write a sentence outline of this essay. What is the value of making such an outline? Do you suppose Mr. Russell made an outline before writing this essay? If not, why not?

2. What are Mr. Russell's arguments in favor of "useless" knowledge? When does he start presenting them? What does he deal with in the earlier part of the essay before arguing positively for "useless" knowledge? What is the value of such procedure?

3. Mr. Russell begins his essay with a brief historical survey. How does he tie that survey in with the rest of the essay?

4. Make a close rhetorical analysis of the last paragraph of this essay, noting the use of repetition, parallelism in structure, rhythm, alliteration, phonetic harmony or dissonance, and any other elements that you think noteworthy. How are all these elements related to the function and purpose of the paragraph?

5. Go through several paragraphs of this essay, noting how many sentences begin with a word, phrase, or clause other than the subject and its modifiers. Classify these introductory elements under such heads as simple inversions, conjunctions, participial clauses or phrases, subordinate clauses, etc. On the basis of this evidence, can you make any generalizations about Mr. Russell's sentence structure?

6. In parts of this essay there is a certain witty maliciousness of tone. How is it achieved? Select specific examples from the text.

7. In arguing for the usefulness of "useless" knowledge, does Mr. Russell display a logical contradiction?

8. This essay is given connotative richness by the many allusions to literature and history. How many of them meant something to you? Did

you resent looking them up in the dictionary? If you had to look up most of them, did you conclude therefrom that this essay is addressed to a more mature audience and that you should not be asked to read it? Whether you so reacted or not, what objections can be urged against such a reaction?

WRITING ASSIGNMENTS

1. Write an account of your own experience with "useless" knowledge.
2. Write an essay around this statement by Mr. Russell in paragraph 12: "The amusements of modern urban populations tend more and more to be passive and collective, and to consist of inactive observation of the skilled activities of others."
3. Write a familiar essay on the pleasures of rumination.
4. In paragraph 20 Mr. Russell remarks that "The attempt to escape from pain drives men to triviality, to self-deception, to the invention of vast collective myths." Write a serious analysis of one of those forms of escape.
5. Write a research paper on one of the following: René Descartes, Robert Burton, Francis Bacon, Thomas Hobbes, Henri Bergson.